History of Education
Volume 2
1973

History of Education
Volume 2

Volume 2 of the journal *History of Education*

Editor: Malcolm Seaborne

 DAVID & CHARLES: NEWTON ABBOT

0 7153 6227 5

Set in Imprint
and printed in Great Britain by
Latimer Trend & Company Ltd Plymouth
for David & Charles (Holdings) Limited
South Devon House Newton Abbot Devon

Number 1   Volume 2 1973   January

Contents

Contents

History of Education
The Journal of the History of Education Society

Classics in Education

LAWRENCE A. CREMIN
GENERAL EDITOR

The Classics in Education series presents the sources of our educational heritage. Many of the volumes combine selections from important documents with readable, up-to-date discussion of their place in the history of educational thought and their bearing on recent theory and practice. Others are reprints of monographs that have significantly affected contemporary historical interpretation. All of the Classics offer fresh perspective on current educational policy.

For further information write to:

TEACHERS COLLEGE PRESS
c/o Eurospan, Ltd
3 Henrietta Street
London WC2 E8LU

TEACHERS COLLEGE PRESS
Teachers College, Columbia University
New York, NY

D. J. BRYDEN

A Didactic Introduction to Arithmetic, Sir Charles Cotterell's 'Instrument for Arithmeticke' of 1667

ON 28 November 1677, Robert Hooke visited Sir Joseph Williamson and noted in his diary: 'spak there of Arithmetick Instrument, and saw Sir Joseph's, after the china manner and Neipeir's bones.'[1] What Hooke saw was an example of the *Instrument for Arithmeticke* invented some ten years earlier and in which interest may have been re-awakened following the publication that year of an instruction-book describing its use. The title-page of this work indicates the potential of the instrument and a full transcription is therefore given: 'ARITH-METICK/ By Inspection./OR,/ So easy a way, to learn and use that Art,/ *That even those who can neither write nor/Read*, have been thereby taught all the general/Parts of it./(*They being reduced to Numeration*)/ As also to summ Accounts, and work the Rule of *Three.*/LIKEWISE,/ skilful Artists may save much Time and Pains/in great CALCULATIONS./ And in Extracting the *SQUARE & CUBE ROOTS.*/By help of an *INSTRUMENT*/Which for easiness of Carriage, of Price, and of Pra-/ctice, is the most convenient yet Extant./[rule]/Invented by Sr. C. C. Knight, *Anno 1667, and then/made for him by* Robert Jole./[rule]/ Whose humble request hath obtained his leave to Print/this Direction for the use of it, and to see both at/his Shop the Sign of the *Globe* against the/*Feathers* Tavern near *Fleet-Bridge.*/[rule]/Psal.90.v.12./ *Teach me so to number my dayes that I may apply my heart/to Wisdome.*/ Printed by *H. B.* for *R. Jole* near Fleet-Bridge, 1677.'[2]
Immediately following the title-page is printed:

An Advertisement. HEre might have been expected the Print of the Instru-ment, but in regard the Beads & Tablets are movable it could not well be Exprest: wherefore I thought good to Advertise that this instrument, or any

5

other Mathematical Instrument, in Silver, Brass, Ivory or Wood, are well made by Robert Jole at the Globe, over against the Feathers Tavern in Fleet Street near Fleet Bridge.

Lack of an illustration to accompany the instruction-book is mitigated by the existence of a number of surviving instruments.[3] A more or less complete example (illustrated on p 41) was recently presented to the Royal Scottish Museum, Edinburgh. It has the maker's name 'Robert Jole fecit' punched on the side and is equipped with a thin brass strip or 'remover' engraved: '*Instrument for Arithmeticke invented by S[r] C.C. 1667*' and on the reverse: '*Robert Jole att y[e] Crowne Nere y[e] new Exchainge fecit*'. This 'remover' not only provides an immediate link with the instrument whose use is described in the instruction-book but also allows this particular example to be dated between 1667 and 1671.[4]

Sir C.C., the designer of the *Instrument for Arithmeticke*, may be identified as Sir Charles Cotterell (1612?–1702), Master of the Ceremonies to Charles I and Charles II. Well known in court circles as a linguist, Cotterell translated a number of works, being identified in the first editions by his initials alone.[5] The attribution is more substantial than this, for in a letter of 1705 Leibniz mentions Cotterell among other earlier designers of calculating machines.[6] The author of *Arithmetick by Inspection* is, however, unknown. The title-page does not credit the text to Cotterell, it only acknowledges his permission to print. Neither is Jole credited with authorship, he is merely responsible for the publication and sale. Another hand wrote the instructions, apparently at Jole's request,[7] but there are no clues to his identity.

The *Instrument for Arithmeticke* is in the form of a two-part box-wood compendium held together with brass clasps. The inside of the lid (illustrated on p 42) is fitted with wires and beads as a bead-abacus, while the base forms a tabulet for a set of 'Napier's bones'. Two accessories are provided, a strip of brass used to move the beads on the wires of the abacus, the *remover;* and a strip of brass pierced so as to act as a cursor for the 'Napier's bones', the *ladder.*

The early history of the abacus is somewhat obscure and it may be that the Chinese *suan phan* bead-abacus and European instruments of differing forms have separate ancestries.[8] By the seventeenth century, with the adoption of the 'Italian method' of arithmetic and book-keeping in western Europe, computation by line-abacus and counting-board was abandoned, except among the barely numerate and as an initial aid in the teaching of numeration.[9] In the second half of the seventeenth century the Chinese bead-abacus attracted some attention in Europe;[10] one was described, illustrated and compared with the classical Roman instrument by Robert Hooke in 1686,[11] and it may be indicative of contemporary English ignorance of the bead-abacus that an example of Russian origin was thought worthy of inclusion in the Tradescant collection of rarities.[12]

As we have seen, in 1677, Hooke briefly described Cotterell's instrument as 'after the china manner'; presumably the wires strung with beads were the significant attributive feature. However, on the Chinese bead-abacus each wire has five beads and a centre bar with two further beads, while on the *Instrument for Arithmeticke* there are nine beads and no centre bar. This is closer to the Russian bead-abacus or *schety* which has no centre bar, and on whose full rows there are either nine or ten beads, depending on whether the older Russian alphabet numerals or the Western (Hindu-Arabic) numerals were used. This may suggest that the design of Cotterell's device was influenced by knowledge of the *schety*, perhaps even directly from seeing the example in Tradescant's Museum at South Lambeth. Against this supposition must be set the fact that in operation the wires on the Russian *schety* are horizontal, while on the *Instrument for Arithmeticke* the wires are vertical, as in the Chinese *suan phan*. The instruction-book for the *Instrument for Arithmeticke* gives no hint as to the origins of the instrument beyond the title-page attribution of the invention; indeed, the word abacus is nowhere used. Also absent is any reference to Napier whose *Rabdologiae* of 1617 explained the use of calibrated rods to undertake multiplication, division and the extrac-tion of roots, and though Leybourn's popular English exposition, *The Art of Numbering by Speaking Rods, Vulgarly termed Nepeir's Bones,* was published in 1667, the same year as Cotterell's invention, neither of the terms 'speaking rod' or 'Napier's bones' is present in the text. Hooke, as we have seen, noticed the similarity immediately. This is not to imply that the author deliberately repressed any reference to the sources from which the inventor of the *Instrument for Arithmeticke* drew his inspiration; *Arithmetick By Inspection* is primarily a text to instruct and initiate beginners in arithmetic through the use of the instrument. Neither should Sir Charles Cotterell be suspected of overt plagiarism. His design shows originality in adapting two existing calculating aids, and as the instructions explicitly show, adapting them for the specific purpose of teaching arithmetic to 'even those who can neither write nor Read'. That the stress on the didactic and even the heuristic nature of the *Instrument for Arithmeticke* was due to Cotterell and was not a new emphasis decided upon by the writer of the instruction-book, is apparent from the Latin inscription on the lid of the pre-1671 instrument in the Royal Scottish Museum (see p 41):

Qvae terrere solent ab amore matheseos illa.
Hic dat perspicve concipienda visus.
Segnius irritant animos demissa per avres.
Qvam qve sunt ocvlis subjecta fidelibus et qve
Ipse sibi tradit spectator.[13]

This inscription suggests that Cotterell's inspiration for the *Instrument for Arithmeticke* may have come directly from John Napier, for facing the first page of the text proper of the latter's *Rabdologiae*, set between type ornaments, is the couplet: '*Quae terrere solent ab amore Matheseos illa. Hoc porvo invenies esse remota libra*'.[14] Furthermore, the final device described in that book (apparently ignored by contemporaries) is a form of tabular arithmetic with the four basic arithmetical operations and the extraction of roots performed on a line-abacus or a chess-board, '. . . simply by the motion of counters, . . . which may be considered an amusement rather than a labour'.[15]

The instruction-book for the *Instrument for Arithmeticke* begins by assuming that the teacher may have a pupil who can neither read nor write, it therefore starts with numeration.[16] This is taught using the left-hand wire on the abacus, the nine beads, alternately black and white, being pushed across the centre line one after another to stand by the digit representing the number. Addition and subtraction, the carrying and borrowing of tens is then introduced and illustrated by examples to be worked through on the abacus. The wires are calibrated in Roman numerals from left to right, I, X, C, etc to represent units, tens, hundreds, etc. By reversing the abacus, calibrations for computation in £ s d can be used. The next step, the association of the process of successive addition with multiplication, is introduced by a worked example.

A printed multiplication table with a capacity of 9×9 precedes the next chapter which points to the similarity of the former with the unacknowledged 'Napier's bones' in the tablet. The use of the 'bones' for multiplication is explained and multiplication with numbers of two or more digits is taught, using the abacus to add the partial-products of each multiplying digit. A chapter explaining and teaching the method of division using the tablet and 'bones' together with the abacus is followed by a chapter on the 'Rule of Three', a topic so loved by all writers on elementary arithmetic.[17] The printed 'Fore Rule' and 'Backe Rule' pasted into the base of the tablet are to assist the beginner in correctly arranging the three known digits given in such questions in order to find the fourth. The 'Fore Rule' is used when, by inspection, the answer will be less than the given digit of the equivalent denomination and the 'Backe Rule' when the answer is expected to be greater.[18]

The explanation of the use of the *Instrument for Arithmeticke* as an introduction to elementary arithmetical techniques is spread over forty pages of text, but as the author writes, '. . . [it is] necessary for me to condescend to the capacity of the meanest choosing rather to be tedious to some than not plain to all',[19] and here the instruction book should have ended, 'but the earnest importunity of the maker of it hath prevailed with me beyond my intention to add what follows in favour of the ingenious Reader'.[20] What follows doubles the size of the work and in two prolix chapters describes the use of the instrument for extracting square and cube roots. The author is clearly dubious of the necessity of writing this section and Jole's intervention as commissioner of the work is crucial. Here the instrument-maker, seeking the widest possible sales for his work, is wishing to demonstrate to those who have already learnt and mastered arithmetic by the traditional written methods, that the *Instrument for Arithmeticke* is worthy of their attention. Not only is the instrument an introductory teaching aid and of assistance in working the fundamental arithmetical operations of addition, subtraction, multiplication and division, but it is asserted that it can also be used for more complex procedures.

Neither the *Instrument for Arithmeticke* nor any other seventeenth-century arithmetical calculating machine received uncritical approbation from mathematically competent contemporaries and Robert Hooke's sceptical analysis may be taken as typical of the savants' opinions.

> The best way for addition and subtraction is by setting down the numbers on paper, and proceeding as in common arithmetic; both these operations being quicker and much more certainly done than by any instrument whatsoever: for, first, the numbers may be writ down in half the time they can be set on any instrument; and, secondly, they remaining altogether in view, may be quickly added or subtracted, and the sum or remainder set down; and if there should be any mistake in the first, they can be presently run over again (which is not a quarter part of the trouble of the operation) whereas by an instrument to examine an operation over again, the whole trouble of the operation is performed; and a man is much more subject to miss in putting the key into the right number, than he is in setting down the figure to express it; and therefore, for those kinds of operations in arithmetic, an instrument is wholly insignificant, and at best will come short of common counters.[21]

This passage begins Hooke's brief but fairly comprehensive outline of the state of the development of the mechanical calculator; but Hooke, like many subsequent writers, failed to distinguish explicitly two essentially separate traditions. I wish to maintain that it is incorrect to consider what I shall call quasi-mechanical calculators such as Cotterell's *Instrument for Arithmeticke*, the Marquis of Worcester's *Arithmetical Instrument*[22] or Sir Samuel Morland's two *Akrithemetic Instruments*,[23] in the same light as the work of Pascal,[24] Leibniz[25] and even Hooke himself.[26] The latter all made serious attempts to design and construct mechanical calculators able to undertake some or all of the primary arithmetical operations. Genuine usefulness, complete reliability and absolute accuracy in computation were of primary importance. In contrast it is possible to distinguish in Britain other design criteria, motivated less by potential scientific usefulness and rather more by social and educational demands coupled with commercial possibilities. These quasi-mechanical calculators were manufactured for sale to beginners in arithmetic and to those with some knowledge but limited abilities, to whom the assistance of a calculating instrument had considerable appeal. In seventeenth-century England, mathematical skills were being accepted as an essential part of a gentleman's attainments, but the educational background was such that John Wallis looking back on tuition in the Cambridge colleges in the early years of the century wrote: 'I had none to direct me, what books to read, or what to seek or in what method to proceed. For mathematics, (at that time with us) were scarce looked upon as academical studies, but rather mechanical; as the business of traders, merchants, seamen, carpenters, surveyors of lands, or the like; and perhaps some almanac-makers in London.'[27] At a more mundane level John Aubrey opined that 'A barre-boy at an Alehouse will reckon better and readier than a Master of Arts in ye University', and further noted that he had known 'young persons of great quality at ye Academie in Paris that at 18+ years old knew not how to cast up pounds shillings & pence, as [methodically] they ought'.[28]

Sir Samuel Morland's *Instrument for Addition and Subtraction* of money was mechanically trivial (the technically difficult but essential problem of carrying tens, so brilliantly solved by Pascal with the *sautoir*, was not attempted) and the new *Multiplying Instrument* was no more than a clever variation on 'Napier's bones', yet both machines were of potential interest to a far wider audience than the ingenious scientific tool that Leibniz was attempting to construct. To this larger market struggling to master the apparent difficulties of written arithmetic Sir Jonas Moore could write:

> If any Gentlemen or other, especially Ladies, that desire to look into their disbursements, or layings out, and yet have not time to practise in numbers,

they may from Mr. *Humphrey Adamson* dwelling near *Turn stile* in *Holbourn*, have those incomparable Instruments, that will shew them to play Addition and Subtraction in l.s.d. and whole Numbers, without Pen, Ink, or help of Memory; which were the invention . . . of Sir *Samuel Moreland*. . . . Multiplication by memory is fit for those that have constant practice but for certainty and ease no invention ever came near that of the Lord *Napair* by Rods, made either of Wood or Ivory, Sir *Samuel* Moreland has devised a neat way upon Circles, but vastly chargeable, and that has been the reason why they have not been so well known.[29]

For multiplication and division, Hooke too praised 'Napier's bones', as the 'plainest, shortest and exactest method', but he roundly dismissed all the various adaptations of the principle;[30] and of Morland's instrument merely noted that it was 'very silly'.[31] But Hooke was too able an arithmetician to be in any way considered as typical of the users of such quasi-mechanical calculators. He would have had no time, for example, for the *Rotula Arithmetica* invented by the Scots arithmetic teacher George Brown:

> . . . to Teach those of a very ordinary capacity who can but read figures to Add, Subtract, multiply and divide in the space of four hours, tho' they are not otherways able Readily to condescend, whether seven and four be Eleven or Twelve.

Neither would Hooke have upheld the claim that the *Rotula Arithmetica* was:

> . . . very usefull, If not necessary for the ablest accomptants. There being nothing yet found comparable to it, not only for dispatch and Certainty, But for freeing the mind from all that Rack of Intortion to which it is obliged in long additions.[32]

Cotterell's *Instrument for Arithmeticke* with its abacus and 'Napier's bones' was also intended for use beyond the initial teaching role, to 'Summ Accounts, work the Rule of *Three*' and 'save much Time and Pains in great CALCULATIONS'[33]—a not implausible assertion, for in the hands of a skilful operator the abacus is both accurate and rapid, even rivalling the modern mechanical calculator.[34] Seventeenth-century English mathematicians and the majority of teachers of arithmetic laid great stress on achieving competence in written methods—so that today the visitor to eastern Europe is initially surprised to observe the widespread and effective use of the abacus (known in Britain and western Europe only as a child's toy) for adding up bills.[35] Many a seventeenth-century gentleman needing to undertake the simpler arithmetical processes, if only to compute his personal accounts, struggled with the unfamiliar and tiresome written arithmetic, unwilling to lose face by turning to the demoted line-abacus and counters. The quasi-mechanical calculator offered a respectable alternative, with the advantage that such devices claimed to transfer the trivial but irksome and apparently difficult arithmetical tasks from the fallible individual wielding a pen to the infallible machine. In this context Samuel Pepys' disparaging remarks on Morland's *Arithmetick Instrument*, 'very pretty, but not very useful'[36] may be interpreted in one of two ways. It may be the comment of one whose arithmetical competence[37] leads him to feel such a gimcrack totally unnecessary, or it may imply that in practice Pepys found that the instrument did not allow him to dispense with pen and paper. A nineteenth-century device whereby 'a person who can only read figures, may by this help add up a bill with as much accuracy as a mathematician' received the approbation of the Society of Arts[38] and rightly so for such a proto-cash-register was an idea worthy of support. However, it, and its seventeenth-century precursors, the quasi-mechanical calculators, are less part of the history of mechanical computing and more an interesting stage in the development and spread of numeracy.

The possibility of mechanical calculators, initially explored in the seventeenth century and continued through the next, was proved viable in the mid-nineteenth century when economic factors and improved manufacturing techniques allowed designs to be reliably translated from prototype into commercial production. Sir Charles Cotterell's *Instrument for Arithmeticke* (together with other English quasi-mechanical calculators of the period), if part of that tradition, is a very distinct part. A separate trend can be distinguished embracing instruments which *either* asserted their great didactic potential in teaching elementary arithmetic *or* were aimed at a wider market than the absolute beginner, by claiming to transfer common and trivial arithmetical tasks from the fallible individual to the infallible machine; *or both*; but neither assertion can be accepted at its face value. While there are good and bad ways of teaching every subject, claims that understanding and knowledge can be attained with astonishing speed rarely, if ever, prove generally valid. The genuine teaching machine is an innovation of the last two or three decades and, prior to this, the primary role of mathematical calculating devices lay in aiding the mathematically competent. There is no doubt that there were many with limited mathematical skills eager to own and use the latest 'inventions' that the teachers of mathematics designed both to advertise their own expertise and to assist their pupils in the solution of problems; however, neither the usefulness nor the educational value of many of these devices, and the quasi-mechanical calculators in particular, can be readily evaluated. The ease and speed which one teacher insisted could be achieved with the aid of his 'invention', would frequently be disputed by his rivals,[39] though such evidence is inherently tendentious. The opposing opinions of William Oughtred and of Richard Delamain, as expressed in the course of a virulent public quarrel over priority of invention, illustrates two contrasting contemporary views of the educational and practical value of calculating and computing instruments. Oughtred, the mathematician, stoutly maintained that thorough comprehension of the theory was absolutely necessary; while for Delamain it was sufficient to be able to manipulate an instrument to attain the desired result, and furthermore by providing a visual representation of the problem the instrument led to a a quicker and better understanding than the abstract mathematical presentation. Oughtred, as reported by his pupil William Forster, insisted:

> That the true way of Art is not by Instruments but by demonstration: and that it is a preposterous course of vulgar Teachers, to begin with Instruments, and not with the Sciences, and so in-stead of Artists, to make their Schollers only doers of tricks, and as it were Juglers: to the despite of Art, loose of precious time, and betraying of willing and industrious wits unto ignorance and idlenesse. That the use of Instruments is indeed excellent, if a man be an Artist: but contemptible, being set and opposed to Art. And lastly, that he meant to commend to me the skill of Instruments, but first he would have me well instructed in the Sciences.[40]

main, in reply, maintains:

A Didactic Introduction to Arithmetic 15

... For none to know the use of a *Mathematicall Instrumen*, except he knowes the cause of its operation, is somewhat too strict, which would keepe many from affecting the *Art*, which of themselves are ready enough every where, to conceive more harshly of the difficulties, and impossibilities of attayning any skill therein, than it deserves, because they see nothing but obscure propositions, and perplex and intricate demonstrations before their eyes. . . . a doctrinall proposition laid first open to the *eye*, and *sense*, and well perceived enters more easily the dore being opened, than if the intellect by the strength of its active sense, should eliciate, or screw out the meaning by a long excogitated operation . . .[41]

The inscription on the *Instrument for Arithmeticke* in the Royal Scottish Museum[42] indicates clearly Cotterell's implicit adherence to Delamain's views on a question which educationalists continue to debate. The author of the instruction-book is equally committed: 'This Instrument presents the Eye with numbers ready cast, which gives them up so to the understanding, and thereby eases it very much of those difficulties, that trouble the brains of most, and do much to discourage all Learners.'[43]

Whipple Museum of the History of Science
University of Cambridge

References

1 H. W. Robinson & W. Adams (eds), *The Diary of Robert Hooke 1672–1680* (1935), 330–1.
2 *Arithmetick by Inspection* . . ., London (1677).
3 (a) Royal Scottish Museum (1969. 28).
(b) Museum of the History of Science, Oxford (Lewis Evans Collection 2369). Incomplete, only the tabulet base with engraved paper of instructions and 19 'Napier's bones' survive; described in E. M. Horsburgh (ed), *Handbook of the Exhibition of Napier relics and of books, instruments and devices for facilitating calculation*, Edinburgh (1914), 18–19.
(c) Whipple Museum of the History of Science, Cambridge (1025; Trinity College, Scattergood Collection) very incomplete, only a clasp, the 'ladder' and 10 'Napier's bones' survive.
(d) Whipple Museum of the History of Science, Cambridge (1587; previously in a private collection and sold by Sotheby & Co, *Catalogue of Scientific Instruments, Watches and fine Clocks 27.10.1969*, lot 6.) Incomplete, lacking all the 'Napier's bones'.
4 In 1670 Jole's address was 'the Crown, over against Durham Yard in the Strand', see S. Jones, *A Guide to the young Gager* (1670), 65. That this is clearly the

same address as 'ye Crown Nere ye new Exchainge' is apparent from maps of the area. Some time in late 1670 or early 1671 Jole moved to the Sign of the Globe in Fleet Street, see R. T. Gunther, *Early Science in Oxford*, I, Oxford (1923), 179, paying watch rate in the ward of Farringdon Without, second precinct, St Bride's Parish, Fleet Street, for the year ending September 1771, see Guildhall, London, MS 6613/1 (unpaginated).

5   *Dictionary of National Biography*. See: *Cassandra Heroine of Romance . . . rendered into English by a person of Quality* (1652), the translator's preface signed 'C.C.'; H. C. Davila, *The Historie of the Civill Warres of France* (1647), the licence attributes the translation to William Aylesbury though the monogram on the title-page is of the initials W.A. and C.C.; the preface to the second edition (1678) attributes the bulk of the translation to Sir Charles Cotterell and the title-page monogram is of the initials C.C.; *The Spiritual Year—or Devout Contemplations digested in Distinct Arguments . . .* (1693) makes strong allusions to the translator (Cotterell) in the preface, but does not name him.

6   Leikniz-Archiv der Niedersächsischen Landesbibliothek, Hannover, *L.Br. 146, f5ʳ–6ᵛ, Letter, G. W. Leibniz to C. Gaze, Hanover, 23.6.1705*, '. . . Avant que de finir puisque vous parlés de Machines Arithmetiques, et entre autre de la Vostre, differente de celles de Monsieur Pascal, de M. le Chevalier Coterel, de M. Grillet; a qui j'adjoute celle de feu M. le Chevalier Samuel Morland . . .' I am indebted to Dr L. von Mackensen for this reference. E. G. R. Taylor, *The Mathematical Practitioners of Tudor and Stuart England*, Cambridge (1954), 254, records Sir Charles Cotterell, 'flourished 1667' as the 'designer of an early calculating machine for adding and multiplying of a type designed by Robert Hooke and Samuel Morland'. In fact what little is known of Hooke's arithmetical engine suggests that the design had a strong affinity with that of Leibniz and certainly not with that of Morland. Cotterell's design differs from both. It is apparent that Professor Taylor had not seen an example of the instrument nor examined a copy of the instruction-book: and regrettably no evidence is given to support her assertion.

7   *Arithmeticke*, op cit (2), 40.

8   G. Sarton, *Introduction to the History of Science*, I, Washington (1927), 757. J. Needham & Wang Ling, *Science and Civilisation in China*, III, Cambridge (1959), 80.

9   D. E. Smith, *History of Mathematics*, II, New York (1925), 177–90, and J. M. Pullan, *The History of the Abacus* (1968), 42–70, 94–101.

10   Needham & Ling, op cit (8), 80.

11   R. Hooke, 'Some Observations and Conjectures concerning the Chinese Characters', *Phil Trans R Soc Lond*, XVI (1686–92), 66–7.

12   *Musaeum Tradescantianum, or a Collection of Rarities preserved . . by John Tradescant*, London (1656) [I have used the Old Ashmolean Reprint No 1, Oxford (1923), 54], 'Beads strung upon stiffe wyers, and set in four-square frames wherewith the Indians cast account'. The Tradescant collection, acquired by Ashmole, went to Oxford in 1683. This abacus, presently on display in the Founder's Room of the Ashmolean Museum, is not Chinese as has been suggested, see R. T. Gunther, *Early Science in Oxford*, I, Oxford (1923), 126. Dr W. F. Ryan suggests that it is Russian in origin, probably brought to England by John Tradescant the elder who visited Russia in 1618: see W. F. Ryan, 'John Tradescant's Russian Abacus', *Oxford Slavonic Papers* (forthcoming). I am indebted to Dr Ryan and Mr G. L'E Turner for these references and notes.

13   In translation reads: 'There are those who are accustomed to make arithmetic

frightening through very love of the subject. This [instrument] provides a readily understood explanation. Things that have been taken in through the ears animate the mind more sluggishly than things that have been observed by attentive eyes; these the pupil absorbs for himself.' I am indebted to Mrs P. M. Atkins and to Dr M. A. Hoskin for their comments on this passage. The claim that learning and understanding are best attained through the visual rather than the aural sense is also found in the introduction to *Arithmetick by Inspection*.

14 J. Napier, *Rabdologiae, seu Numerationis per Virgulas Libri duo: Cum Appendice de expeditissimo Multiplicationes promptuario. Quibus accessit & Arithmeticae Localis Liber unus*, Edinburgh (1617), *Sig* *6ᵛ.

15 Ibid, 113–14.

16 This was not unusual, M. H. Curtis, *Oxford and Cambridge in Transition 1558–1642*, Oxford (1959), 245, notes that '. . . instructors in mathematics could not count on their pupils having any knowledge of Arabic numbers, to say nothing of simple arithmetical operations performed in such notation'.

17 *Arithmetick*, op cit (2), 35. 'The reason of this Name is because that three Numbers being given, by them the fourth is found; and that only by Multiplication and Division'.

18 The example of the 'Fore-Rule' is of a merchant buying 2,148lb of cinnamon for £537, wishing to calculate how many pounds an additional £426 would buy. The answer 1,704lb is incorrectly given on the tabulet as 1,074lb, the engraver transposing two digits. The error is not mentioned in the printed corrigenda, nor corrected on either the Cambridge or Oxford instruments. On the Edinburgh instrument there is a manuscript correction.

19 *Arithmetick*, op cit (2), 2.

20 Ibid, 40.

21 R. Hooke, 'concerning arithmetical instruments' (1673), in T. Birch, *The History of the Royal Society of London*, III (1757), 86.

22 E. Somerset (Second Marquis of Worcester), *A Century of the Names and Scantlings of such Inventions* . . . (1663). [I have used the edition addended to H. Dircks, *Life and Times and Scientific Labours of the Second Marquis of Worcester* . . . (1865).] Item 84 [512], 'An Instrument whereby persons ignorant in Arithmetick may perfectly observe Numerations and Substractions of all Summes and Fractions.'

23 S. Morland, *The Description and Use of two Arithmetick Instruments* (1673). See also H. W. Dickinson, *Sir Samuel Morland, Diplomat and Inventor 1625–1695* (Cambridge, for the Newcomen Society, 1970), 29–31. For the traditional English view which incorporates Morland's work into the general history of the calculating machine see A. Wolf, *A History of Science, Technology and Philosophy in the 16th and 17th Centuries* (2nd revised edition, ed D. McKie, 1950), 560–3.

24 R. Taton, 'Sur l'invention de la machine arithmetique', *Revue d'Histoire des Sciences*, XVI (1963), 139–60, and J. Payes, 'Les examplaires conservés de la machine de Pascal', ibid, 161–78.

25 W. Jordan, 'Die Leibniz'sche Rechenmaschine', *Zeitschrift für Vermessungswesen*, XXVI (1897), 289–315, and L. von Mackensen, 'Zur Vorgeschichte und Entstehung der ersten digitalen 4-Spezies-Rechenmaschine von G. W. Leibniz', *Studia Leibnitiana Supplementa*, II (1969), 34–68.

26 Leibniz was the motivation for Hooke's brief incursion into the design and construction of calculating machines, but the latter's initial enthusiasm was not maintained; see Birch, op cit (21), III, 73, 75, 77, 87; Robinson and Adams, op cit (1)

entries in 1673 for 22 January, 2, 4, 5, 26 February, 3, 5, 8, 11, 20 March; R. Hooke, *Animadversions on the first part of the Machina Coelestis* (1674), 45; and J. Pell's Mathematical Papers in British Museum, Addit MS 4422, f78.

27 T. Hearne (ed), *Peter Langtoft's Chronicle*, I, Oxford (1735), cxlvii–cxlviii, cited by Curtis, op cit (16), 244–5.

28 Bodleian Library, *MS Aubrey 10*, f29a and ibid, f35a. I am indebted to Mr A. J. Turner for this reference.

29 J. Moore, *A Mathematical Compendium* (2nd edition, 1681), 20–1. I have not seen the first edition which appeared in 1674 under the editorship of N. Stephenson, who published a subsequent edition in 1679; but this comment apparently appears in that edition, see Taylor, op cit (6), 219.

30 Hooke, op cit (11), 66.

31 Robinson & Adams, op cit (1), 25; 'silly', probably in the sense, 'trifling, unsophisticated, simple', *OED*.

32 Scottish Record Office, *Privy Council Register of Acta* (PC 1.51), 1.12.1698. The text of this act is printed in G. P. Insh, *School life in Old Scotland*, Edinburgh (1925) 80–2. See also D. J. Bryden, 'George Brown, Author of the Rotula', *Annals of Science*, 28 (1972), 1–29.

33 *Arithmetick*, op cit (2), *tp*.

34 Needham & Ling, op cit (8), 75; citing T. Kojima, *The Japanese Abacus, its Use and Theory*, Tokyo (1954).

35 Personal communications of Dr M. B. Hesse, Mr G. L'E Turner and others.

36 H. B. Wheatland (ed), *The Diary of Samuel Pepys*, VII (1896), 363.

37 On Pepys' earlier lack of arithmetical skills see M. H. Nicolson, *Pepys' Diary and the New Science*, Charlottesville (1965), 8–10.

38 J. Goss, 'A Mechanical Instrument to Work Addition of Numbers with accuracy and dispatch', *Trans Soc Arts*, XXX (1813), 161.

39 See for example, J. Paterson, *A New Prognostication for the year of our Lord 1683*, Edinburgh (1683), 12; 'Such as desire the Mathematical Arts, or Instruments theie to belonging, especially a Spiral Line, which I have so framed that you may work more Arithmetick in an hour than any other in two days with the Pen, and that exactly . . .', and compare the comment of J. Forbes, *The Mariner's Everlasting Almanack*, Aberdeen (1683), 48.

40 W. Oughtred, *The Circles of Proportion and the Horizontal Instrument* (1632, trans W. Forster), preface, *Sig A4^r*.

41 R. Delamain, *Grammelogie, Or the Mathematical Ring* (2nd edition, 1633?), appendix, *Sig A8^r–B1^r*.

42 See (13) above.

43 *Arithmetick*, op cit (2), 3.

Acknowledgement

The author is indebted to Mr A. J. Turner for his comments on an earlier draft of this paper.

For plates, provided by the author, see pp 41–2

NANCY BALL

Elementary School Attendance and Voluntary Effort before 1870

WHEN the report of the Newcastle Commission argued that compulsory education was un-English and unnecessary, it was expressing a view widely held in educational circles. Compulsion, in the words of W. J. Kennedy, HM Inspector of Schools, was opposed 'to the genius and temper of our people'.[1] Moreover, although it was admitted that the 'perishing and dangerous' classes presented special problems, most middle-class Victorians could scarcely credit that the 'industrious' poor would be so blind to their own interests as to reject the manifest benefits of education once they became aware of them. School promoters, it was believed, had only to offer an education which parents would see to be of value and attendance problems would disappear. Consequently, the fundamental need was to provide efficiently organised facilities for education.

This view, the assumption behind the education bills of the fifties, was challenged in 1857, immediately after the failure of Sir John Pakington's bill, at a conference organised by Canon Moseley, who had been from 1844 to 1855 the most influential member of HM Inspectorate. The conference committee, a distinguished body, reflected every shade of educational opinion except the Catholics and the secularists. Prince Albert presided. Public administration, past and present, was represented by Lansdowne, Cowper-Temple and Kay-Shuttleworth, two senior inspectors (Temple and Cook) and the assistant secretary of the Department. There were representatives from the National Society, the British and Foreign School Society and the Wesleyan Education Committee; and the high churchmen Lord Lyttelton and Bishop Wilberforce sat with Baines, Samuel Morley and the Halifax mill-owner Edward Akroyd. Their thesis, which is the subject of this paper, was as follows:

That the main defect in the present state of popular education in this country is not so much the lack of schools, as the insufficient attendance of the children of the working classes (many never coming at all, and most others being withdrawn before they have had time to derive much benefit), is a truth which has for some years past been impressing itself more and more upon those who are best informed on the subject.[2]

In his report on the educational census of 1851 Horace Mann, having argued that one in six of the population was of school age, calculated that about 28 per cent (850,000) of the age group was not being educated.[3] Surviving figures for specific localities suggest that this was an under-estimate. At Winchester in 1847, 774 children between the ages of 6 and 14 were in school, 108 working and 223 neither at school nor at work. In Manchester, the Statistical Society reported in 1851 that of children aged between 3 and 10 years, 21,774 were at school and 22,096 (excluding those sick or at work) were not; while a house-to-house visitation of two wards, St Michael's and St John's, counted 12,372 children aged between 3 and 14 of whom only 4,249 were in school. Twenty years later, the investigation of 1870 into education in four major provincial centres, showed, according to Mann's criterion, only about 60 per cent of the potential school population to be on roll in Birmingham, Liverpool and Manchester, with Leeds only slightly better at 65 per cent.[4]

It would be natural to assume that the facts just stated illustrate the general inadequacy of voluntary provision. This was certainly the case in some areas, but the position was more complex than appears at first sight. The five public church schools in Winchester, with 370 vacant places, would by themselves have held not only the 223 absentees mentioned above, but half the 291 infants between 2 and 5 years old who were not in school. In national terms, inspected schools with, in 1859, accommodation for 1,111,102 children, had 748,164 in average attendance; in 1869, with accommodation for 2,011,214, an average attendance of only 1,245,027.[5]

Although denominational rivalries had led to the founding of some unnecessary schools, this does not adequately explain the discrepancy between attendance and accommodation. In 1853, for a total of 18,090 Catholic children in Manchester and Salford, of whom 960 were estimated to be in private schools, there were 4,073 places available in Catholic day schools. Even allowing for the fact that the attendance of Catholics was especially affected by poverty, it might be assumed that there would have been no difficulty in filling these places. Yet only 3,340 were occupied. If the largest and only over-crowded school (St Patrick's) be excluded, the figures become still more striking—756 vacant places out of a total of 2,991.[6] These figures may serve to show that the problem of getting children into school and keeping them there could not be solved simply by opening schools run on principles acceptable to parents.

Numbers on roll and average attendance figures give little indication of the amount of schooling actually taking place. A register covering 15 of the 18 months between June 1855 and December 1856, surviving from Winston, Co Durham (average attendance 32), shows 72 children passing through the school, of whom 17 remained on the books throughout. Of the 60 whose names appear during the first 6 months, only 28 attended for more than 50 per cent of the time. Of the rest, 15 made fewer than one-fifth of possible attendances.[7]

A constant source of educational difficulty was the short stay of pupils in one school; an average of $8\frac{1}{2}$ months at St Philip's, Birmingham, for instance, in 1856, and 6 months in Sheffield in 1857. Of 94 boys who left Derby British school (average attendance 150) between January and June, 1848, only 4 had attended for more than 4 years and 33 for over a year. All the rest had been in the school for less than a year—16 for less than 3 months.[8] Two well-known schools showed a similar pattern—the National Society's school in Westminster, with an average attendance of 330, admitted 444 boys during 1847; in 1858 Borough Road (average attendance 603) admitted 728.[9] Few of the birds of passage finished their education when they left; they simply moved elsewhere, to bring down the attendance percentages of another school. For example, of 14 children admitted to Henley National school (Warwickshire) in 1868 whose previous career is recorded, 10 came from Henley British school. Often they came back again, to confuse the figures still further. Eight of the 72 children at Winston school in 1855–6 were re-admitted during the period, one of them twice. At Melton Mowbray (Leicestershire) in 1852, of 152 entrants, 59 were re-admissions.[10]

A problem resulting from these migrations was that of assimilating children of very different ages. Walditch school (Dorset), for instance (average attendance under 40), had between 1862 and 1869 to absorb 28 children under 4 years old, 29 of between 4 and 6, 31 between 7 and 10, and 7 aged more then 10 years.[11]

In spite of the minority of late entrants, there were few older pupils in the schools. This fact is too well known to need emphasis; the official figures for inspected schools showed 70 per cent of all pupils to be under 10 years old in the late fifties and sixties.[12] John Flint, formerly a National Society organising master, presenting evidence to the conference of 1857 on non-grant schools in Derbyshire, pointed out that the extent of early leaving depended on the demand for labour. In the mainly agricultural deaneries of Alfreton, Ashbourne and Eyam, the percentages of pupils over 10 years old were 35, 31 and 34 respectively. In the Wirksworth deanery, which contained lead mines and cotton mills, the figure was 21 per cent, falling to 19 per cent and 13 per cent in Ockbrook and Derby, centres of the silk, cotton and hosiery trades.[13]

But although the demands of agriculture in pastoral districts like Derbyshire were relatively low, this was not true of the country as a whole. In lowland England seasonal work was demanded of children from the age of seven. Schools made some attempt to adjust to this. The farther north the rural school, the later was the date of the summer (harvest) holidays, except for the hopping districts of Kent, which were the latest of all (mid-September to October). But holidays could not provide for all farming exigencies. There were sudden drops in attendance at the beginning and end of harvest, for haymaking, bird-scaring and, most universal of all, planting the family garden in spring. By the time he was nine or ten years old, a boy could find agricultural employment all the year round and consequently left altogether.

Some industries also provided seasonal or occasional work, but in general they either took the children from school altogether or occupied some part of their time each week. The half-time system in the textile districts was a statutory regularisation of this and the Mines Act of 1860 attempted, ineffectually, to extend some control to collieries. Elsewhere there was no regulation of employment at all until the sixties, and the laments of educationists over the dire social consequences make melancholy reading. In the Potteries, 75 per cent of children left school before the age of ten; in south Staffordshire the figure was 84 per cent. The gun trade of Birmingham produced little workmen, ten or twelve years old, 'loud in voice and truculent in manner; having no respect towards person or sex . . .' In Sheffield most boys left school before they were ten and 'at once *"become men"*, and imitate the vices and follies of those that are grown up'.[14] The leather, hosiery and gloving trades of the Midlands, which were still largely domestic, involved regular absence when the children collected the materials and returned the finished work, as well as early removal. The rural industries of lace-making and straw-plaiting were exceptional in employing children almost from infancy; some school promoters, in desperation, sponsored lace and straw-plaiting schools in the hope of ensuring that the children at least received a few hours' teaching a week.[15]

By the late fifties, even to many who objected to direct compulsion, the case for extending factory legislation seemed strong. The result was the Children's Employment Commission and the series of acts extending the half-time system piecemeal during the sixties. If those who blamed poor attendance wholly on the demands of employers were right, these acts should have made radical changes in the schools. But the effect was surprisingly small; the experience of these years proved that the half-time system by itself would never solve the attendance problem.

Other causes of absence existed, perhaps the more exasperating in that they were less rational than the desire to earn money. Previously, schooling had been only for a minority; now, strong social pressures persuaded a large section of the population that they were under some sort of obligation to send their children to school. But the conviction did not go deep. A state of affairs existed in which lateness was so habitual that children could not even be punctual on inspection day[16] and inevitably this casual attitude extended to actual attendance. The migration between schools already noted was admittedly sometimes the result of a well-founded dislike of inefficiency. But often the motive was simply curiosity about a new school; pique—'Punish little Jack or Bill for any fault, and immediately he will be transferred in state by his affronted mother to the opposition school';[17] debts in school pence, or the prospect of lower (or occasionally higher) fees; unwillingness to have the child at home during the holidays; or just the desire for a change. When removal was so easily justified, mere absence scarcely needed explanation. Sunday school treats, circuses, hiring fairs, races and 'watching the soldiers' perpetually emptied schools. Among less conventional causes were a heatwave, during which the children were basking in the sun; attendance at a dancing school (involving ten weeks' continuous absence); and 'the cheap trip to Sheffield to view the spot of the late awful catastrophe' (the Bradfield reservoir disaster). The attitude of many parents was summarised by a Kentish mother with a nice turn of phrase: 'On Monday he was kept at home on her business. Yesterday (Wednesday) for her pleasure. She is quite tired of sending him, because the Master makes so much bother when he is absent.'[18]

Although there were conscientious parents whose children were regular attenders, there was certainly much indifference. The willingness of Lancashire parents to leave their children to arrange their own education, reported by two inspectors and the secretary of the Manchester and Salford Committee, was confirmed by the schoolmaster of Waterside, Colne—'Believe in some cases the School fees had been given to children either to spend or to attend school as they chose'. A similar complaint came from the Midlands—'The children of Melton Mowbray know they may come to school or stay away, learn or not learn as they please and children do not often learn for the pleasure of doing so.'[19] Such indifference bred contempt and a number of parents seem to have had little control over their children—'He would not come'; 'he would not get up'; 'she had told him to come but he *wouldn't*'; were excuses sometimes found. A schoolmaster en-

gaged in the uphill task of taming the boys of a new industrial settlement (Witton Park Ironworks, Co Durham) repeatedly complained of
parental helplessness—'the usual "Witton Park" experience,' he said
of one father, 'He could not manage him.'[20]

Bishop Wilberforce once warned parents, at the opening of War-
grave school (Berkshire), against 'a burning fever which shows itself
in great earnestness on the child's behalf, and . . . a low fever which is
a carelessness as to whether the child is at school or not'.[21] In many
cases it must have seemed that they suffered from both at once, as at
Witton Park, where on 27 May 1867 the master received the following
letter:

> Sir,
>   My son, George E Green, has been poorly last week, and I kept him at
> home, and by, examining his reading, and writing too, I find he is getting
> on very badly, and especially when I look at the time he has been at school,
> between five and six years, I don't know where the fault is, whether it is on
> him, or on his teacher, I am
>   Yours,
>   E. Green

In his reply, the master retorted that George was admitted in 1865
and attended seventeen times before leaving. He was re-admitted in
March 1867 and, in all, had been present on ninety-eight occasions
since January 1865. Since March, he had arrived on time once. On
the previous Thursday he had been eighty minutes late in the morning
and sixty-five in the afternoon! It is unlikely that this reply, though
unanswerable, did much to mend matters. In such circumstances the
chances of solving the attendance problem by voluntary effort were
slim.

Apart from paying the fees of individuals or providing some free
places, few school managers attempted to remedy what the British and
Foreign committee once described as the grievous neglect of the very
destitute poor,[22] many of whom never set foot in elementary schools.
The problem, to officials as to school promoters, seemed to be to
encourage pupils on roll to attend more regularly to a more advanced
age. Treats, special privileges and attendance prizes were common
(including sometimes actual payments from the capitation grant to

those who earned it). Since managers lost money, not only in fees but in grants, as a result of irregular attendance, some tried the effect of financial sanctions, but with little success. Most of the rules ordering pence to be paid during absence unless pupils were sick, or charging special fees for re-admission seem to have been dead letters from the start; the committee at Foots Cray (Kent), in rescinding one such rule, remarked that as parents would not pay, there was a danger of attendance diminishing still further.[23] In general, managers trusted to exhortations to parents, verbal or written, and to visiting of absentees, which was usually delegated to monitors or pupil-teachers although sometimes committee members and teachers went round. In one or two Anglican schools scripture readers or district visitors acted virtually as attendance officers.[24]

The use of the school as a centre of welfare activities was not primarily intended to stimulate attendance, but could often serve that purpose. Samuel Best, the rector of Abbott's Ann (Hampshire), who made membership of his village provident society compulsory for all schoolchildren, adjusted the premiums payable according to the child's attendance record.[25] This refinement was uncommon, but the penny clubs, shoe and coal clubs and savings banks attached to schools must have done something to reconcile parents to school attendance. However, since their success depended upon the funds contributed by patrons, it was related to a factor which, though not easily identifiable, certainly affected attendance in individual schools—the attitude of squire, parson or employer. In a stable community, dominated by persons interested in the school, regular attendance could pay dividends in terms of the present position of the parent and the future prospects of the child. The desire to 'get a good place' was probably the biggest single factor in keeping village girls in school, since its achievement usually depended on the parson's wife or the ladies from the big house. The influence of the Wenlocks on their East Riding estates is a case in point.[26] There was exceptional regularity at the Kay-Shuttleworths' school at Habergham (Lancashire) which gained the biggest capitation grant in the country in 1855. The only genuinely rural school amongst the six receiving the largest grants in that year was Acton, near Nantwich, which for two generations was under the patronage of the squire's wife, Mrs Tomkinson and her daughter, Mrs Tollemache, who made it 'a model school in all respects'.[27]

A similarly paternalistic attitude was expected of industrialists. An Inspector's report of 1866 urged the owners of Witton Park Ironworks to use their authority to end the bad attendance in the school. In Teesdale the London Lead Company demanded certificates of six years' school attendance from boys entering its service, and appeals to the company's agent brought an instant improvement in attendance at local schools. Such action was possible, however, only where choice of employment was limited. Messrs Marshall of Leeds were zealous promoters of attendance and their huge school admittedly gained one of the six largest capitation grants in 1856, but this was only in respect of 188 children out of an average attendance of 899, which does not suggest great regularity; movement to another place of work to escape pressure was too easy.[28]

A by-product of the feeling of responsibility amongst some of the wealthy was a series of experiments in voluntary half-time schemes intended to keep older children in school. It appears to have developed naturally from experience of running industrial schools for boys. The practical training which such schools provided was intended to appeal to parents and thus counteract irregular attendance; and in some cases the boys received direct payment for their work. They were, however, expensive to run and disliked by farmers. Moseley had therefore suggested in 1849 that the same result might be obtained at less trouble and expense if schoolmasters were to act as agents in arranging half-time work for boys over ten years old. This suggestion was amplified in 1851 by J. P. Norris, HM Inspector for the North-West Midlands, who pointed out that work in the fields provided a real instead of an artificial industrial training. By this time such a scheme was already operating successfully at Betley, on the Staffordshire-Cheshire border —'an excellent discipline for rather naughty, active, spirited boys'.[29] The major problem was to find enough farmers willing to co-operate; many were unsympathetic, and small farmers, who needed boys only occasionally, could scarcely be expected to fit in. Home farms and estate gardens were a different matter; and Norris succeeded in interesting a number of the gentry of his district.

In Staffordshire Lord Hatherton employed 30 estate boys between 11 and 15, who attended school from 6am to 8am daily; while the interest of another Staffordshire magnate, the Lord President, Granville, accounts for the fact that in 1854 the capitation grant was extended to boys over 10 attending for 88 days only, provided they were under a half-time scheme approved by HM Inspector. The Tollemaches of Acton and Tarporley in Cheshire allowed 2 days' absence a week provided the boys were gardening and the girls washing, cleaning or nursing at home. At Acton, Mrs Tollemache, besides herself employing 6 boys half-time all year and 8 more from June to September, sent 14 others to local farmers for varying periods. Elsewhere in Cheshire half-time schemes were introduced, as at Rostherne and Oulton; and, in Shropshire, at Ellesmere and Myddle. At Hagley (Worcestershire) Lord Lyttelton permitted boys over 12 to attend his school on alternate weeks. This, he told the Newcastle Commission, meant that at any one time there would be 12 or 13 boys in school who would otherwise have left.[30]

Outside the west Midlands, versions of the scheme were tried at Terling (Essex) by Lord Rayleigh, in Hertfordshire by Lord Cowper, at Kiddington (Oxfordshire), and at Ruddington (Nottinghamshire) by Charles Paget, MP, who described his plan to the Social Science Congress of 1858. The most interesting feature at Ruddington was that some of the parents joined in, by pairing off their children, so that there were not only 16 children working on two farms but a number of others sewing stockings (Ruddington was in the hosiery district) or helping with housework in pairs. The conference of 1857 devoted a good deal of attention to voluntary half-time schemes;[31] but inevitably the experiment remained one which only a minority was prepared to undertake in the face of hostility from farmers.

Some government support was given to two other plans for encouraging attendance, originating from officials. The first was suggested by Tremenheere, the commissioner for mines. He subscribed to the view that education produced submissive and industrious work-men and consequently was anxious to encourage boys to stay on at school. In 1850, therefore, he persuaded twenty-three firms in south Staffordshire to set up 'The Iron and Coal Masters' Association for the Encouragement of Education . . . in the Mining Districts' which offered substantial money prizes on the results of general examinations of children over the age of eleven, who had attended regularly for two years. In the first year £160 was subscribed for this purpose and the Education Department was invited to co-operate by allowing its in-spectors to act as examiners. This involved Norris who, by writing a series of special reports upon this and other schemes between 1852 and 1856, became the recognised expert on the subject.[32]

Of all the educational innovations of the mid-nineteenth century this was the most widely supported. Prize schemes mushroomed during the next few years. By 1857 eleven had been started in mining districts; many of the Anglican diocesan boards had taken over the idea, as had the Birmingham Educational Association and private individuals like Bernhard Samuelson in the Banbury area. In Norris's district the LNW Railway established a scheme in its schools in Crewe, as did the trustees of the Weaver Navigation in theirs, where canal-boat child-ren were already recognised as creating a special attendance problem. W. J. Kennedy remarked in 1857 on the furore being excited in favour of prize schemes, and the largest claims were made, not only for their moral effects on prizewinners but for their success in raising attendance figures.[33]

In 1855 Tremenheere suggested that the Education Department should subsidise the schemes; but Norris protested heatedly. They were, he said, so popular that there was no difficulty in raising funds. Their value would go if parents once thought that part of the money came from government; employers would no longer be exhibited in a friendly attitude towards their employees; there would be no more of the annual cheers for the masters which rejoiced Norris's heart as much as they surprised industrialists who happened to be present.[34]

Tremenheere's idea was rejected. Norris's remarks suggest that he was already valuing prize schemes for their contribution to social order rather than for their effect upon attendance. The Victorian belief in competition ensured that they would continue to flourish, but as time went on there was less emphasis on their original purpose. They had always had their critics. It was alleged that most of the prizes went, not to the families of miners or ironworkers, but to lower middle-class children who would have stayed at school anyway. In 1858 Edward Akroyd pointed out the inconsistency of offering parents 'the bribe of good wages to take their children from school' and then of subscribing 'for money prizes as a higher bribe to tempt parents to send their children back again to school'. The Newcastle Commission concluded that they had no effect on the bulk of the school population. As Parson Bull said, 'As to the Prize Scheme, what has it to offer to the dead? What to the educationally defunct at between 7 and 13? Secure time for education, and the scheme may succeed.' The weakness of prize schemes, founded to improve attendance, lay in the paradox that if they were to affect the majority of children, attendance must already have been improved.[35]

The second suggestion came from Frederick Watkins, HM Inspector, partly as a result of a proposal by some Bradford schoolmasters that certificates of merit should be issued to children leaving school at thirteen years of age after two years of satisfactory attendance and progress. The idea was accepted officially in 1855 on the grounds that such certificates might help to prolong attendance. The age was to be twelve; the pupil was to have attended the same school for three years, to have reached the standard demanded of stipendiary monitors, to be regular, punctual, clean and well-conducted. The certificates, designed in the Science and Art Department and surmounted by the motto 'Well begun is half done', were to be issued by managers and countersigned by one of Her Majesty's Inspectors, who would 'say a few words of advice and encouragement' to the recipients. Their real value, of course, depended on the co-operation of employers. If, as the rector of St Philip's, Birmingham, pointed out, they were publicly accepted 'as passports to . . . employment', 'a sterling value may be given to these bits of paper which will make all the difference in the world'.[36]

Unfortunately this was what employers in general would not do. Watkins complained in 1858 of the chairman of a railway company who looked at a certificate and said he 'did not understand at all what it was all about'. Certificates continued to be issued but, as one inspector remarked in 1861 when recording that he had signed 293 since 1856, most of the recipients would have stayed without them.[37] They are mentioned fairly frequently in school records, but always in schools of repute, providing for boys prepared to stay until thirteen or fourteen before going on to clerkships. To such a boy a Scholar's Certificate, framed and glazed by his proud parents, was a fitting conclusion to an industrious school career, as in the case of John Harrop of Dukinfield (Cheshire), 'a sharp intelligent and a thinking boy—made the Certificate a subject for a lesson—Character—Formation of being my chief aim. The boy is now engaged in a large iron firm near Manchester.'[38] But there are few instances of a certificate affecting a boy's prospects of employment—certainly not enough to induce a change of heart in parents.

A modification suggested in 1856 by Norris had only temporary and local success in Staffordshire. This was to create a register of children who had been in regular attendance at the same school for two years from the age of nine, with re-registration every six months, which employers would agree to consult when looking for labour. The plan was supported by the Duke of Sutherland and Lord Granville and 1,500 names were registered by 1857. But it depended on the voluntary labour of Norris and two friends. He had hoped to make it official, and forty-five out of the fifty-five registrars of births, deaths and marriages in Staffordshire agreed to undertake the work. He found, however, that their intervention would wreck the scheme, so great was working-class hostility towards them; and little more came of it than Kay-Shuttleworth's resolution at the conference of 1857 that registration, certificate and prize schemes were worthy of more extensive trial.[39]

These plans foundered because most employers were no more convinced of the value of education than were most parents. As an inspector remarked in 1864, attendance would soon improve if employers would give preference to holders of Scholar's Certificates. But for twenty years educationists had been begging them to prefer better-educated children without any permanent success. When the secretary of the Manchester Church Education Society tried to persuade manu-facturers to impose educational conditions, he found that they were on the whole willing to display a notice stating their preference for the literate as long as nobody expected them to act upon it. They argued that when labour was scarce there could be no question of implement-ing it; and (taking a high moral tone) when education was not free it would be unfair to penalise those who could not afford it.[40] Most employers interested in education took the more realistic line of pro-viding for their own workpeople. Some, like Akroyd, supported the demand, growing by the middle fifties, for legislation making some sort of educational certificate compulsory for young workers. This had been suggested by Hook in 1846 for factory children and was raised in several forms at the conference of 1857. It received support from teachers and was embodied in Adderley's bill of 1860.[41] Nothing came of it at the time, except for the ineffective use of the certificate in the Mines Act; but ultimately it bore more fruit than most of the expedients described above, since it became the required qualification for exemption under Sandon's Act.

A study of attendance before 1870 illustrates the dangers of basing an educational system upon voluntary action and enlightened self-interest. The grant system was constructed as if, by financial induce-ments, managers could somehow be forced to make children attend regularly. Because the creation of an educated populace was in the general interest, school promoters assumed that, once this was under-stood, employers and parents would co-operate with them to bring it about. Neither assumption was valid. So the school places which promoters laboriously provided remained unfilled and their efforts to extend education were checked. It has not often been recognised how powerfully the existence of half-empty schools must have acted as a deterrent to the establishment of new ones, thus contributing to the failure of the voluntary system and making the 1870 reconstruction inevitable. Even then the authors of the act tried to avoid responsibility for introducing compulsion and only after Mundella's Act did a solution to the attendance problem become possible.

Crewe College of Education

References

1   PP 1861 [2794–I], xxi, Pt I, 300; *Essays upon Educational Subjects, read at the Educational Conference*, A. Hill (ed) (1857), 234.
2   A. Hill, op cit, v–vii.
3   *Census of Great Britain, 1851. Education, England and Wales, Report and Tables* (1854), xiv, xxii–xxvii.
4   C. J. Hoare, *Educational Statistics and Church Union* (1847), 40–1; Manchester Statistical Society, *Children under 15 in Manchester* (1851), tables 6, 7; PP 1870 (91), liv, 2–13.
5   *Report of the Committee of Council on Education* (CCE) (1869–70), viii.
6   PP 1852–3 (571), xxiv, q 1051.
7   Durham Record Office, EP/Wi 87, Winston, C. E., Attendance Register. The second quarter of 1856 is missing.
8   G. A. Yorke, *The School and the Workshop* (1856), 9; A. Hill, op cit, 71; Borough Library, Derby, MS 8028, Derby British Minutes, 1812–57.
9   National Society, *Report* (1847), 12; British & Foreign School Society (BFS), *Report* (1858), 2.
10 Warwickshire RO, Warwick, CR827/10, Henley Admission Register; Leicestershire RO, Leicester, E/MB/B/219/1, Melton Mowbray Church Free, Minutes & Admission Register.
11 Dorset RO, Dorchester, S20, Walditch Admission Register.
12 Annual tables in CCE.
13 A. Hill, op cit, 15.
14 H. Sandford, *The Education of Children Employed in the Potteries*, Stoke (1862), 6; *Education and Labour*, Birmingham (1865), 5; G. Yorke, op cit, 11; A. Hill, op cit, 71, 74.
15 *Monthly Paper* (1851), 4–5; Northamptonshire Society for promoting the education of the poor, *Report* (1855), 11; PP 1863 [3170], xviii, 185, 255; 1864 [3414], xxii, 203.
16 CCE, 1869–70, 248.
17 H. Chester, *Hints on the Building and Management of Schools* (1860), 6–7.
18 Lancashire RO, Preston, SMI/8/1, Heywood, St James's Infant Log Book (LB), 25 May 1864; Westmorland RO, Kendal, Extracts from Staveley school LB, 9 March 1866; Cheshire RO, Chester, SL/45/3/1, Dukinfield, St Mark's Boys' LB, 16 March 1864; Kent Archives, Maidstone, C/ES23/2/1, Bexleyheath LB, 28 September 1865.
19 CCE, 1847–8, ii, 5; 1848–50, ii, 190; PP 1852 (499), xi, q 654; Lancs RO, SMCo/ 11/2, Colne, Waterside National LB, 2 September 1867; Leics RO, E/LB/219/1, Girls' LB, 29 April 1864.

20   Ches RO, SL120/1/1, Weston LB, 27 March 1865, 18 July 1866; Dorset RO, S55, Stoke Abbott LB, 5 December 1866; Worcestershire RO, Worcester, 506 BA 2890/1(i), Evesham National Boys' LB, 19 January 1865; Durham RO, E/SW 44, Escomb & Witton Park LB, 9 September 1863, etc.

21   A. Ashwell & R. Wilberforce, *Life of Samuel Wilberforce* (1880–2), iii, 67.

22   BFS, *Report* (1853), 2.

23   Kent Archives, P101/25/2, Foots Cray & Chislehurst, Minutes, 9.

24   E. Brotherton, *Popular Education and Political Economy*, Manchester (1864), 19; Derby Library, MS 980, All Saints Infants LB.

25   S. Best, *A Manual of Parochial Institutions* (2nd ed, 1849), 25–7.

26   See T. Bamford, *The Evolution of Rural Education, 1850–1964*, Hull (1965), 21.

27   PP 1856 (61), xlvi; CCE, 1863–4, 115.

28   Escomb & Witton Park LB Report, 1866; Durham RO, E/SW 55, Harwood-in-Teesdale LB, 21 June 1865, 28 September 1865; PP 1861 [2794–II], xxi, Pt II, 397–402; D. Rimmer, *Marshall's of Leeds, 1788–1886*, Cambridge (1960), 105–9, 217; PP 1857 Sess I (38), xiii.

29   CCE, 1848–50, i, 13; 1851–2, ii, 395–8; 1852–3, ii, 461–2.

30   CCE, 1853–4, ii, 516–18; 1855–6, 383–4; 1857–8, 420–3; Public Record Office (PRO), 30/29, Granville Papers, Box 23, Pt I, 19 April 1854; PP 1867–8 [4068], xvii, 147; 1868–9 [4202] xiii, 78; 1861 [2794–V] xxi Pt V, 277.

31   PP 1867–8 [4068] xvii, 148–9; CCE, 1856–7, 437; *Report of an Educational Conference in the Oxford Diocese* (1856), 33; C. Paget, *Results of an Experiment on the Half-time System* (1859); A. Hill, op cit, 250–63, 382.

32   PP 1851 [1406], xxiii, 3–8; CCE, 1852–3, i, 345–52.

33   A. Hill, op cit, 173–93, 230; BFS, *Report* (1860), 43; CCE, 1853–4, i, 415–18.

34   PRO 30/29, Box 19, Pt I, 19 February 1856.

35   *Educational Guardian* (1859), 13–14; E. Akroyd, *On Factory Education, and its Extension*, Leeds (1858), 19; PP 1861 [2794–I], xii, Pt I, 222; [2794–V], xxi, Pt V, 185; 1864 [3414–I], xxii, 162.

36   CCE, 1853–4, ii, 162–3; 1855–6, 27–30; PP 1859, Sess I [2463], xxi, 79; G. Yorke, op cit, 18.

37   CCE, 1858–9, 53–4; 1861–2, 49.

38   Dukinfield, St Mark's Boys' LB, 11 November 1863; *Educational Record* (1854–7), 177.

39   J. P. Norris, *Education in Staffordshire* (1857); A. Hill, op cit, 204–15, 381–2; PRO 30/29, Box 23, Pt I, 21 May 1855, Pt II, 9 April 1856.

40   CCE, 1864–5, 32; C. Richson, *A Sketch of Some of the Causes which, in Manchester, induced the Abandonment of the Voluntary System . . .* (1851), 35–7.

41   E. Akroyd, op cit, 16–17; W. F. Hook, *On the Means of Rendering more Efficient the Education of the People* (1846), 20; A. Hill, op cit, 75, 222, 263, 349; *Papers for the Schoolmaster* (1855–6), 229–31 (Memorial of the Northern Association of Certificated Schoolmasters); M. Seaborne & Sir G. Isham, *A Victorian Schoolmaster*, Northampton (1967), 8.

DAVID ALLSOBROOK

The Reform of the Endowed Schools: the work of the Northamptonshire Educational Society 1854–1874

THE nature of the opposition to the work of the Endowed Schools Commission has been characterised in general terms, but hardly analysed.[1] The indiscretions of Lyttelton and Hobhouse before a meeting of the Social Science Association in 1869,[2] the religious controversies of the time, the Radical content of the Taunton report, the greater political importance of the 1870 Act, Matthew Arnold's picture of middle-class resistance to state intervention,[3] the pressure group of the HMC; all these items have a clear bearing on the problem of the failure of an attempt to make the endowed schools, in a limited sense, part of a national system of education after 1868. But perhaps this complex problem has been over-simplified by treating it almost exclusively at a national level, with some reinforcement in the form of arbitrarily selected and isolated local examples. Wading through a sea of histories of endowed grammar schools, each with its marginal reference to the Schools Inquiry Commission, historians seem to have overlooked the possibility of there being local associations with which the Commissioners may have corresponded constructively.

Such associations did exist. Before the Select Committee in 1873, Douglas Close Richmond, then Secretary to the Commission, on being asked by Thomas Acland for information about correspondence between the Commissioners and district and county committees, replied, 'There is a committee formed in Leicestershire; there is one of which we have lately received information in Northants; there was one . . . in Gloucestershire; there is one, as you may be aware, in Devonshire, and there has been one such association . . . in Yorkshire.'[4] It may seem surprising, in the light of preponderant evidence of opposition, that Richmond also remarked on the generally favourable attitude of such committees to the Commission's work of reform.

The implication of Richmond's answer was that these committees were *ad hoc* bodies, especially since he stated that schools' trustees were represented in the case of Gloucestershire. The Gloucestershire committee was a temporary association. In fact it represented the Cathedral Chapter and the City Council of Gloucester, and prepared a scheme, after the 1869 Act, for dealing with the Cathedral school, the Crypt school and Sir Thomas Rich's Blue Coat school. But, as the official historians of Gloucestershire education have said, 'nothing came of it'.[5] The Devonshire committee was presumably based on the Devon County School Association, established under the guidance of Canon Brereton, Earl Fortescue, and the same Thomas Acland who was questioning Richmond. The association in 1858 had set up a school for the sons of farmers at West Buckland, and this was a model for a number of subsequent experiments with middle-class schools in Yorkshire, Suffolk and Surrey.[6] The Yorkshire committee had been mentioned by Canon Hugh Robinson, later to serve as an Endowed Schools Commissioner, in his evidence to the Taunton Commission in 1865; he had said, replying to Lord Lyttelton, 'in connection with some gentlemen in the county a scheme was drawn up for a county school in Yorkshire which is not carried out now, but is in abeyance'.[7] In Northamptonshire, though the County Committee of 1872 took the form of a temporary co-operation among parties interested in secondary education, it too had its roots in a long-standing organisation whose purpose had been the reform and supervision of the endowed schools over a considerable area extending beyond the boundaries of the county.

At a meeting in Northampton on 28 August 1854, the county branch of the National Society transformed itself into the Northamptonshire Educational Society by adopting the recommendations of a report embodying new rules and aims. The report was presented by the Rev Lord Alwyne Compton, academically the most successful of any noble family until that time, and later to be bishop of Ely. The aim of the committee had been 'To consider the best means of improving and extending education in the diocese [of Peterborough] either by the establishment of training, reformatory or middle schools or other institutions as well as by the appointment of diocesan inspectors.'[8] In considering the future supervision of the agencies of formal education in a large area, the society was reflecting the opinions, during the middle decades of the century, of a number of HM Inspectors, opinions recorded in the minutes of the Committee of Council. At this time some of the Inspectors, such as Sandford, Morrell, Kennedy and Norris,[9] were lacing their comments on the operation of schools in their areas with recommendations for the establishment of a truly national system of education, embracing the concept of education for the lower middle, or upper working classes. Their remarks were surely read with interest by the Anglican members of the Northamptonshire Society.

Compton reported the society's concern for middle-class education in the county, and the heavy charges to which the middle class were liable for schooling, in the absence of efficient provision. However, he was sure 'that the endowed grammar schools and hospitals which exist in many large towns would, if properly managed, serve, in great measure, to supply this want'. The society 'might, in many cases, lend a helping hand in this work'.[10]

As a result of this report, three committees were set up by the newly-constituted society: the first for the education of the poor, the second for industrial schools, and the third to 'promote Education among the Middle Classes'. The first action of the Middle Schools Committee, at its meeting in December 1854, was to ask advice of the headmasters of two of the Woodard schools, at Shoreham and Hurstpierpoint, about the expense of school management.

The task facing the committee was considerable. In the county there were twelve schools in 1854 which could still be called 'grammar' schools, with a handful of others, like Little Harrowden, Pytchley and Burton Latimer, which had given up any attempt to provide education in Latin and Greek and were being conducted as elementary

schools. The Court of Chancery had already been active in modifying
the charters of two schools, at Kettering and Blakesley. The members
of the committee, throughout its existence until 1874, were pre-
ponderantly Anglican clergy, some of whom were trustees of local
schools, with some prominent laymen, like H. P. Markham, the clerk
of the peace.

The committee was confronted, not only by the general disrepair
of local endowed schools, but also by a particularly bitter current
crisis on their own doorstep in Northampton. Earlier in the year, the
headmaster of the grammar school, Charles West, had petitioned the
Court of Chancery about the state of the school and a diminution in
his salary of late years.[11] During this controversy Markham was con-
currently a member of the Middle Schools Committee and of the
Grammar School Committee of the Town Charities, and was therefore the chief intermediary on behalf of the society when they tried to
help the grammar school. The society suggested hiring a house to
accommodate 200 scholars, and recommended that the reformed
school should be subject to a conscience clause and include the teaching of mathematics. Finally a meeting was arranged between the
grammar school trustees and the Middle Schools Committee in February 1856. A scheme was fashioned on this occasion which would
have given the committee peculiar privileges: in return for a donation
of thirty guineas the society would have the right to appoint a life
governor to the board of the new school. The proposal came to nothing,
however, and the business of scheme-making dragged on until 1864,
when the Charity Commission accepted another plan.

The committee had more success in connection with the decayed
school at Guilsborough. A new scheme was before Chancery from
1855 to 1857, and in the latter year, to help the governors out of a
temporary financial difficulty, the committee presented a subscription
of £30 to the school. Compton, on behalf of the society, attended
several meetings of the governors at which plans for a new school
building were approved. The Rev Robert Isham, chairman of the
Guilsborough trustees, and a member of the Middle Schools Committee, had enlisted the assistance of several other members in preparing

the scheme for the school in 1856. (See p 43 for a photograph of the former grammar school at Guilsborough.)

In June 1856 the committee received a petition from the newly appointed governors of Kettering grammar school, for which a scheme had been approved in Chancery in 1854. The governors lacked £300 of the sum required for providing a proper school house. The committee sent £25. (The new building, now replaced, is shown on p 44.) In the same month, the committee received a request from the Fellows of Magdalen College, Oxford, for some suggestions as to the reorganisation of Magdalen College school, Brackley, in the south of the county. The committee replied suggesting that some provision should be made for agricultural and scientific instruction, in addition to classics, mathematics and modern languages. Also, several committee members promised money: the Earl of Ellesmere £50, Earl Spencer £25. The society itself would provide £25 annually and appoint two of its members as inspectors. The Fellows, however, thought the sums promised too small to give the committee the right of inspection and interference, and negotiations were abandoned. The society's liberal inclinations were similarly frustrated in the case of the decayed school at Clipston, near Market Harborough. (This school, which survives as a primary school, is shown on p 43.)

The record of the Middle Schools Committee thus far was hardly one of glittering achievement, but at least it was an attempt to carry out in a systematic and economical way the aims set before the members in 1854. There was now a body keeping, as far as possible, a watching brief over the work of the county's endowed schools. In a more positive sense, the committee served as an encouragement and powerful ally in dealings with agencies of the central government, whose interest in education *per se* was insubstantial: the Charity Commission and Chancery were more concerned to provide for efficient financial administration of schools, than for the suitability of their educational aims and resources.

The main achievement of the committee, however, lay in a field other than that of verbal and financial encouragement. Its members must have been among the first groups interested in secondary education who became seized of the importance of examinations in maintaining high standards of efficiency in endowed schools.

In 1857, Thomas Acland, MP for North Devon, and later a member of the Taunton Commission, had helped to initiate a scheme for holding a voluntary examination at Exeter for boys at grammar and private schools in Devon, Cornwall and Somerset, on the principle that boys should have some common standard against which to measure their progress, and that parents should have some means of comparing schools. Two inspectors, one of them Frederick Temple, another Taunton Commissioner, were seconded by the Committee of Council to assist in the work. Acland and Temple were anxious to develop the scheme on a national scale before the evidence of the first experiment was available. Despite High Anglican opposition, the support of Oxford University was enlisted, and Temple later persuaded Cambridge to join the scheme. A link had been forged between the two great universities and the endowed middle-class schools.[12] The relative success of the examinations was an important presupposition for the discussions of the Taunton Commission.

Already, in June 1856, the Northamptonshire Middle Schools Committee had passed a resolution recommending that the society should institute annual prizes for the grammar schools of the county 'to be adjudicated by some person of the society'. Then, in July 1857, three months after Temple had first begun to enlist the universities' support, the committee resolved that it would gladly co-operate with the universities in the proposed scheme of examinations for the Middle Classes. In December, copies of the examination regulations were sent by the committee to the masters of the various schools in the county. The committee was also keen to make Northampton one of the first centres for the Oxford Examinations.

The response to the committee's enthusiastic preparations was disappointing. Notices had been sent to eleven schools, two of these, Oakham and Uppingham, outside the county; but only one, Kettering, replied. Even here, the master, a Cambridge man, vaguely suggested that his scholars would probably be entered for the examinations of his

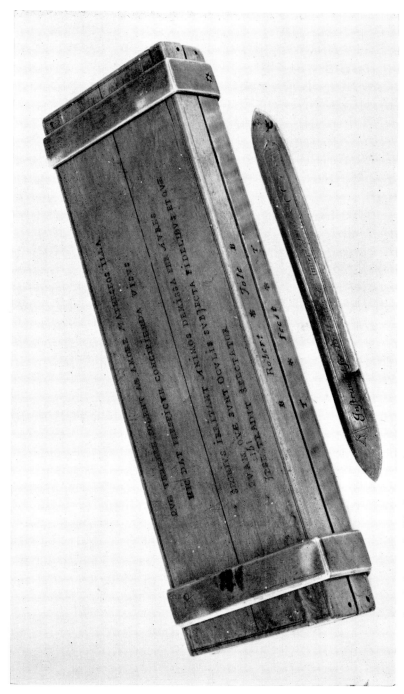

Inscription on the lid of a pre 1671 example of Sir Charles Cotterell's 'Instrument for Arithmeticke', with the maker's name and a brass 'remover' (Crown copyright and by permission of the Director, Royal Scottish Museum, Edinburgh)

See Bryden, 'A Didactic Introduction to Arithmetic', pp 5–18

42

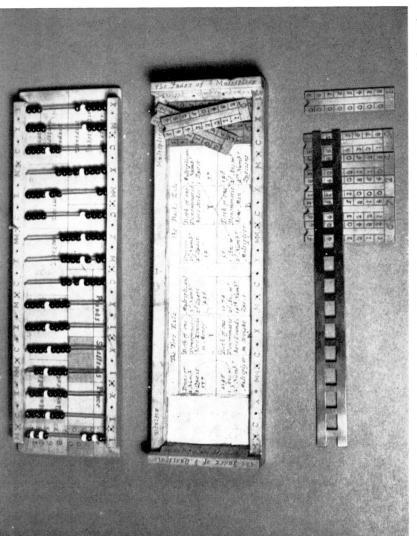

The bead-abacus, tabulet, ladder and 'Napier's bones'. The latter arranged for 7 ×67249, with the result (470743) set on the upper parts of the right-hand wires of the abacus. (Whipple Museum of the History of Science, Cambridge)

See Bryden, 'A Didactic Introduction to Arithmetic', pp 5–18

The former grammar school at Guilsborough, built 1668
(National Monuments Record)

The former grammar school at Clipston, built 1667
See Allsobrook, 'The Reform of the Endowed Schools', pp 35–55

*Kettering Grammar School, rebuilt 1856 and now replaced
(reproduced by permission of the Headmaster)*

See Allsobrook, 'The Reform of the Endowed Schools',
pp 35–55

old university at the more convenient Bedford centre. Nevertheless, the first examinations were held at Northampton in December 1859, the seventeen candidates coming from Guilsborough school and from two private schools in Northampton. No candidates passed with honours, but the committee were sanguine: 'There can be no doubt that their very failure has proved the necessity of this probation of the middle class education of this district and of giving it every stimulus in our power of persevering in this important and discriminating test. It is far better to know our shortcomings than to go groping on in self-satisfied blindness.' The examination was 'the tribunal to which all middle class education will appeal for its character'.[13] The 1861 committee report stated that the examinations 'seem generally overcoming the indifference with which they were at first received', and by 1867 there were 130 candidates from the county, nearly half of them from endowed schools.

It is interesting that, with the exception of Guilsborough, most of the candidates in the first few years were supplied by private and commercial schools. Three of the headmasters of such schools were in fact co-opted on to the Middle Schools Committee in 1866. One of these, William Kingston, who had begun his career as a commercial master at Oundle School under Stansbury,[14] was thanked in the 1859 report 'not only for the interest shown and co-operation afforded (the committee) in the whole organisation of the local arrangements, but also for his great kindness and hospitality in accommodating many of the distant candidates in his own house during the week of the examinations'.

A system of rewards for candidates who gained honours was started in 1864: prizes of £2 for Seniors, £1 for Juniors. It was resolved that, since the Oxford Delegacy had refused to provide ornamental borders for certificates, the society should provide them from its funds. A prize-giving day, presided over by the bishop, became an annual event of the society after 1865.

The question of religion as a subject for examination caused some concern. In a letter to the Rev H. J. Barton, secretary to the committee, in February 1862, Acland admitted that it was a thorny problem. His remarks perhaps reflect some of the difficulties he and Temple encountered at Oxford when proposing to establish the examinations. 'There are a great many obstacles in Oxford to diluting "Rudimenta fidei" into Scriptural religion without the Catechism, and if Rud. fid. means what the Church means, it is difficult to make it count on marks. I admit the system is not working as well as might be wished.' (The remainder of the letter consists of advice to Barton on an agricultural sewage problem.) The committee seem not to have been concerned later when candidates were permitted to opt out of the religious section, though they did recommend that an equivalent section on secular knowledge should be substituted.

The committee also anticipated the Taunton Report on the issue of girls' education. In 1864 they considered the question of 'admitting females to the local examinations' and desired 'to express their approval of that course and their hope that the universities will make arrangements for carrying it into effect'.[15] In the same year they supported Miss Emily Davies's petition on the matter to Cambridge. In 1871 a Ladies' Committee was formed, and the girls' examinations had become established by 1874, with thirteen candidates.

So the county which T. H. Green[16] inspected on behalf of the Taunton Commission in 1865 and 1866 already possessed an embryonic educational administration which, though predominantly Anglican, was generous in outlook, and might be ready to assist considerably in co-ordinating any work of reform which the central government might propose in secondary education. Compton anticipated the findings of the Taunton Commission by making his 1868 report to the society a review of the past thirteen years work. The committee had extended its influence in connection with examinations to twenty-three schools in the area, including schools outside the county at Lutterworth, Leicester, Spalding, Buckingham and Market Harborough.

The first sign of a clear commitment to dealing with the three commissioners appointed under the 1869 Act was shown by the committee at their meeting on 3 December 1870. The Rt Hon George Ward Hunt, MP, took the chair: he had been Chancellor of the Exchequer in the last Derby-Disraeli administration, and was later to be First Lord of the Admiralty in the 1874–80 ministry. Another Tory MP, Albert Pell, was present. The secretary gave a very detailed summary of the Taunton findings relating to Northamptonshire, and took up some of the broader issues raised by the 1867 report, asking finally, 'is it desirable to attempt to create a voluntary "Provincial Authority" with a view to organising, and, in some respects, super-intending, the secondary education of the county?'.[17]

Discussion followed, and it was unanimously agreed 'that the Secretary be instructed to write to the Clerk of the Trustees of each of the Endowed Schools in Northants, asking them to call meetings of the Trustees and to convey to them the invitation of this Committee to send a representative . . . of their several bodies to confer with this Committee on 9th January, 1871, at Noon, respecting the propriety of taking some steps to meet the impending action of HM Commissioners'. Letters were sent to nineteen schools in the county.

Although representatives of only seven schools attended, the sentiment of the subsequent meeting was such that it resolved to petition the High Sheriff to call a County Meeting to consider the operation of the 1869 Act, and, 'if such a meeting see fit, to appoint a Committee to examine into the requirements of the County in respect of Middle Class and Higher Education, and into the meeting of such requirements'. Such county meetings were uncommon. Their history is probably rooted in the medieval grand jury, and they seem to have been convened at moments of national, rather than local, emergency, such as the Northampton meeting for the purpose of military recruitment during the French Revolutionary Wars.

The High Sheriff, Sir Geoffrey Palmer, called the County Meeting for 2 March 1871.[18] It may fairly be called representative of the leading figures in the public life of the county and diocese. Most of the great families were represented, with a large collection of Anglican clergy and a sprinkling of leading businessmen. Palmer explained the purpose of the meeting which, he said, 'had nothing to do with the Act of 1870, which related to the elementary schools'. He hoped he was not expected to say anything on the subject himself, for he was quite ignorant of it.

Dr Magee, Bishop of Peterborough, spoke first. His speech was a

considered defence of the Commissioners' declared intention of modifying endowments where necessary. His chief presupposition, shared
by the six later speakers, was that the Commissioners, when they
visited the county, should not be treated as interlopers, but, on the
contrary, should receive, in the conduct of their essential task, the
benefit of the deep local experience of secondary education and its
administration which existed in the county. He thought that where a
clear religious prescription was attached to an endowment, it should
be respected. But he said that 'the living would be in a state of continual slavery to the departed' if certain due and just modifications
were not made: 'There would be a tyranny of the dead over the needs
of the living.' He 'could not help thinking such co-operation on the
part of those in the county of Northampton who were trustees in the
schools would make the operation of the Act not only better and wiser,
but smoother and happier'. Those who knew the real wants of the
county should deliberate and advise upon the sacrifices which might
have to be made. They should meet the Commissioners and help
them.

H. O. Nethercote spoke, standing in for Lord Henley, one of the
Tory MPs for Northampton. As a trustee of Clipston school, he could
say that it needed 'the waters of the commission to cleanse the Augean
stables of which he had the misfortune to be one of the grooms', and
he hoped that when the stream did come, 'it would come with such a
force that it would carry away himself and his helpmeets'. The Rev
Lord Compton then moved the resolution, 'That the Endowed
Schools Act of 1869 provides the machinery by which the secondary
education in the county may be largely improved and extended.' He
knew the county's schools were inefficient, with the result that those
(presumably, in his eyes, the middle class) who were supposed to
benefit by them sent their children to private schools. Hunt, seconding
Compton's resolution, also argued for assisting the Commissioners:
he thought some people's pride might be hurt in consequence of the
final schemes, but in the long run a greater amount of good might
accrue to the county as a whole.

G. Stopford-Sackville, MP, resolved, 'That a committee be appointed to examine into the requirements of the county in respect of secondary education, and into the means of meeting such requirements.' He too confessed his ignorance of the working of these schools, but suggested as models for their reform those 'in Suffolk and Sussex', presumably the Suffolk county school at Framlingham and the Woodard schools, 'which had been found both useful and efficient'. Pickering Phipps, the brewer, seconding the resolution, said that it was of the greatest importance, now that elementary education had been so much improved, that an equal provision should be made for the classes immediately above the class for whom elementary education was intended.

Finally, the Rev Canon Broughton, Vicar of Wellingborough and a Diocesan Inspector, moved that the suggested committee should include the Lord Lieutenant, the Bishop, Earl Spencer, the Marquis of Exeter, the Duke of Grafton, Hunt, and other worthies. Seconding Broughton's motion, Mr Toller of Kettering said that 'it was very questionable whether endowments were good things or not. It was a question too, in his mind, how far individuals had the right to say how money left by them should be dealt with a thousand years after they were dead, and there could be no doubt that in such cases the Legislature had a perfect right to interfere.' All the resolutions were carried.

This unique county gathering had reached a surprising degree of unanimity. There was agreement on the necessity for revising the terms of endowments, and, if necessary, for transferring or re-applying them; and, most important, for assisting, rather than blocking, the work of the Commissioners. Perhaps most surprising of all, a bishop had declared himself, with one significant qualification, in favour of radical reform of endowments; and a leading member of a Conservative government had warned that it would be necessary to accept the general restructuring of endowments if county education were to prosper.

It should be remarked that the only member of the county's extensive Nonconformist communities who was noted as being present at the meeting was Mr Toller, a prominent Kettering Baptist. Nevertheless,

Green, in 1866, had observed in Wellingborough, a strongly Congregationalist town, the presence of a Nonconformist on the board of school trustees, and the son of a local minister attending the school. The Middle Schools Committee had been generous in their attitude to Dissent since 1854, notably recommending the insertion of a conscience clause in the Northampton charter in 1855. Their plans for assisting in the reform of Clipston school in 1859 had been baulked by the rector who, despite, or perhaps because of, the presence of a large Baptist community in the village, had refused to consider a scheme containing a conscience clause. Perhaps in general the power of Nonconformist opposition has been over-emphasised in relation to middle-class education. Several witnesses before the Taunton Commission in 1865 suggested that, even where conscience clauses operated in Anglican foundations, dissenters did not, in most instances, bother to withdraw their sons from religious instruction. The quality and perhaps the commercial value of the education seems to have counted for more, in certain cases, than religious distinctions.[19]

The three Commissioners summarised the difficulties attending their work in an interim report to the Privy Council in 1872. They concluded, 'Our experience in attempting to work the Act has shown that the country was hardly prepared for its reception.' Any proposal for organic upheaval, like the joining together of endowments, had been met with passionate resistance. They did mention the intelligent encouragement they had already received from county committees in Devonshire, Yorkshire and Gloucestershire, but 'we have not had to wait till suitors come to us for assistance, but to take the initiative in bringing the law to bear on them'.[20] At that point in time, the commissioners had not visited Northamptonshire, and their published comments must have encouraged the Northamptonshire Committee as they prepared their own scheme. Certainly, Northamptonshire was going against the grain of what have been considered the general attitudes to the Commissioners' operations.

The committee's final report,[21] embodying their detailed seven-page scheme, was presented to a meeting at the George Hotel, Northampton, in September 1872. It was sub-titled, 'Recommendations to be submitted to Her Majesty's Endowed Schools Commissioners'. First, they outlined the principles on which they had based their suggestions: 'That existing educational endowments or endowments convertible to educational purposes, ought to be so employed that every portion of the county should have within its reach sufficient efficient Schools of such grades as it required; while at the same time Endowments should, as far as possible, be retained in the localities to which they belong.' And they implied acceptance of the notion of an 'educational ladder', suggested in the Taunton Report, by recommending 'that it should be possible for a scholar to rise through the whole gradation of Schools, from the elementary to the highest grade'.

Their grading of schools followed closely that used by Green in his official survey and by the Commission in its Report. The committee suggested two first-grade schools, at Oundle and Peterborough, the latter serving as a semi-classical school since this 'would probably meet the requirements of such a locality as Peterborough better than a more entirely classical curriculum'. Second-grade schools should be set up in Northampton, Wellingborough, Kettering, Brackley and Guilsborough, and there should be second-grade girls' schools at Northampton and Daventry. In considering Northampton 'it would probably be desirable to create in it more than one school for Boys of this grade, if there did not exist several Private Schools more or less corresponding to this description'. Their experience with Mr Kingston probably led them to trust private adventure schooling more readily than the Taunton Commissioners had been willing to do. They noted that in Northampton there were non-educational endowments of over £5,000. They saw Brackley school, commanding an important position in the south of the county, as a second-grade, semi-classical school, serving large areas of three adjacent counties.

The committee's report also recommended that there should be sufficient numbers of third-grade schools, which should be 'in reach of as many parents as possible, for those who send their children to them can seldom afford to pay boarding fees'. Such schools for boys were recommended for ten towns and villages, including Northampton, Peterborough and Wellingborough, and for girls in three towns.

Entry to these schools for free scholars should be, as Taunton had
suggested, according to merit, 'account being taken of conduct as well
as intellectual attainment', and competition should be confined to the
elementary pupils of the towns. 'There should also be in these third
grade schools a certain number of Exhibitions conferring free or
comparatively free places in second grade schools.' They felt that the
conversion of existing apprenticeship and dole money to the use of
these schools would be far more advantageous to the poor of the
towns than the present application of non-educational endowments.
In the area of Peterborough, they thought that if there was any difficulty over creating a girls' school, a higher department might be
attached to one of the town's elementary schools.

They concluded that 'the schools thus indicated', together with
schools just outside the border of the county, 'would constitute, in
addition to the elementary schools, an Educational System for the
county which would be fairly complete'. They reiterated the idea of
a 'ladder' by suggesting that 'vitality and effectiveness' would be increased by exhibitions existing in every school 'in such proportions
that it would be possible for Boys of ability and good conduct to pass
from the lower to the higher schools'. However, these 'helps' should
be concentrated in the lower parts of the system: the universities
themselves provided many scholarships; 'but, as the grades descend,
it becomes desirable that the Exhibitions should be numerous; for
the number of competitors for them grows larger, and their influence
upon the working of the School becomes more certain; while at the
same time, the cost of them, taken accordingly, diminishes'. The
awards need not always be in money: they might provide free lodging
or free travel to and from school—'indeed, their form could hardly
be too elastic'. They recommended amalgamation of endowments,
similar to those suggested by Green, wherever necessary.[22]

The scheme is most impressive, and was evidently informed by
twenty years' experience of dealing with matters of secondary education. It had been drawn up essentially by long-standing members of
the Middle Schools Committee. It showed, on the one hand, a close
study of the main recommendations of the Taunton Commission and

the way in which these had been reflected or diffused in the 1869 Act and on the other, an intimate knowledge of the financial and educational needs and resources of the county. Just as the county, through the Middle Schools Committee, had anticipated and attempted to meet the need for reform after 1854, so now, in 1873, this newly constituted committee was, in a far-seeing and liberal way, preparing to advance in conjunction with agents of the central government.

The bleak story of the abandonment of the scheme is recorded in a note scribbled by the Rev William Bury, the current secretary, in the minute book of the Middle Schools Committee; the note is undated, and is the last entry: 'Subsequently an enquiry held at Northampton by an Assistant Commissioner with a view to applying the Scheme to Northampton—Representations from Northampton strongly opposed—no further action taken—a reaction against the aims of the Commission set in. Powers under the Endowed Schools Act transferred to the Charity Commissioners—County Scheme fell through.— W.B.'[23]

Compton, presenting the Middle Schools report in April 1876 said, 'the scheme was submitted to the Endowed Schools Commissioners, who expressed their approval of it in most complimentary terms. Since then a change of Government resulted in a change in the character of the Commission, and nothing further has transpired concerning the above-mentioned scheme.'

The abandonment of the scheme marks the beginning of the ossification or decline of a number of the county's schools. The process of decay which the Middle Schools Committee had done something to arrest, continued. Oundle, oblivious of scheme and committee, began to consolidate its development as a separate public school; Wellingborough school developed similar tendencies; Northampton school's uncertain progress continued till it gained some constitutional security under the title 'Northampton and County Modern and Technical School' in 1894. By 1900, Guilsborough had declined to the level of an elementary school.

Just as the concept of a national system of education embracing secondary schools moved from the area of possibility back into the realm of the ideal after 1874, so efforts to co-ordinate and improve secondary education in Northamptonshire proved fruitless with the shelving of the county scheme. Nevertheless, a prosperous county, still predominantly agricultural, mixed in religion, had shown that it might be possible to arrange a coherent system of education over a relatively large area.

The sequence of events which led up to the founding of the County Committee in 1872, and the apparent enthusiasm with which a well-informed group of local educational dignitaries went about the work of scheme-making, raise certain interesting questions about the sub-sequent fate of the three-man Commission. The doom of the Com-mission was, in retrospect, sealed already in 1869; the terms of the act made certain, not only that the Commissioners would be a tem-porary body, but also that they would have only a fraction of the time actually needed for completing their task: Hobhouse and Lyttel-ton had been aware of the impossibility of completing the work even before they began, in 1869.

Also it could be presumed that the nature of the opposition to the Commissioners' work was public knowledge, even before they pre-sented their report in 1872. And it is hardly conceivable that the machinations of Thring and his HMC colleagues would have been unknown to the County Committee by 1872, particularly since, at various times, Uppingham, Oakham and Oundle had come within the Middle Schools Committee's sphere of influence over examinations. Perhaps it may be possible to modify, at a later stage, the accepted picture of a steady build-up of opposition to the Commissioners' work, culminating in the Conservative party's abandoning the Commission in 1874. Certainly, a group comprising Conservative politicians (one of whom held office under Disraeli in 1874) and influential Anglican clergy, seemed unaware that they were involved in a delicate political issue in 1872.

University College, Cardiff

References

1 Two notable exceptions are: (i) F. E. Balls, 'The Endowed Schools Act 1869 and the Development of English Grammar Schools in the Nineteenth Century', *Durham Research Review*, vol V, no 19 (September 1967), 207–16; and vol V, no 20 (April 1968), pp 219–29; and (ii) B. Simon, *Studies in the History of Education, 1780–1870* (1960), 318–36.

2 Quoted in P. H. J. H. Gosden, *The Development of Educational Administration in England and Wales*, Oxford (1966), 68.

3 Matthew Arnold, 'A French Eton', in *Matthew Arnold and the Education of the New Order*, Peter Smith and Geoffrey Summerfield (eds), Cambridge (1969), 31.

4 Select Committee appointed to inquire into the operation of the Endowed Schools Act 1869, (1873), 8–9.

5 A. Platts and G. Hamilton, *Education in Gloucestershire, A Short History*, Gloucestershire County Council (1954), 16.

6 Earl Fortescue, *Public Schools for the Middle Classes* (1864), 7–9.

7 Evidence of Canon H. G. Robinson to the Schools Inquiry Commission, 31 May 1865, SIC Report, vol IV, 621. Robinson had been Principal of York training college until 1863.

8 Printed Report of Special Committee of Northants Educational Society (1854), 10–18, Northants County Record Office, Box 306.

9 Minutes of Committee of Council, 1855–6, 359; 1868–9, 201–2.

10 Loc cit.

11 PRO file ED27/3672; also T. C. Lees, *A Short History of Northampton Grammar School*, Northampton (1947), 53.

12 W. R. Ward, *Victorian Oxford* (1965), 280–2.

13 Annual Report of Middle Schools Committee, 1959, 33–4. Printed copy in Middle School Minutes.

14 W. G. Walker, *A History of Oundle Schools* (1956), 353.

15 Minutes of Middle Schools Committee, 9 January 1864; and Annual Report of Middle Schools Committee, 1874.

16 *Report of Schools Inquiry Commission*, vol XII, South Midlands Division, 1868.

17 Middle Schools Committee, 3 December 1870.

18 Verbatim report of the meeting, taken from *Northampton Mercury*, 9 March 1871, included in Middle Schools Minute Book.

19 See particularly evidence of Sir E. C. Kerrison, for Suffolk County School, *Schools Inquiry Commission Report*, vol IV, 652; and of Rev J. S. Howson, headmaster of Liverpool College, ibid, 291–2.

20 *Report of the Endowed Schools Commissioners to the Lords of Her Majesty's Privy Council on Education* (1872), 37–8.

21 Printed copy of the County Scheme in Middle Schools Committee Minute Book.

22 Green's recommendations for the Towcester-Blakesley area, *Schools Inquiry Commission Report*, vol XII, 316–17; 371–2.

23 The governors of Northampton School were pressing for a new scheme which would have divided the school into upper and lower departments. Details in the *Annual Report* of Northants Educational Society, 1876.

For plates of the endowed school buildings at Clipston, Guilsborough and Kettering, see pp 43–4

ALAN SIMON

Joseph Chamberlain and Free Education in the Election of 1885

I

THE General Election of 1885 was the first to be fought on the new and enlarged franchise introduced by the Third Reform Act, which had effectively almost doubled the electorate. The extended campaign was very largely dominated by the so-called 'Unauthorised Programme' put forward by Joseph Chamberlain, then one of the most prominent figures in the Liberal party. One of the chief items in this programme was the concession of free primary education; and it is with Chamberlain's advocacy of this and the opposition which it aroused that this paper is concerned.[1]

The particular interest of this episode lies in the fact that free education, as Chamberlain defined it in 1885, was considerably more moderate and flexible than has been generally supposed. What Chamberlain tried and failed to do was, in a sense, to take education out of politics. His advocacy of free education was not, as was supposed then and later, inspired by a desire to damage the denominational system. On the contrary, his proposal was an honest and well-intentioned if unrealistic attempt to separate altogether the whole question of free schools from the perennial religious question. As such it failed. But nonetheless his attempt to commit the Liberal party to free education, his definition of it, and the reactions which it aroused constitute an interesting and significant episode in the educational history of the later nineteenth century.

II

With the passing of Sandon's Act in 1876 the education question had entered a relatively quiescent stage. 'I can't find out that there is any stir in the country', Chamberlain noted at the time. 'When this Bill is passed my impression is that the Education fight is over for the next seven years.'[2] But by the time of the run up to the election of 1885 the situation was becoming fluid once more. Among the more militant Nonconformists the ultimate aim of an educational system 'universal, unsectarian, compulsory and free' to be achieved by the 'painless extinction' of the voluntary schools still remained; and the 1870 Act, in that, in their view, it had buttressed the position of the voluntary schools, remained only a temporary compromise. As *The Radical Programme* put it,[3] it was 'a truce and not a peace which was concluded, and the Liberal party expressly reserved its right to reopen the question when a favourable opportunity should offer'. Equally, on the other side of the fence, the denominationalists were becoming increasingly vocal about their dissatisfaction with the working of the 1870 Act which, despite the further concessions made in 1876, was seen as operating against the interests of the voluntary schools. The rapid extension of the school board system was seen as a breach of the Government's initial pledge that the system was intended to 'supplement' the voluntary schools rather than to replace them. These grievances were thrown into sharp relief by the creeping financial crisis which developed from the late 1870s onwards.

The existing agricultural depression had, by 1885, been reinforced by an acute industrial depression, which in turn seriously affected the level of subscriptions to the voluntary schools. By the mid 1880s they were in fact in a very critical position indeed. Costs were rising sharply while subscriptions were tumbling. Thus, while in 1878 subscriptions had averaged 8s 1¼d for each child in average attendance, this had dropped to 7s 3d by 1880 and to 6s 8½d by 1884.[4] With these declining assets they had to face the competition of the board schools with the education rate behind them, enabling them to spend considerably more and to compete more than effectively with the voluntary system. Thus, the amount spent per head in 1885 was as follows:[5]

Church of England schools	£1 – 15 – 10¼
Wesleyan schools	£1 – 16 – 2¼
Roman Catholic schools	£1 – 12 – 7¾

British etc	£1 – 17 – 4
Board schools	£2 – 5 – 4

With these costs, the subscriptions per head received by each denomination in 1885 were as follows:[6]

Church of England schools	7/1¼
Wesleyan schools	2/5½
Roman Catholic schools	6/9¾
British etc	5/7½

The declining financial position revealed by these figures manifested itself also in the declining rate of school building. Thus, while the voluntary schools had taken considerable advantage of the year of grace given to them by the 1870 Act, the rate of school building declined drastically from the later 1870s onwards,[7] while that of the school boards was rapidly increasing. Thus while in 1876 there were only 1,596 board schools to 12,677 voluntary schools, the figures had become 3,692 as opposed to 14,370 by 1881 and, by 1885, 4,295 to to 14,600.[8] In other words in the period between 1881 and 1885 the building of new schools by the school boards had increased at double the rate of that of the voluntary schools. While in 1876 board schools had accounted for just 11·2 per cent of the total, by 1885 they accounted for 22·7 per cent; and, while the total number of board schools had nearly trebled since 1876, the number of voluntary schools had increased by just 15 per cent.

It was against this background of steady and persistent decline that Manning launched his campaign for rate-aid for voluntary schools with an article in the December 1882 number of the *Nineteenth Century*,[9] which demanded in addition a royal commission to examine the working of the Education Act. 'There is danger in delay', he concluded, 'that every year will spread more widely schools without religion and starve out the Christian schools of England. It is now or never.' In 1884 he founded the Voluntary Schools Association in order to campaign for these two demands.[10] Its initial meeting was held in June 1885 when Manning urged resistance to the school boards.[11] Clearly, irrespective of Chamberlain, education was in any event going to become an issue in the forthcoming general election.

III

A few weeks after the appearance of Manning's article Joseph Chamberlain made a speech in Birmingham.[12] Although little noticed at the time, it was of considerable importance in that it demonstrated how far he had moved from his position of the early 1870s, and foreshadowed the much more moderate line which he was to take two years later. The 1870 Act, against which he had contended so bitterly, was described as 'a great measure', which had conferred 'benefits more lasting and more important than those which have followed any other legislation of our time'. Listing the benefits which it had brought in Birmingham, he concluded that the act had achieved:

> . . . neither more nor less than a great revolution affecting all our social prospects and conditions, and in view of such a change as that I confess I am less inclined now to go back upon the defects and omissions of the Act of 1870 than I am to congratulate all who were concerned in that measure, beginning with its author, down to those who took the smallest part in the agitation which made the introduction of the measure possible.

Both in tone and spirit this speech, with its compliment to Forster who had been the subject of his most violent attacks, marked a considerable change in emphasis. In fact for Chamberlain, in education as with disestablishment, effectiveness predominated over doctrinal considerations. His initial objection to the Education Act had stemmed not so much from a doctrinal objection to denominational education as such as from his belief that 'thoroughly satisfactory education can never be secured through the agency of the sects'.[13] Hence, by the mid-1880s, the considerable social progress achieved by Forster's Act largely nullified, so far as he was concerned, his original objections to it. The abolition of school fees appeared the next immediate practical measure. It was in this spirit that he approached the issue of free education in 1885.

Free education as put forward by Chamberlain during his extended electoral campaign was by no means so straightforward a matter as is commonly supposed. What he set out to do when he advocated free education was to divorce the issue altogether from the question of school boards versus denominational schools; to argue, in effect, that free education was an entirely separate matter and that it could be conceded without in any way prejudicing any other question. But, in the circumstances of 1885, such an ambition simply illustrated the triumph of hope over experience. In essence, what he had to do was to convince the denominationalists that his scheme would not in any way affect the security of their schools, while at the same time reassuring his Nonconformist supporters that it would not in any way strengthen the voluntary system. Equally he had to reassure the voters at large that it would be financially painless. In all the circumstances it was something of a tightrope strategy.

The complications were obvious. Recognising them Chamberlain initially took refuge in vagueness. As he put it to Jesse Collings towards the end of September, 'All I want to do is to get the principle of Free Ed[ucatio]n established, and I don't want to dwell on the method.'[14] This was an aspiration rather than a viable policy. However, during the early part of his campaign, he clearly hoped to get through it without antagonising either side. Thus, initially, he failed altogether to make clear whether his proposal of free education applied to the voluntary schools or not, or where the money was to be found. The relevant chapter in *The Radical Programme*[15]—which he 'partly wrote and wholly supervised'[16]—was a masterpiece of imprecision. Extending over forty-three pages it did not at any stage make clear whether the proposal applied equally to both systems (except in so far as its failure to mention the point at all implied that it did), while its discussion of the financial aspects was ambiguous and inconclusive.

With this vagueness it was left to those concerned to draw their own conclusions. Thus the *Tablet*, for the Catholics, had no hesitation in concluding that the proposal applied only to board schools, and therefore carried obvious implications for the voluntary schools which, it concluded, 'must be either instantly and heavily subsidised anew, or else closed. But as it is an avowed part of the Radical programme to destroy the Denominational system, we may presume that they would refuse to sanction the further application of public moneys to what they would describe as sectarian uses.'[17] Chamberlain's major speech at Warrington on 8 September hardly cleared the confusion since it was interpreted by different observers in diametrically opposite ways; although the words themselves were specific enough:[18]

> Now I think there exists some misconception as to the scope and nature of the proposal we make on this point. I see sometimes a statement that it would destroy the denominational schools and put an end to religious education. These are questions of grave importance which, some day or other—perhaps at no distant day—will be discussed on their own merits. But I wish to say, that they are altogether outside and apart from the particular proposal I am making. You might free the schools tomorrow without in the slightest degree affecting the denominational system. . . . At the present time the total of fees receivable in all the schools of England and Wales amount to a little over a million and a half, and I believe an addition to the income-tax of three farthings in the pound, as one method of providing the money, would be sufficient to throw open tomorrow every schoolhouse in the land, leaving all other and collateral questions entirely unprejudiced and untouched.

This was surely clear enough, and the *Tablet* certainly accepted it as such. It was 'a pronouncement which we have long wished to hear from his lips. . . The moment the proposal becomes universal and is extended to cover both systems impartially our special and separate opposition ends.'[19] The *Catholic Times* however was less impressed. For them free education, as Chamberlain expounded it, meant 'the forcible de-Christianising of the future generation by the State, the usurpation by the State of the rights of conscientious parents, and the tyrannous imposition of taxes upon the majority of the people of this kingdom in order to pay for the godless instruction of the children of the minority'; and its readers were exhorted to 'endeavour energetically to defeat every Parliamentary candidate who declares his adhesion to this odious item in the Radical programme'.[20] On the other side of the fence the *School Board Chronicle*, while admitting that Chamberlain's words made clear that his proposal applied equally to both systems, preferred to believe that he had not meant what he said. Such a proposal, it argued, would be 'so huge an advance on the lines of the State endowment of the denominational system that it is not likely to be proposed by the former chief of the Executive Committee of the National Education League . . . Mr. Chamberlain is not the man to propose to put new blood into the denominational system and to raise up fresh barriers against the progress of school boards'.[21] This effectively highlighted Chamberlain's dilemma: to too many people the fact that the champion of the League should be proposing a further substantial subvention to the denominational system without simultaneously insisting on public control appeared inconceivable.[22]

Meanwhile on the question of the cost Chamberlain continued to shift ground. Thus at Glasgow on 15 September and at Inverness three days later he hinted at the eventual use of the revenues of the Church in order to finance the scheme.[23] But since the Glasgow speech also explicitly ruled out disestablishment as a matter for the next parliament the question remained unanswered. Another suggestion came from his close colleague, Sir Charles Dilke, who argued in favour of the concession of a national tax to the local authorities for the purpose.[24] 'You made a capital speech,' Chamberlain told him, 'and . . . I approve every word of it.'[25] Thus, by the early part of October, he had endorsed in rapid succession three separate methods of financing free education. This hardly helped to clarify the situation.

At Bradford on 1 October Chamberlain once again made it crystal clear that he intended his proposal to apply to both systems equally, and to be completely divorced from the wider issue of the voluntary system versus school boards. As he put it:[26]

> The existence of sectarian schools supported by State grants is no doubt a very serious question in itself, and one which some day or another ought to receive consideration. Whenever the time comes for its discussion, I for one shall not hesitate to express my opinion that contributions of Government money, whether great or small, ought in all cases to be accompanied by some form of representative control . . . But this is a question which can be treated by itself. It is independent of that which I have brought before you, and it seems to me that it should not be mixed up or confused with the just claims of the working classes to a free education in all the common schools of the country.

This clear statement, taken together with the Warrington speech, ought to have made the position perfectly clear. However, the *Church Times* took the view that the object was to 'supplant the voluntary schools', while the 'necessary result of [free education] would be to force all children into Board Schools and to shut up almost all others'.[27]

The *Nonconformist* on the other hand regarded the proposal as one for 'concurrent endowment to which many Nonconformists would have grave objections'. The issue of free education was intimately linked with that of disestablishment, and in proposing it on its own Chamberlain was 'putting the cart before the horse'.[28] Much more important however was the attitude of Chamberlain's own National Liberal Federation which, after a debate in the afternoon of 1 October, just before Chamberlain's address in the evening, decisively rejected his scheme.[29] The official resolution, as put forward by Jesse Collings, declared 'That, in the opinion of this meeting, the public elementary schools of this country should be free and placed under the management of duly elected representatives of the people, and that any deficiency caused by the abolition of fees in the schools under the control of the ratepayers should be supplied from the national exchequer.' This, following Chamberlain's policy, placed the question of the freedom of the schools over and above that of taking over the denominational schools. As Collings explained it:

> The principal difficulty was the existence of the denominational schools, but they could not allow this great national work to be retarded for any consideration whatever. When the time came for dealing seriously with the Church they would disestablish the schools at the same time.

But for the National Liberal Federation, born, as it was, of the National Education League, Chamberlain's proposal was unacceptable. Alfred Illingworth, a prominent Nonconformist (and Forster's co-member at Bradford), immediately proposed and carried an amendment which reversed the order of the official resolution, making it read, 'That, in the opinion of this meeting, the public elementary schools of this country should be placed under the management of duly elected representatives of the people, and that they should be made free and that any deficiency should be made good out of the national exchequer.' This effectively pulled the rug from under Chamberlain. It was in fact a clear demonstration that his own creation was not prepared to support him in his attempt to deal with free education as an isolated subject; thus making nonsense of his attempts to reassure the denominationalists. Hence the *Tablet*, which had welcomed the Warrington speech, promptly back-tracked. The resolution, it noted, 'clearly restricts State payment to State schools', while it doubted whether Chamberlain 'could carry his party with him in extending state payment of fees to voluntary schools; and if he did it is pretty certain that such a measure would raise such an agitation in the country as in a very few years to lead to its repeal'.[30]

Clearly as a result of this vote the whole situation remained ambiguous. Chamberlain appeared to be saying one thing, the National Liberal Federation another. Were fees to be remitted in both types of school or in board schools alone? And were the voluntary schools, if they were given a state grant in lieu of fees, to be taken under public management or not? In the immediate aftermath of the Bradford conference speeches from a number of leading Liberals reflected this ambiguity.[31] Hence the situation had to be clarified. On 13 October an exchange of letters between Chamberlain and the dean of Wells was published.[32] The dean's letter raised the two specific questions: was the principle of free education to apply to the voluntary schools, and how was the scheme to be financed? Chamberlain's reply clearly reflected the influence which the Bradford meeting had had on him. He made it clear that the ultimate aim was to finance free education from the revenues of a disestablished and disendowed Church of England, but since 'the delay may be considerable', his view was that:

> ... all schools, voluntary as well as Board Schools, should at once be made free and that to meet the cost an additional grant should be provided from the Consolidated Fund. It would be a matter for consideration whether this grant should take the form of a capitation grant calculated on the average amount of the fees, or of an additional grant for results calculated so as to amount, on the average, to about the same sum now received from the parents.
>
> So far I believe that we shall be in complete agreement, but, as I explained at Bradford, I am personally desirous of going further. I think that the present position of the voluntary schools is anomalous, and that in every case there ought to be some popular representative control of the schools during school hours, leaving the use of the buildings at all times, except those when secular instruction is being given, to the subscribers and voluntary managers.

The last paragraph was clearly a genuflection towards the majority at Bradford. But it still stopped a long way short of the views of most of his followers. As a whole, it was a compromise, and the most ineffective compromise of all. The denominationalists were not conciliated since public control was clearly implied at some future date. Thus the *Church Times* described the proposal as 'a bait which cannot conceal the hook from any but the dullest eye'.[33] Equally the Nonconformists were unappeased. As the *Nonconformist* warned, they would 'hardly at this time of day consent to a scheme which would in effect create a new endowment of religious teaching and give a fresh lease of life to the established Church'.[34] A week later it was even more explicit, describing itself as 'surprised and alarmed' at Chamberlain's proposal to 'promote the abolition of fees all round without making it a condition that the voluntary schools shall be brought under a greater degree of public control . . . the effect must necessarily be to improve the position of the denominational schools'.[35] Quite apart from the Conservative and clerical attacks to which Chamberlain's scheme was subjected, the half-heartedness, if not active hostility towards it, among his own Radical and Nonconformist supporters, was a major factor to be reckoned with.

That there would be opposition from the Nonconformist side was clear from the first; Chamberlain however seems to have underestimated its full extent. 'I am told there will be trouble about free schools', he told Collings at the end of September. 'The Noncon feeling is against further grants.'[36] On his own home ground the *Birmingham Daily Post*, under the editorship of J. T. Bunce, formerly a prominent figure in the League, came out firmly in opposition, arguing that 'if persisted in, such a proposal would split the Liberal party into irreconcilable sections'.[37] When Chamberlain made a strong protest, Bunce reiterated that his proposal would be 'strongly opposed by a large section of the Nonconformists'.[38] Equally Mundella, the former Vice-President of the Council and a very recent convert to the idea, found himself up against the same difficulties. 'It is a fact,' he told Chamberlain, 'that some of my best supporters who are radical on other questions, are not yet convinced about Free Schools and I shall have to put forth all my powers of reasoning and persuasion to satisfy them.' The Nonconformists were 'very uneasy'.[39] Lyulph Stanley epitomised the attitude with which Chamberlain had to contend. 'He

loves "Free Schools" much,' Mundella noted, 'but he hates denominationalism more.'[40] In his own constituency at Sheffield he found
strong opposition on the issue.[41] Schnadhorst made no secret of his
doubts about the policy;[42] and in the immediate aftermath of the
Bradford conference Lord Richard Grosvenor (the chief whip) told
Gladstone that Schnadhorst had 'advised Chamberlain that free
education is *not* a good horse to ride, it is not popular with the noncons
so J.C. will drop it I expect'.[43] Alfred Illingworth, who had led the
opposition at Bradford, took the matter one stage further by writing a
letter to John Bright for transmission to Gladstone. The Federation,
he wrote, had:[44]

> . . . endeavoured by a mild amendment to the 'cut and dried' scheme pre-
> sented to the Conference to give a caution to Chamberlain and Jesse Collings
> as to the mode in which the thing ought to be dealt with. Surely we are not
> called on *just now* to take up & hunt this newly-started hare. . . . Good men
> from all parts are writing to me in great anxiety & I am troubling you to let
> Mr. Gladstone know that there is not & cannot be unanimity among Radicals
> if *free* schools are to be rushed thro' without a scheme of popular control
> over sectarian schools going forward at the same time.

'Chamberlain's path in the matter of Free Education, should he
continue to tread it,' Gladstone noted with some satisfaction, 'is by
no means a smooth one. I think he will pull up.'[45] His own election
address, published in mid-September,[46] had made no secret of his
distaste for the concept of free schools; the section dealing with the
subject was, for Chamberlain, the 'worst passage' of an altogether
unsatisfactory manifesto.[47] When Chamberlain, on 24 October, sent
him a list of the Scottish Liberal candidates who, to his knowledge,
were pledged to free education, claiming at the same time that almost
every Liberal candidate in London was 'pledged to the principle' and
that the same was 'true of the great majority of candidates in agricultural districts', Gladstone's reply was to emphasise the significance
of Illingworth's opposition.[48] 'I entirely accept your view as to the
importance of Illingworth's opposition,' Chamberlain replied. 'It is
not numerically great but it represents the most active section of the
Nonconformists. I hope to be able to modify or even to avert it, but
in any case all I ask for myself in this matter is full permission to

express my own view by vote and speech.'[49] Clearly, in the circumstances of the time, there was no chance of Chamberlain carrying his party with him on the issue of free education, as he had defined it. Still less was there any chance of his convincing his opponents.

IV

As far as the clerical opposition was concerned it was confined almost exclusively to the Catholics. Early in October, in an article in the *Dublin Review*, Manning set out the two questions for parliamentary candidates which he had put forward in his article of December 1882. These were:

1. Will you do your utmost to place voluntary schools on an equal footing with board schools?
2. Will you do your utmost to obtain a Royal Commission to review the present state of education in England and Wales and especially the Act of 1870 and its administration by the School Boards?[50]

This virtually amounted to a 'Catholic manifesto'[51] and with it the Catholic offensive was fairly launched. To see the issue of free education simply as a matter of economics or public policy was, the *Tablet* warned, a 'fool's paradise. . . . The destruction of the Denominational system is the final object, and the freeing of the schools is the chosen means';[52] while the *Catholic Times* denounced 'the aggressive Radical clique, who are doing their best to undermine the basis of society, to banish religion from the land, to usurp the rights of parents in regard to the proper education of their children, and to paganise the rising generation'.[53] Manning himself preached a series of three sermons on the education question,[54] while the *Tablet* had, by the middle of November, sent out 40,000 copies of Manning's article and circularised all the London candidates with his two questions—the replies to which were printed in their last issue before the opening of the polls.[55] Finally, on 2 November, the day of the School Board elections, a manifesto signed by all the Catholic bishops appeared,[56] the language of which was even stronger than that of Manning's article. It claimed that the exclusion of the voluntary schools from participation in the education rate was 'glaring in its inequality and injustice . . . [and] threatens the extinction of the voluntary and Christian schools of the country'. The bishops, it summed up, 'cannot confide in any candidate for a seat in Parliament who will not engage himself to do his utmost to protect liberty of conscience and to redress the present glaring inequalities by providing for the just maintenance of Christian and voluntary schools as the growth of the people shall require'.

The result of the London School Board election was hailed as a triumph by the *Tablet*,[57] while Mundella from Sheffield reported 'a crushing School B[oar]d defeat here. . . . The drum ecclesiastic is at work.'[58] However, the aims of the Catholic hierarchy were fixed higher than the School Board's. Manning's two questions clearly pointed in favour of Catholics voting for Conservative candidates, and several bishops instructed their flocks quite simply to 'vote Conservative'.[59] Thus the Bishop of Salford declared:[60]

> The time is near for a hand to hand struggle with the doctrinaires and the representatives in this country of the principles of the French Revolution. They are bent on establishing State supremacy over education, on making the religion of children a civil disability, on driving Christ out of the school room, and repeating in England the course of despotism which has been adopted in France. Our people need no word of warning as to how they should vote.

Another bishop was similarly emphatic. Commending Manning's questions the Bishop of Northampton declared:[61]

> The proposal is that all Schools, Board and voluntary, should be free and under the management of the school boards and that we, the bishops, priests and people of God's Church should give up all control over the management of our schools, leaving the children of God and of the Church, the children for whom Jesus Christ suffered and died, to be brought up in schools where the name of God and that of His Son are never heard. Here we detect the cloven foot of the enemy of God and man, and therefore we reject the proposal of 'free' education. . . . Let your support, dear children in Jesus Christ, depend upon the answers given.

'To Catholics of course,' the *Catholic Times* proclaimed in its last issue before the opening of the polls, 'the all-absorbing question is that of the safeguarding of our schools against the insidious attacks of the

Radicals . . . Our people need no word of warning. They know to whom they ought to give their votes and for whose success they ought to work.'[62] Although the *Tablet* had wavered briefly early in September the Catholic opposition to free education has been vigorous and consistent. For them, as for the Nonconformists, Chamberlain's plan was equally anathema.

V

Manning's campaign was effectively backed by the Conservatives, who seized on the issue in order to consolidate their denominational support. Thus Lord George Hamilton, a former Vice-President of the Council, announced that 'the real object is not free schools, but the destruction of voluntary and religious schools', which, he argued, would cost £6 millions[63] (the next day he increased his estimate to £7 millions, before settling for the even more alarming 'several millions').[64] For Edward Stanhope it would 'put an end to the voluntary schools and largely increase the rates'.[65] W. H. Smith aired another fear: 'Free Education is merely the thin end of the wedge, and with the extinction of the voluntary schools will come purely secular teaching and all religion will be banished from our schools.'[66] 'The Conservatives,' Cross insisted, 'are determined to maintain the voluntary schools and to help them as far as they can.'[67] Salisbury privately gave evidence of this. 'The Education Act of 1870,' he told Manning on 6 November, 'was a clumsy compromise, intended rather to give time for the enemies of religious education to gather their strength than to effect any just and permanent settlement of the question. I earnestly hope that it will be possible to review the arrangement in a sense favourable to religious teaching.'[68] Shortly afterwards Cross announced the Government's decision to set up the Royal Commission for which Manning had asked;[69] a decision welcomed by Manning 'with the greatest joy and hope'.[70] One, at any rate, of his two demands had been conceded.

The line of opposition to Chamberlain's proposal from the Conservative party had paralleled that of Manning and the Catholics.

But the hostility with which free education had been received by Non-conformists, Catholics and Conservatives was not, however, counter-balanced by any great enthusiasm among the more secular Liberals. Here, Chamberlain's most important conversion was that of A. J. Mundella, who had been Vice-President of the Council from 1880 to 1885; a conversion, however, which appears to have owed as much to political as to educational considerations. 'I have had Mundella down here,' Chamberlain wrote to Dilke from Birmingham on 10 October. 'He is all right & will go strongly for Free Schools.' But, he added, 'The "distinguished convert" has his price which he asks with really touching naivete. He must be in the Cabinet next time. I told him he would be "if he was a good boy".'[71] Mundella certainly did his best to earn his place, proselytising hard and bombarding Chamber-lain with letters. On 21 October he devoted a long and closely argued speech to the subject which, however, to Chamberlain's indignation, was very badly reported.[72] None the less, the support of an ack-nowledged educational expert was of some importance.[73]

However, generally speaking, so far from being regarded as a major rallying cry, the proposal of free education tended to be seen largely as a minor question of administration. Thus *The Times*, which was almost unwaveringly hostile to Chamberlain at this time, regarded it as 'the least objectionable of Mr. Chamberlain's proposals', and as 'mainly a question of expediency, convenience and expense'.[74] Among Liberals only Goschen and Leonard Courtney took a high doctrinal line on the subject,[75] while the remainder of Chamberlain's former cabinet colleagues were not prepared to man the barricades against it. Among the electorate as a whole two other considerations would appear to have counted. Chamberlain himself had summed up the first of them some twelve years earlier when he told Morley, 'Education for the ignorant cannot have the meaning that belonged to bread for the starving.'[76] The issue of school pence could simply not be elevated to a high moral principle; and particularly not when, on top of all the other difficulties it raised, was the question of finance. For Mundella in particular the fear of a reaction against education brought about by an increase in the rates had always been a serious fear.[77] Hence

Chamberlain's repeated concern to reiterate that the cost would fall on the exchequer rather than the rates.[78] However, in the circumstances of 1885 the cost of such a scheme represented a powerful argument against it. As the *Pall Mall Gazette* put it, 'People are hard-up just now. Business is depressed, and an endless vista of new rates and taxes to enrich the Have-Nots at the expense of the Haves is not exactly calculated to arouse a keen enthusiasm among the householders for the Radical leader.'[79] However estimates of the cost might vary, the fact remained that Chamberlain's proposal involved the expenditure of a substantial amount of public money at a time when the bulk of the voters were suffering the effects of an acute economic depression. This must surely have been not the least of the factors which made it electorally unpopular.

Thus, altogether those who championed free education in the constituencies found themselves at a disadvantage. Dilke, fighting an uphill battle in Chelsea, warned Chamberlain that the idea was 'unpopular'; by the end of his campaign he was conceding that free education was not 'a matter which is likely to be carried out in the next few years'.[80] Similarly Mundella, who had campaigned in his own constituency in Sheffield and a wide area around, found it 'a decided hindrance'.[81] It is clear from a study of Chamberlain's own speeches during the last six weeks of the campaign that he too recognised that free education had become an electoral liability. The last occasion on which he dealt with it at any sort of length was in a speech of 14 October.[82] Thereafter in only one of the remaining ten speeches he made did it receive more than cursory attention. At Evesham on 16 November[83] he reiterated once again that 'free education may be created tomorrow and neither the existence nor the position of the voluntary schools would be affected in the slightest degree'. But it was hardly likely by that time that the clerics would be convinced or the Nonconformists converted.

As the borough defeats poured in, Chamberlain recognised that free education had proved a failure. 'I put my money on free schools', he told Labouchere, 'but judging by London the electors do not care much about it.'[84] To Harcourt he was even more despondent, 'The boroughs do not care for our present programme and I confess I do not know what substitute to offer them.'[85] One (unidentified) former Liberal MP, who had supported free education against the advice of his local party and had gone down to defeat, wryly summed up:[86]

> The working men said 'We have to pay for educating our own children. Why should we pay for educating other people's?'. The Nonconformists vowed they would not free the schools if it involved the voting of another penny of public money to denominational institutions, and the Churchmen . . . would have none of it.

VI

Free education therefore proved an electoral failure. There were too many disparate interests to be placated, and it was impossible to placate them all simultaneously. Two main points emerge from this episode. First, it illustrates a certain degree of naïvete. Thus Chamberlain appears initially to have assumed that he could get through an election campaign dealing with the highly loaded issue of education, primarily by issuing ringing declarations in favour of free schools and avoiding having to 'dwell on the method'.[87] But the matter was far too complex for that. What he failed to realise was that, for the denominationalists, his past would always make him suspect; while his assumption that he could carry the National Liberal Federation—the product of militant Nonconformity—with him on a policy of providing further subsidies for the denominational schools without, at the very least, setting a firm date for their takeover, was, to put it no higher, excessively optimistic—and, in the event, decisively disproved. But, secondly, what is even more important is the fact that he should have made such a proposal at all, running, as it did, directly counter to the most fundamental tenet of Nonconformity.

In the first place it should be noted that his proposal in 1885 was rather less clear cut than he subsequently made out. Thus he told Harcourt in 1890 that he had believed 'for years' that 'the possession of the field by the denominational system, largely extended as it was by Forster's legislation, made it practically impossible to demand the abolition of the Voluntary Schools & that our policy as Educationalists was to treat Free Education as a separate matter which might be conceded without affecting the relative position of Board & Denominational Schools'.[88] Similarly, when Salisbury's government introduced free education the following year, he claimed, 'That is the proposal which I made in 1885, and that is the proposal which the Government make now.'[89] However, while technically quite correct, this cannot be regarded as altogether true. In the proposal put forward by the Unionist government there was no question whatever of an eventual takeover of the voluntary system by the school boards; indeed a large part of the explanation of the Conservative party's abandonment of some cherished prejudices in making the proposal was precisely to avoid such a contingency, whereas in 1885 it had been clearly implied. This was a vital distinction. Thus, while arguing that the question of free education should be utterly divorced from that of the denominational schools, Chamberlain had clearly and explicitly reserved his position on the latter. Ultimately he was, in fact, quite prepared to accept the full logic of the Nonconformist position. As he told Harcourt in the immediate aftermath of the Bradford conference, 'The Non. Cons. want to accompany [free education] with representative control of all schools during school hours. I agree with them and probably the next Parl[iamen]t will be ripe for this.'[90] This is, in fact, clear evidence that he was still some way from having achieved that philosophic acceptance of the permanence of the denominational system at which he had arrived by 1890.

Other evidence also points in the same direction. Thus at the end of September 1885 he told Collings, apropos of the Nonconformist revolt:[91]

> The Noncon feeling is against further grants. But they are wrong for if an average grant were made the Denominational schools would suffer as their fees are higher than the average. . . . I should like to give something like 2d per head to all children in average attendance where the schools are made free. This would leave the denominationalists with increased subscriptions to find.

Without attaching too much importance to a single letter it is worth looking more closely at what this suggestion entailed. In 1891 3d per head per week was allowed on the calculation that it would cost

10s a year. Thus, on those figures, Chamberlain's proposed 2d a week would have meant allowing 6s 8d only—while, of course, simultaneously prohibiting the charging of further fees. This would, as he recognised, have had a very serious effect, as the following figures listing the average fee charged per head in each category of denominational schools in 1885 clearly demonstrates:[92]

Church of England schools	10/8
Roman Catholic schools	9/5½
Wesleyan schools	16/1
British etc	13/7¾

Hence, clearly, had they been allowed only 6s 8d per head in lieu of fees, the denominational schools would have had to make up a fairly substantial difference from voluntary subscriptions—and, moreover, to do this at a time when their subscriptions had been declining steadily over a period of years. Free education on that financial basis would, in effect, have amounted to imposing a further considerable levy on the voluntary system, with obvious implications for its survival.

However, even allowing for his commitment to the principle of eventual popular control, Chamberlain's proposal in 1885 was a pretty remarkable one. The key here lies in a phrase in his letter to Harcourt quoted above: '. . . our policy *as Educationalists* was to treat Free Education as a separate matter'. Chamberlain, in fact, approached the issue of free education purely in terms of its educational merits. The abolition of fees was good in itself; hence it should be carried through without being confused with or in any way prejudiced by the wider issue. This proposal marked a logical development from his speech (already quoted) at the beginning of 1883, in which, to all intents and purposes, he had largely repudiated the attacks he had made on Forster and the 1870 Act on the grounds of its subsequent effectiveness as an educational measure. What mattered was the effectiveness and availability of education; doctrinal considerations came a poor second. But in the circumstances of 1885 simply to ignore, as he did, the doctrinal considerations involved was an impossible line to take; and one on which he could not carry even his own section of the

Liberal party. Lyulph Stanley's attitude, as described by Mundella, was that of virtually all of them—'he loves "Free Schools" much but he hates denominationalism more'.[93] In one sense Chamberlain's proposal was solid pragmatism; in another, given the limits of the possible, it was idealism of the purest kind.

One final question remains to be dealt with: how far can it be said that Chamberlain's campaign for free education in 1885 helped towards its adoption six years later? Certainly his campaign helped to make the question an important political issue, but it would seem clear that, in the short term, its principal effect was to emphasise the difficulties which it raised. Immediately after the election, the Conservatives redeemed their commitment and set up the Cross Commission. Heavily weighted with denominationalists the majority report came down decisively against free schools.[94] However, the authors of the minority report, who included Lyulph Stanley and R. W. Dale, equally refused to support free education on the ground that 'no scheme consistent with the maintenance of the voluntary schools has been presented to us'.[95] Only one member of the commission—Sidney Buxton—was found to advocate the scheme which Chamberlain had put forward in 1885.[96] The decision of the Conservative government in 1891 to propose the measure would appear on balance to have been less a genuflection towards Chamberlain than a move to save the voluntary schools from an incoming Liberal government. As Salisbury made clear in the autumn of 1890 the principal reason for the government's change of attitude was to prevent a future Liberal government from attempting to destroy the voluntary schools by carrying free education for the board schools only.[97] It represented, in effect, a recognition of the fact that the Liberal party after 1886 had adopted the full logic of the Nonconformist position and that they were now insisting, as Chamberlain had not done, that free education must be accompanied immediately by popular control. For if Chamberlain's campaign had demonstrated one fact beyond any doubt it was that there was no possible via media where the question of education was concerned; and that it could not, however well intentioned such an aim might be, be separated from the religious issue. Since the majority of clergy were against the Liberal party in any event it followed logically that, on education, they should have the wholehearted support of the Nonconformists. Hence, from the mid 1880s the polarisation of the two parties on the education question began, the Liberals taking their stand firmly on the Nonconformist position. This was a new departure. Hitherto, whatever the views of the Nonconformists, the Liberal leadership as a whole had been as tender to the voluntary system as the Conservatives. Now all that was changed.

References

1   The principal MS source for this article is the Joseph Chamberlain Papers in the possession of the Birmingham University Library. I am grateful to the librarian for permission to quote from them.
2   Chamberlain to Morley, 11 July 1876, JCP5/54/112.
3   *The Radical Programme with a preface by the Rt. Hon. Joseph Chamberlain, M.P.* (1885), 213. This was a reprint of a series of articles which had been appearing in the *Fortnightly Review* since the summer of 1883, setting out the Radical viewpoint over the whole field of domestic policy. The article on education was by John Morley.
4   Cross Commission Report, 1.537.
5   Ibid, 1.530.
6   Ibid, 1.519.
7   The figures are as follows: (ibid, 1.537)
       1878   506   1882   51
       1879   416   1883   70
       1880   154   1884   89
       1881   189
8   Ibid, 1.521.
9   Cardinal Manning, 'Is the Education Act of 1870 a just law?', *Nineteenth Century*, xii (December 1882), 958–68.
10 V. A. McClelland, *Cardinal Manning; His Public Life and Influence 1865–1892*, Oxford (1962), 83.
11 *The Times*, 25 June 1885, 4f.
12 *Birmingham Daily Post*, 16 January 1883. (Press cutting in JCP4/3.)
13 Chamberlain to Morley, 14 August 1873, JCP5/54/10.
14 Chamberlain to Collings, 27 September 1885, JCP5/16/108.
15 *The Radical Programme*, 213–56.
16 Chamberlain to R. W. Dale, 29 April 1891, Peter Fraser, *Joseph Chamberlain: Radicalism and Empire* (1966), 144.
17 *The Tablet*, 15 August 1885, 242–3.
18 *Speeches of the Rt. Hon. Joseph Chamberlain*, Henry Lucy (ed) (1885), 190.
19 *The Tablet*, 12 September 1885, 401–2.
20 *Catholic Times*, 11 September 1885, 5c.

21 *School Board Chronicle*, 12 September 1885, 256–7.
22 It has also appeared inconceivable to a number of later historians. Thus M. Cruickshank, *Church and State in English Education* (1963), 56, states that the proposal applied to board schools only, while C. H. D. Howard, 'Joseph Chamberlain and the "Unauthorized Programme" ', *Eng Hist Rev*, lxv (1950), 477–91, writes that Chamberlain's proposal was 'taken to mean that fees should be abolished in the board schools only'. See also McClelland, *Manning*, 82.
23 Lucy, 204, 215–16.
24 *The Times*, 7 October 1885, 10a–e.
25 Chamberlain to Dilke, 7 October 1885, S Gwynn and G. Tuckwell, *The Life of Sir Charles Dilke* (1917), ii, 190.
26 Lucy, 234–5.
27 *Church Times*, 2 October 1885, 733–4.
28 *Nonconformist*, 1, 8 October 1885, 938, 952.
29 *The Times*, 2 October 1885, 7a.
30 *The Tablet*, 10 October 1885, 560.
31 *The Times*, 6 October 1885, 6c–e; 8 October 1885, 6a–e; 12 October 1885, 8a–d; 13 October 1885, 12a–c.
32 Ibid, 13 October 1885, 4a–b.
33 *Church Times*, 23 October 1885, 803.
34 *Nonconformist*, 15 October 1885, 997.
35 Ibid, 22 October 1885, 1020–1.
36 Chamberlain to Collings, 27 September 1885, JCP5/16/108.
37 *Birmingham Daily Post*, 25 September 1885, 4b–c; 29 September 1885, 4b–d.
38 Chamberlain to Bunce, 30 September 1885, JCP5/8/79i; Bunce to Chamberlain, 3 October 1885, JCP5/8/79ii.
39 Mundella to Chamberlain, 11 October 1885, JCP5/55/8.
40 Mundella to Chamberlain, 13 October 1885, JCP5/55/9.
41 Mundella to Chamberlain, 15, 28 October 1885, JCP5/55/10, 11.
42 Harcourt to Chamberlain, 30 September 1885, JCP5/38/34.
43 Grosvenor to Gladstone, 6 October 1885, British Museum (Gladstone Papers), Add MSS 44316, f43.
44 Illingworth to Bright, 21 October 1885, GP Add MSS 44113, ff221–2.
45 Gladstone to Granville, 24 October 1885, *The Political Correspondence of Mr. Gladstone and Earl Granville, 1876–1886*, A. Ramm (ed), Oxford (1962), ii, 412.
46 *The Times*, 19 September 1885, 8a–d.
47 Chamberlain to Collings, 20 September 1885, JCP5/16/107.
48 Chamberlain to Gladstone, 24 October 1885, GP Add MSS 44126, ff112–13; Gladstone to Chamberlain, 25 October 1885, *Joseph Chamberlain, A Political Memoirs*, C. H. D. Howard (ed) (1953), 131–2.
49 Chamberlain to Gladstone, 26 October 1885, ibid, 132–3.
50 McClelland, *Manning*, 84.
51 *Pall Mall Gazette*, 10 October 1885, 3.
52 *The Tablet*, 17 October 1885, 601–2.
53 *Catholic Times*, 6 November 1885, 4.
54 Ibid, 16, 23, 30 October, 3.
55 *The Tablet*, 7 November 1885, 721; 21 November 1885, 819–20.
56 *The Times*, 2 November 1885, 9f.
57 *The Tablet*, 7 November 1885, 749–50.
58 Mundella to Chamberlain, 8 November 1885, JCP5/55/12.

59   *The Tablet*, 17 October 1885, 598; 14 November 1885, 769; 21 November 1885, 806; 28 November 1885, 871–3.
60   Ibid, 21 November 1885, 832–3.
61   Ibid, 21 November 1885, 832–3.
62   *Catholic Times*, 20 November 1885, 5d–e.
63   *The Times*, 2 October 1885, 8c–d.
64   Ibid, 3 October 1885, 7b–c; 24 October 1885, 6e.
65   *The Times*, 13 October 1885, 7e–f.
66   Ibid, 14 October 1885, 6a–c.
67   Ibid, 9 October 1885, 6f.
68   Quoted in C. H. D. Howard, 'Manning and Education', in *Manning; Anglican and Catholic*, J. Fitzsimons (ed) (1951), 104.
69   McClelland, *Manning*, 85.
70   Manning to Cross, 13 November 1885, British Museum (Cross Papers), Add MSS 51274 unf.
71   Chamberlain to Dilke, 10 October (1885), British Museum (Dilke Papers), Add MSS 43886, ff232–3 (misplaced).
72   *Sheffield Independent*, 22 October 1885, 2a–g. W. H. G. Armytage, *A. J. Mundella, 1825–1897* (1951), 230. *The Times*, 22 October 1885, 10f. Chamberlain to Mundella, 23 October 1885, Armytage, 231.
73   See speeches by Sir Henry James (*The Times*, 15 October 1885, 7a–c), and Harcourt (ibid, 24 October 1885, 10a–d).
74   Ibid, 18 September 1885, 9b; 13 October 1885, 9d.
75   Ibid, 8 October 1885, 6a–e; 6 October 1885, 6c–e; 6 November 1885, 13f–14a.
76   Chamberlain to Morley, 19 August 1873, Garvin i, 146.
77   Armytage, *Mundella*, 231; Mundella to Chamberlain, 4 October 1885, JCP5/55/7.
78   Lucy, 216; *The Times*, 7 October 1885, 10b–f; 17 November 1885, 10a–c.
79   *Pall Mall Gazette*, 7 November 1885, 1.
80   Dilke to Chamberlain, 19 November 1885, JCP5/24/145; *The Times*, 19 November 1885, 11a.
81   Mundella to Gladstone, 15 December 1885, GP Add MSS 44258, ff211–14.
82   Lucy, 243–5.
83   *The Times*, 17 November 1885, 10a–c.
84   Chamberlain to Labouchere, 4 December 1885, A. L. Thorold, *The Life of Henry Labouchere* (1913), 246.
85   Chamberlain to Harcourt, 6 December 1885, JCP5/38/146.
86   *Pall Mall Gazette*, 8 December 1885, 2.
87   Chamberlain to Collings, 27 September 1885, JCP5/16/108.
88   Chamberlain to Harcourt, 26 February 1890, JCP5/38/197a.
89   Hansard, 3rd ser, ccliv, cc 1759–60.
90   Chamberlain to Harcourt, 5 October 1885, JCP5/38/144.
91   Chamberlain to Collings, 27 September 1885, JCP5/16/108.
92   Cross Commission 1.519.
93   Mundella to Chamberlain, 13 October 1885, JCP5/55/9.
94   Cross Commission Final Report, IV, 198–200.
95   Ibid, IV, 249–50.
96   Ibid, IV, 250.
97   *Annual Register, 1890*, 82.

SOL COHEN

New Perspectives in the History of American Education 1960–1970

My education owed a great deal both to their teaching and to their work. ... both have not only taught us that the historian's first duty is to be sincere; they fully appreciated that the very progress of our studies is founded upon the inevitable opposition between generations of scholars. Therefore, I shall be keeping faith with their teaching in criticizing them most freely wherever I may deem it useful; just as I hope, some day, that my pupils will criticize me in their turn.[1]

History is subject to generational changes; our perspectives and our understanding of the past tend to shift as successive generations of historians come to maturity. The changing circumstances of society alter the formative experiences of historians, whose subsequent work often reflects their changing assumptions and values. The particular question asked, the particular types of research undertaken, the particular forms of evidence used, also have much to do with ways in which approaches to the past are transformed.[2]

SINCE it was introduced as a specialty in American teacher-training institutions more than three-quarters of a century ago, the history of American education has had a promising future and a disappointing present. This is not to say there is not a voluminous literature on the subject. There is. Unfortunately, too much of it, at least as conceived by American historians, is parochial, anachronistic, and out of touch with main currents of contemporary scholarship. This was the gist of three important essays which broke new ground in the late fifties and early sixties; the Fund for the Advancement of Education's *The Role of Education in American History*; Bernard Bailyn's *Education in the Forming of American Society*; and Lawrence Cremin's *The Wonderful World of Ellwood Patterson Cubberley: An Essay in the Historiography of American Education*.[3] These three publications help to construct a platform from which we may survey this past decade.

In 1953 the Ford Foundation's Fund for the Advancement of

Education, never before interested in the subject, appointed a pres-
tigious committee of historians to study the historiography of American
Education. Their call for action came out four years later. The
committee was unanimous in its contention that relative to its importance in the development of the nation, the history of education in
America has been shamefully neglected by American historians. The
consequences of this neglect have been serious, affecting adversely the
planning of curricula, the formulation of policy, and the administration of educational agencies in the continuing crisis of American education.[4] The committee urged historians to devote themselves to close
monographic study of the role of education, formal and informal, in
American history, and called for a new history of American education
which would break from particularised and institutional history, and
which would concern itself with the broader subject of the impact of
education upon society. The committee recommended that historians
'approach education saying: here is a constellation of institutions . . .
What difference have they made in the life of the society around
them?' The committee urged historians to investigate the influence of
education upon such matters as economic development, the building
of new communities on the frontier, social mobility, assimilation of
immigrants, and the development of political values and institutions.[5]

In his seminal essay, the first fruit of the Fund's call, Professor
Bailyn brought together two papers; the first a lengthy critique of
American educational historiography; the second, a provocative revisionist interpretation of colonial educational history. At a time of
deep public concern over the schools, Bailyn charged, 'the role of
education in American history is obscure. We have almost no historical
leverage on the problems of American education.'[6] Why? Because men
like Ellwood Cubberley who have taught the history of education—
and written the textbooks—viewed the subject not as an aspect of
American history writ large, but rather as a device for communicating
an appropriate ideology to a newly self-conscious profession. As a
consequence, the history of American education suffers not from
neglect but from distortion. As a corrective to this myopic point of
view Bailyn urged, in a widely quoted dictum, that historians think

of education 'not only as formal pedagogy but as the entire process by which a culture transmits itself across the generations'.[7] Bailyn subsequently sketched a history of education in the colonial and Revolutionary periods which took into account changes in the family, religious life, the apprenticeship system, race relations, and economic development, as crucial determinants of the transmission of culture from generation to generation.

Lawrence Cremin continued the historiographical dialogue in his essay on Cubberley. Like a number of other early American educational historians, Cubberley had little professional training in history. His major area of training (and expertise) was not history but school administration. But he worked within a fairly well-formulated tradition. As a former public school superintendent, Cubberley found especially congenial the accounts of schools and schoolmen written by pioneer school administrators like Henry Barnard, James Wickersham, George Martin and the Rev A. D. Mayo, for whom educational history was the history of the public school realising itself over time: 'the moral of educational history is the common school triumphant, and with it, the republic'.[8] Activists all, they believed that a recital of past victories would unite and inspire a new profession. Cubberley stayed in this tradition with his extremely influential *Public Education in the United States* (1919). While acknowledging Cubberley's astounding industry, and his service to the profession, Cremin concludes that Cubberley's historiography had helped to produce a generation of American schoolmen unable to comprehend—much less contend with —the great educational controversies which beset America in the decades following World War II.

In his assessment of Cubberley's work, Cremin takes issue with Bailyn on one important point. Cubberley was not so much in isolation from the mainstream of American historiography as Bailyn maintained. Which is to say, while early twentieth-century studies of the history of American education lacked brilliance, the general study of American history also tended to suffer from similar problems and inadequacies. (And, vice-versa, some educationalists like Paul Monroe could, on occasion, write exemplary history.)[9] Still, Cremin agrees

with Bailyn that Cubberley committed many sins against Clio: the
sin of anachronism, by looking for the seeds of the public school in
the colonial period; the sin of parochialism, by confusing education
with schooling, hence writing a narrow history of the institutional
evolution of the schools; and the sin of evangelism, by seeking to inspire
teachers with professional zeal, rather than attempting to understand
what really happened. Cremin closed his essay with encouragement
for efforts which attempted to assimilate the history of American
education to the model provided by social and cultural history. His
Bancroft Prize-winning *The Transformation of the School: Progressivism
in American Education, 1876–1957* (1961), exemplified just such a
history (as does his most recent *American Education: The Colonial
Experience, 1607–1783*).[10]

The past decade has witnessed a surge of writing in the history of
American education; broadly conceived, closely allied with the fields
of social and intellectual history, imaginative and mature in its use of
the tools and apparatus of historical scholarship. Bailyn's *Education in
the Forming of American Society*, and Cremin's *The Transformation of
the School* provided the inspiration. Bailyn and Cremin have, in the
past decade, been followed or accompanied by many others. The new
historians of education, whether on school of education faculties or
history faculties, have eschewed writing about the public school as if
it were unequivocally progressive and historically inevitable. Their
writing has sought not to instill professional pride, but rather to
analyse institutional adaptation to social change, and to emphasise the
relation of pedagogical ideas and practices to social, economic, and
political contexts. Berenice Fisher's history of industrial education,
Michael Katz's reinterpretation of the common school movement,
Ruth Elson's analysis of nineteenth-century American schoolbooks,
Rush Welter's depiction of the relation between education and political
thought, Edward Krug's history of the high school, the work of
Frederick Rudolph and Laurence Veysey in the history of higher
education, Claude Bower's history of progressive education during the
Depression, and Maxine Greene's Parringtonian analysis of the schools
from the angle of vision of creative writers, come to mind.[11] And

recently some of the discipline's more venturesome practitioners have demonstrated how methods and insights borrowed from the social sciences can provide significant new approaches to their enterprise. Teaford uses demographic tools in a sophisticated way to analyse change in Puritan education.[12] In the hands of Fishlow, educational history becomes economic history; in Bidwell's hands it almost becomes sociology.[13] Tyack and Katz borrow concepts from political science as well as sociology in their studies of educational bureaucracy and school centralisation.[14]

There are three, or at least three, legitimate conditions for re-interpretation in history: one, the discovery of new source materials; two, the impact of new theories, new methods, new academic disciplines; and three, the asking of new or different kinds of questions of the historical data, old or new. In general, an artificial conception of the nature of public education prevails in America. There is a tendency to believe that educational policy-making is dictated only by the loftiest democratic values, or by advances in the Science of Pedagogy, or by the inexorable finger of Progress, or by some process of ratiocination uncontaminated by profane motives. But education is a field supremely loaded with value. The schools serve social interests, social purposes, even social prejudices. Education is an arena in which competing interests jostle for power and influence. Yet we know little about such important matters as: Who has the power? Where is power located? How is it exercised? Whose interests are served? Within the past decade, however, American historians have begun to study the political and social conditions of the school's existence and presuppositions. They have begun to ask new sorts of questions, questions having to do with power, strategies, stakes, interests. Tyack, in his study of educational bureaucracy in Portland, and Katz in his study of bureaucracy in Boston, are explicitly concerned with questions of power and control. Sol Cohen has explored the strategies used by groups who wish to influence school decision makers.[15] Raymond E. Callahan has critically examined school administrators as an interest group in his *Education and The Cult of Efficiency*.[16] Further, historians of American education are now not only asking new questions, different questions, tough-minded questions of the data of educational history, but, like Vincent Lannie in his studies of Catholic education, and August Meier and Edgar Toppin in their studies of early Negro militancy in the field of public education, are bringing to their work an awareness of the racial, ethnic and religious conflict with which American history is permeated.[17]

The older style in the historiography of American education was one of attachment to the idea of the public school. There was a consensus, a shared loyalty, a common commitment to the public school system. The new historians of American education are largely emancipated from inherited loyalties concerning public schools and school reforms and school reformers. The departure from orthodoxy is represented by their critical attitude toward many of the educational crusaders and educational crusades of the past. Tyack sees the efforts of American school reformers in the early national period as aimed at using the schools to inculcate a patriotic homogeneity.[18] Messerli portrays Franklin with at least one wart—xenophobia where German immigrants to Pennsylvania were concerned.[19] Especially have new approaches to the common school movement led to fresh and even startling conclusions. Thus, Fishlow questions whether there was 'a common school crusade' in the 1830s and 1840s. But Katz questions the conventional wisdom about the whole common school movement, concluding that it served the interests of a minority at the expense of the majority.[20] While Taylor points out that in the South the common school was erected as the buttress of regional orthodoxy rather than the palladium of the republic, as Jefferson would have it.[21] Nor are later reform movements faring better. Through his study of Thorndike, Karier is beginning to unravel the tangle of élitist practices and egalitarian professions which characterise so much of American education, while Strickland and Burgess are doing the same through their study of G. Stanley Hall.[22] There are even the beginnings of a less pious and more critical approach to Dewey.[23] To cite a few more examples. Bowers has attempted to disentangle the dogmatisms of social philosophy which made up much of the dialogue about American educational progressivism in the thirties.[24] Cohen describes the functions of industrial education in impeding the social mobility of the 'new immigrants'.[25] This is not to imply that the new historians of American education speak with one voice. Timothy Smith argues brilliantly from archival records here and abroad, and from interviews with immigrants, that the public schools eminently suited immigrant needs and aspirations.[26]

Many relatively new or hitherto overlooked subjects, or subjects which American educational historians had taken for granted have recently been given unexpected historical dimensions: college athletics,[27] the role of schoolbooks in the transmission of culture,[28] the education of women,[29] rural education reform,[30] federal aid to education,[31] and the role of the courts in education.[32] State and local educational history have demonstrated they can still be productive.[33] The influence of foreign educators like Herbart and Montessori is coming under renewed scrutiny.[34] Biography is flourishing.[35] Attention is being paid to hitherto overlooked educators—Kingsley, Bagley, Demiashkevich, and to early educational innovators like Maclure, Thoreau and Alcott.[36]

Education, as Bailyn stated, is more than formal schooling. Indeed, formal schooling accounts for a relatively small part of the cognitive development of the child. Neil Sutherland has observed that 'the child's attitude, personality, and his life in his family and its wider environment, are more important factors in governing what he learns and how he uses what he learns than are curricula, textbooks, teachers, school administrators, and school boards'.[37] The history of the family in America, long a gaping lacuna in our knowledge, has lately become a 'high priority' field. For example, John Demos and Richard Storr have persuasively illustrated the possibilities for educational history when views of the child and the history of the family are imaginatively joined to the story of the schools.[38] While Calhoun speculates in a trenchant way about the learning that goes on in city streets.[39]

Today the American Negro is no longer the 'invisible man'. Of the history of Negro education in the South there is now considerable knowledge. Bullock's history of Negro education in the South from 1619 to the present has illuminated Negro strategies in exploiting a dual educational system.[40] Harlan has described a pioneer experiment in school desegration in New Orleans during Reconstruction.[41] Toppin has analysed some early successes of the strategy of peaceful, non-direct protest on behalf of equal schooling in Atlanta.[42] And we are beginning to learn about education in the black ghettoes of the North. Tyack has raised significant questions about the attitudes of Northern Blacks as well as Whites toward school integration.[43] Meier and Rudwick have reminded us that Negro direct action on behalf of equal educational opportunity in the North has a long history.[44] James McPherson takes a contemporary issue, that of black power v white expertise, and uses it to explore the dilemmas of leadership in Negro higher education in the late nineteenth century.[45]

Traditional fields and subjects are still being explored, but the questions being asked and the methods employed to explore them are quite different from those of the past. Thus Wilson Smith analyses the connection between Harvard College, Puritan ideology, and early patterns of recruitment into the professions, and the low estate of teachers in the Colonial period.[46] Teaford, by investigating the role of English and other modern subjects in the Puritan curriculum, provides a fresh approach to the study of the decline of classical education in the same period.[47] Timothy Smith, instead of decrying the crucial role of the Protestant sects in establishing the common school system, closely examines the reasons for their involvement with the public schools.[48] Messerli, writing of Mann's childhood, modifies a legend; writing on Mann's college years, he sheds light on the old-time college as well as on Mann's subsequent life and career.[49] Wiebe, tracing the social functions of the American public school from the early nineteenth century to the present, implies there has been no fall from a time when the public schools stressed development of intellectual abilities or the transmission of the inherited cultural tradition; the schools have always been delegated broad social responsibilities.[50]

The newer tendencies in American educational history, however, are not without their pitfalls. Thus, social science and behavioural science concepts—status anxiety, identity crisis, symbolism, ideology,

social class, motivation, socialisation, though fruitful of new and helpful interpretations, will have to be used with caution.[51] And broaden-
ing the scope of educational history to include its interrelations with
'the rest of society', as Bailyn has urged, may prove as barren as the
old, narrow institutional history. This approach opens up new perspectives, but it also tends to deify 'society'. Indeed, Veysey recom-
mends eliminating the concept of 'society' from the historian's thinking. This would serve, as he rightly points out, to bring into sharper
focus 'the myriad competing groups, factions, and individuals who
in fact form the stuff of any society'.[52] Nevertheless, it is clear that
the history of American education is coming of age. There are even
the beginnings of historiographical debate within the fraternity.[53]

Despite the renaissance in history of American education of the
past decade, there are still many opportunities awaiting historians.
For example, about private boarding schools we now know something,
thanks to the work of James McLachlan.[54] But we still know little
about the Catholic parochial school system. The Catholic school
played a crucial role in adjusting many newcomers to the city.[55] Other
denominations also operate schools, but Catholic schools comprise
nine-tenths of all private school education in America. The size of
the Catholic system alone should make it a matter of pressing historical
concern. Also, American historians have neglected the writings of
foreign observers of American education, writings which provide a
rich store of information and insights on American schools. In fact,
though all Western nations have had their own variety of such common historical experiences as immigration, urbanisation, industrialisa-
tion, and racial or religious conflict, Americans still neglect the comparative approach to American educational history.[56] Not only does
American educational history neglect any international or comparative
approach, it is just beginning to do justice to American regionalism.
For example, to most historians of education, the American West
might be uninhabited; no Indians, Mexican-Americans, Japanese,
Chinese, Negroes, no cities like Los Angeles or San Francisco or
Seattle; no schools. No region of the United States has been so
neglected by historians of education as the region West of the Rockies.[57]

Regardless of region, we know scandalously little about what it has been like to grow up an Indian and go to school in America.[58] And one of the largest minorities in the United States, the Mexican-Americans, are still largely 'forgotten Americans'. What opportunities await the historian of American education in this field.

Most interpretations of the history of American education are still mainly concerned with the attitudes of upper-class promoters of public schooling. Very little is known about the attitudes toward education of the people whom the reformers quarrelled over. Tyack has observed that the early dominant genre in the history of American education was a version of house history. It was an 'insider's view of the schools, seen from the top down'.[59] Popular education, Tyack suggests, needs to be studied 'from below'. For example, it would be helpful to know what expectations black Americans had about education. Tyack, and Toppin, as well as Meier and Rudwick, have demonstrated that the story is complicated, often involving struggle within black communities, and among different social classes.[60] Then, what might be called the counter-reformist or conservative tradition in American education, still awaits its historian.[61] Furthermore, the effects of education in perpetuating particular class structures has never been sufficiently investigated by American historians and, vice-versa, study of the effects of patterns of social stratification on the structure of education might be profitably pursued. Finally, though progress has been made, historical research on the family is still in an early stage. As Talbott points out, very little is known about the interaction between changes in the family and changes in the structure of education. Did changes in family structure make schools increasingly important agencies of socialisation, or did pressures outside the family, from government or from social and religious institutions, provide the impetus for this shift in educational responsibilities? How has the submission to the discipline of the school altered the experience of childhood and affected adult behaviour?[62] Only in the last few years have such questions begun to receive the attention they merit.

The resurgence of interest in the history of American education is, of course, in part a consequence of trends in the professional study of history; for example, the pervasive influence of the emphasis on inter-disciplinary approaches to the past. But especially the troubled state of contemporary American education is forcing American historians to understand the past in new ways. David Cohen puts it this way:

> In every age there is an impulse to seek in the past an understanding of con-temporary dilemmas and accomplishments . . . This impulse must be par-ticularly powerful in times such as ours, when it seems clear that the society is undergoing wrenching transformations. Whatever we may think of the changes, or of historical inquiry which arises immediately from such potent experience, it seems undeniable that for the next generation at least, much work in the history of education will be given over to efforts to grasp the experience we now live through better by understanding how it all came to pass.[63]

It is likely that research motivated by such concern will in the future generate historical controversy over such issues as the motives of school reformers, the social functions of compulsory public education, the group interests served by school bureaucracies, the role of the schools in promoting equal opportunity, and the role of race, religion and ethnicity in education.

There are some dangers however in this approach to education. Much of the recent history of American education is written by his-torians who are troubled and angry and intensely involved with the issues of our time. Like the radical historians in *Towards a New Past* (Barton J. Bernstein, ed), some of them aim to write usable history which will help us to change our times as much as (or more than) to help us to understand times past. There is a tendency to polarise and simplify, and to drift toward conspiratorial interpretations of events. There is the danger that past ideas and actions may be combined with the moral or social prejudices of the historian to produce a work that distorts the past in an attempt to castigate the past and to lecture the present. A decade hence, will a new generation of American educa-tional historians say of the current generation what Bailyn said of an older generation, 'To these writers the past was simply the present writ small'?

There is the danger then of tendentiousness, of entanglement in partisan commitments in the new, revisionist history of American education. But there is another danger. John Higham's strictures about the homogenising of history should be pondered by all historians of education:

> The emphasis on consensus and continuity has softened the outlines and flattened the crises of American history. A certain tameness and amiability have crept into our view of things . . . The conservative frame of reference is giving us a bland history, in which conflict is muted, in which the elements of spontaneity, effervescence, and violence . . . scholarship is threatened with a moral vacuum.[64]

It is precisely this moral vacuum at which J. H. Plumb directed these eloquent words:

> As the historian has grown mountainous in scholarship, he has shrunken as a man. He has ceased to be a combatant in the battle for truth. Aping a nonexistent Providence, his cult of objectivity has been nothing more than a treason to the intellect. By squeezing morality out of history, he is committing professional suicide, leaving the biting social and intellectual criticism which should be his milieu to the rare satirist or philosopher, the Orwells and the Russells, or to the little reviews . . . What historians have forgotten is that facts, either human or social, become inescapably moral facts.[65]

This neglect of conflict, this indifference to 'moral facts', has left American historians of education largely unprepared to explain the strife and division characteristic of American education today. There is a great need for historical understanding of the problems currently besetting America in the field of education; a great need for some historical leverage on the problems of American education. If historians of American education evade such problems, people will turn elsewhere for answers, and we may qualify for the definition that Tolstoy once formulated for academic historians of his own day: deaf men replying to questions that nobody asked them.

Graduate School of Education,
University of California, Los Angeles

References

1   Marc Bloch on his teachers, Langlois and Seignobos, in his *The Historian's Craft*, New York (1953), 4.

2 Philip J. Greven, Jr, *Four Generations: Of Population, Land, and Family in Colonial Andover, Massachusetts*, Ithaca (1970), VII.

3 Fund for the Advancement of Education, *The Role of Education in American History*, NY (1957); Fund for the Advancement of Education, Committee on the Role of Education in American History, *Education and American History*, NY (1965); Bernard Bailyn, *Education in the Forming of American Society*, Chapel Hill (1960); Lawrence A. Cremin, *The Wonderful World of Ellwood Patterson Cubberley: An Essay in the Historiography of American Education*, NY (1965); also Wilson Smith, 'The New Historian of American Education', *Harvard Educational Review*, 31 (Spring 1961), 136–43.

4 *Education and American History*, 4.

5 Ibid, 9–24.

6 Bailyn, op cit, 4.

7 Ibid, 14. See also Bailyn's 'Education as a Discipline: Some Historical Notes', in John Walton and James L. Kuethe (eds), *The Discipline of Education*, Madison (1963), 131–9.

8 Cremin, op cit, 17, 25.

9 Ibid. And see also William W. Brickman, 'Revisionism and the Study of the History of Education', *History of Education Quarterly*, IV (December 1964), 209–23; Edgar B. Wesley, 'Lo, the Poor History of Education', *History of Education Quarterly*, IX (Fall 1969), 320–42; and Wilson Smith's comments on Bailyn's 'Education as a Discipline: Some Historical Notes', in Walton and Kuethe, op cit, 139–44.

10 Lawrence A. Cremin, *The Transformation of the School: Progressivism in American Education, 1876–1957*, NY (1961); and *American Education: The Colonial Experience, 1607–1783*, NY (1970).

11 Berenice Fisher, *Industrial Education: American Ideals and Institutions*, Madison (1967); Edward A. Krug, *The Shaping of the American High School*, NY (1964); Claude A. Bowers, *The Progressive Educator and the Depression: the Radical Years*, NY (1969); Michael B. Katz, *The Irony of Early School Reform: Educational Innovation in Mid-Nineteenth Century Massachusetts*, Cambridge, Mass (1968); Ruth Elson, *Guardians of Tradition: American Schoolbooks of the Nineteenth Century*, Lincoln, Nebr (1964); Maxine Greene, *Public School And Private Vision*, NY (1965); Rush Welter, *Popular Education and Democratic Thought In America*, NY (1962); Frederick Rudolph, *The American College and University: A History*, NY (1962); Laurence R. Veysey, *The Emergence of the American University*, Chicago (1965).

12 Jon Teaford, 'The Transformation of Massachusetts Education, 1670–1780', *History of Education Quarterly*, 10 (Fall 1970), 287–307.

13 Albert Fishlow, 'The American Common School Revival: Fact or Fancy?' in H. Rosovsky (ed), *Industrialization In Two Systems: Essays in Honor of Alexander Gerschenkron*, NY (1966), 40–67; Charles E. Bidwell, 'The Moral Significance of the Common School: A Sociological Study of Local Patterns of School Control and Moral Education in Massachusetts and New York, 1837–1840', *History of Education Quarterly*, VI (Fall 1966), 50–91.

14 Michael B. Katz, 'The Emergence of Bureaucracy in Urban Education: The Boston Case, 1850–1884', *History of Education Quarterly*, VIII (Fall 1968), 319–57; David B. Tyack, 'Bureaucracy and the Common School: The Example of Portland, Oregon, 1851–1913', *American Quarterly*, 19 (Fall 1967), 475–88.

15 Sol Cohen, *Progressives and Urban School Reform*, NY (1964).

16 Raymond E. Callahan, *Education and The Cult of Efficiency*, Chicago (1962).
17 Vincent P. Lannie, *Public Money and Parochial Education: Bishop Hughes, Governor Seward, and the New York School Controversy*, Cleveland (1968); Vincent P. Lannie and Bernard C. Diethorn, 'For the Honor and Glory of God: The Philadelphia Bible Riots of 1840', *History of Education Quarterly* (Spring 1968), 44–106; John W. Pratt, 'Religious Conflict in the Development of the New York City Public School System', *History of Education Quarterly*, V (June 1965), 110–20; August Meier and Elliott M. Rudwick, 'Early Boycotts of Segregated Schools: One Case of Springfield, Ohio, 1922–1923', *American Quarterly*, 20 (Winter 1968), 744–58; Edgar A. Toppin, 'Walter White and the Atlanta NAACP's Fight for Equal Schools, 1916–1917', *History of Education Quarterly*, 7 (Spring 1967), 3–21.
18 David B. Tyack, 'Forming the National Character', *Harvard Educational Review*, 36 (Fall 1966), 29–41. See also Jonathan Messerli, 'The Columbian Complex: The Impulse to National Consolidation', *History of Education Quarterly*, 7 (Winter 1967), 417–33; Frederick Rudolph (ed), *Essays On Education in the Early Republic*, Cambridge (1965); and Gordon C. Lee (ed), *Crusade Against Ignorance: Thomas Jefferson on Education*, NY (1961).
19 Jonathan Messerli, 'Benjamin Franklin: Colonial and Cosmopolitan Educator', *British Journal of Educational Studies*, 16 (February 1968), 43–59. See also David B. Tyack, 'Education as Artifact: Benjamin Franklin and Instruction of a Rising People', *History of Education Quarterly*, VI (Spring 1966), 3–15; John Hardin Best (ed), *Benjamin Franklin on Education*, NY (1962).
20 Fishlow, op cit, Katz, *The Irony of School Reform*. For an earlier suggestion that the American common school may not have been the spearhead of democracy, see Merle Curti, *The Social Ideas of American Educators*, NY (1935).
21 William R. Taylor, 'Toward a Definition of Orthodoxy: The Patrician South and the Common Schools', *Harvard Educational Review*, 36 (Fall 1966), 412–26.
22 Clarence J. Karier, 'Elite Views on American Education', *Journal of Contemporary History*, 2 (July 1967), 149–63; Charles E. Strickland and Charles Burgess, *Health, Growth, and Heredity: G. Stanley Hall in Natural Education*, NY (1965).
23 Frederic Lilge, 'John Dewey in Retrospect: An American Reconsideration', *British Journal of Educational Studies* (May 1960), 99–111; Richard Hofstadter, 'The Child and the World', *Daedalus* (Summer 1962), 501–26.
24 Claude A. Bowers, 'The Ideologies of Progressive Education', *History of Education Quarterly* (Winter 1967), 452–73. See also Joel Spring, 'Education and Progressivism', *History of Education Quarterly* (Spring 1970), 53–71.
25 Sol Cohen, 'The Industrial Education Movement, 1906–1917', *American Quarterly*, 20 (Spring 1968), 95–110; Sol Cohen, 'Urban School Reform', *History of Education Quarterly*, IX (Fall 1969), 300–4.
26 Timothy L. Smith, 'Immigrant Social Aspirations and American Education, 1880–1930', *American Quarterly*, 21 (Fall 1969), 523–43. See also Smith's 'New Approaches to the History of Immigration in Twentieth-Century America', *American Historical Review*, 71 (July 1966), 1265–79.
27 Guy Lewis, 'The Beginning of Organized Collegiate Sport', *American Quarterly* (Summer 1970), 222–9; Rudolph, op cit, chap 18.
28 Elson, op cit, J. Merton England, 'The Democratic Faith in American Schoolbooks, 1783–1860', *American Quarterly*, 15 (Summer 1963), 191–9; John C. Crandall, 'Patriotism and Humanitarian Reform in Children's Literature, 1825–1860', *American Quarterly*, 21 (Spring 1969), 3–22.

29 Glenda Riley, 'Origins of the Argument for Improved Female Education', *History of Education Quarterly*, 9 (Winter 1969), 455–70. See also Barbara M. Cross (ed), *The Educated Woman in America*, NY (1965).

30 Ann M. Keppel, 'The Myth of Agrarianism in Rural Educational Reform, 1890–1914', *History of Education Quarterly*, II (June 1962), 100–11.

31 John H. Florer, 'Major Issues in the Congressional Debate of the Merrill Act of 1862', *History of Education Quarterly*, 8 (Winter 1968), 459–78; Ambrose A. Clegg, 'Church Groups and Federal Aid to Education, 1933–1939', *History of Education Quarterly*, 4 (September 1964), 137–51; George A. Kizer, 'Federal Aid to Education, 1945–1963', *History of Education Quarterly* (Spring 1970), 84–102; William M. Tuttle, Jr, 'Higher Education and the Federal Government: The Lean Years, 1940–42', *Teachers College Record*, 71 (December 1969), 297–312; William M. Tuttle, Jr, 'Higher Education and the Federal Government: The Triumph, 1942–45', *Teachers College Record*, 72 (February 1970), 485–99.

32 Leonard Levy and Harlan Phillips, 'The Roberts Case: Source of the "Separate But Equal" Doctrine', *American Historical Review*, 56 (April 1951), 510–18; Barton J. Bernstein, 'Plessy vs Ferguson: Conservative Sociological Jurisprudence', *Journal of Negro History*, 48 (July 1963), 196–205; Kenneth O'Brien, 'Education, Americanization and the Supreme Court: The 1920's', *American Quarterly*, 13 (Summer 1961), 161–71; also, David B. Tyack, 'The Perils of Pluralism: The Background of the Pierce Case', *American Historical Review*, 74 (1968), 74–98.

33 Kenneth V. Lottich, 'Educational Leadership in Early Ohio', *History of Education Quarterly*, II (March 1962); Irving G. Hendrick, 'A Reappraisal of Colonial New Hampshire's Efforts in Public Education', *History of Education Quarterly*, VI (Summer 1966), 43–60; John Pulliam, 'Changing Attitudes Toward Free Public Schools in Illinois, 1825–1860', *History of Education Quarterly*, 7 (Summer 1967), 191–208.

34 Harold B. Dunkel, 'Herbartianism Comes to America', *History of Education Quarterly*, 9 (Summer 1969), 202–33; Sol Cohen, 'Educating the Children of the Urban Poor: Maria Montessori and Her Method', *Education and Urban Society*, I (November 1968), 61–79; Sol Cohen, 'Maria Montessori: Priestess or Pedagogue', *Teachers College Record*, 71 (December 1969), 313–26.

35 Geraldine M. Joncich, *The Sane Positivist: A Biography of Edward L. Thorndike*, Middletown, Conn (1968); Jack Campbell, *Col. Francis W. Parker*, Col Univ, NY (1967); Walter H. Drost, *David Snedden and Education for Social Efficiency*, Madison (1967); Lewis S. Feuer, 'John Dewey's Sojourn in Japan', *Teachers College Record*, 71 (September 1969), 123–45.

36 The following are all in the *History of Education Quarterly*: Gurney Chambers, 'Michael John Demiashkevich and the Essentialist Committee for the Advancement of American Education' (Spring 1969), 46–55; Walter Droost, 'Clarence Kingsley—The New York Years' (Fall 1966), 18–34; Erwin V. Johanningmeier, 'William Chandler Bagley's Changing Views on the Relationship Between Psychology and Education' (Spring 1969), 3–27; Lawrence Willson, 'Thoreau on Education' (March 1962), 19–29; Charles Burgess, 'William Maclure and Education for a Good Society' (June 1963), 58–76. See also Charles Strickland, 'A Transcendentalist Father: The Child Rearing Practice of Bronson Alcott', *Perspectives in American History*, III (1969), 5–73.

37 Neil Sutherland, 'The Urban Child', *History of Education Quarterly*, IX (Fall 1969), 305.

38 John Demos, *A Little Commonwealth: Family Life in Plymouth Colony*, NY (1970);

Richard Storr, 'The Education of History: Some Impressions', *Harvard Educational Review*, 31 (Spring 1961), 123–35. See also Strickland, op cit; Bernard Wishy, *The Child and the Republic*, Philadelphia (1968); and Geoffrey H. Steere, 'Freudianism and Child-Rearing in the Twenties', *American Quarterly*, 20 (Winter, 1968), 759–65.

39   Daniel Calhoun, 'The City as Teacher: Historical Problems', *History of Education Quarterly*, 9 (Fall 1969), 312–25.

40   Henry A. Bullock, *A History of Negro Education in the South: From 1619 to the Present*, Cambridge, Mass (1967); August Meier, *Negro Thought in America, 1880–1915*, Ann Arbor, Mich (1963).

41   Louis R. Harlan, 'Desegregation in New Orleans' Public Schools During Reconstruction', *American Historical Review*, LXVII (April 1962), 663–75. See also Harlan's *Separate and Unequal: Public School Campaigns and Racism in the Southern Seaboard States, 1901–1915*, NY (1968).

42   Edgar A. Toppin, 'Walter White and the Atlanta NAACP's Fight for Equal Schools, 1916–1917', *History of Education Quarterly*, 7 (Spring 1967), 3–21.

43   David B. Tyack, 'Growing Up Black: Perspectives on the History of Education in Northern Ghettoes', *History of Education Quarterly*, 9 (Fall 1969), 287–97. See also Tyack's comments in his 'New Perspectives on the History of American Education', in Herbart J. Bass (ed), *The State of American History*, Chicago (1970), 32–4.

44   August Meier and Elliott M. Rudwick, 'Early Boycotts of Segregated Schools: The Case of Springfield, Ohio, 1922–1923', *American Quarterly*, 20 (Winter 1968), 744–58; and by the same authors, 'Early Boycotts of Segregated Schools: The East Orange, New Jersey Experience, 1899–1906', *History of Education Quarterly*, VII (Spring 1967), 22–35; and 'Early Boycotts of Segregated Schools: The Alton, Illinois Case, 1897–1908', *Journal of Negro Education*, XXVI (Fall 1967), 394–402.

45   James McPherson, 'White Liberals and Black Power in Negro Education, 1865–1915', *American Historical Review*, 75 (June 1970), 1357–1379.

46   Wilson Smith, 'The Teacher in Puritan Culture', *Harvard Educational Review*, 36 (Fall 1966), 394–411.

47   Jon Teaford, 'The Transformation of Massachusetts Education, 1670–1780', *History of Education Quarterly*, 10 (Fall 1970), 287–307. See also Frank Klassen, 'Persistence and Change in Eighteenth Century Colonial Education', *History of Education Quarterly*, II (June 1962), 83–99.

48   Timothy L. Smith, 'Protestant Schooling and American Nationality, 1800–1850', *Journal of American History*, 53 (March 1967), 679–95.

49   Jonathan Messerli, 'Horace Mann at Brown', *Harvard Educational Review*, 33 (Summer 1963), 285–311; 'Horace Mann's Childhood: Myth and Reality', *Educational Forum*, 30 (January 1966), 159–68; 'Localism and State Control in Horace Mann's Reform of the Common Schools', *American Quarterly*, XVII (Spring 1965), 104–18.

50   Robert H. Wiebe, 'The Social Functions of Public Education', *American Quarterly*, 21 (Summer 1969), 147–64.

51   Eg, Edward N. Saveth, 'The Problem of American Family History', *American Quarterly*, 21 (Summer 1969), 311–29.

52   Laurence R. Veysey, 'Toward A New Direction in Educational History: Prospect and Retrospect', *History of Education Quarterly*, 9 (Fall 1969), 343–58. See also Talbott, op cit, 142–3.

53 Eg, John W. Pratt, 'Religious Conflict in the Development of the New York City Public School System', *History of Education Quarterly*, V (June 1965), 110–20, and Vincent P. Lannie, 'William Seward and Common School Education', *History of Education Quarterly*, IV (September 1964), 181–92; Michael B. Katz, book review of Claude Bowers' *The Progressive Educator and the Depression*, in *School Review*, 77 (November 1969), 139–43, and Bowers' response in *School Review*, 78 (May 1970), 443–50. Also the exchange between Tamara K. Hareven, 'Step-Children of the Dream', *History of Education Quarterly*, 9 (Winter 1969), 505–14, and Paul H. Mattingly, 'Useful History and Black Identity', *History of Education Quarterly*, X (Fall 1970), 338–50.

54 James McLachlan, *American Boarding Schools: A Historical Study*, NY (1970).

55 See Timothy L. Smith, 'Immigrant Social Aspirations and American Education, 1880–1930', *American Quarterly*, 21 (Fall 1969), 523–43; and Smith's 'New Approaches to the History of Immigration in Twentieth-Century America', *American Historical Review*, 71 (July 1966), 1272–4. See also Neil G. McCluskey, S J (ed), *Catholic Education in America: A Documentary History*, NY (1964). And, of course, Lannie, *Public Money and Parochial Education*, op cit.

56 For examples of what can be done, see Ronald P. Dore, *Education in Tokugawa, Japan*, Berkeley (1965); E. R. Norman, *The Conscience of the State in North America*, London (1968); and C. Vann Woodward (ed), *The Comparative Approach to American History*, NY (1968). See also William W. Brickman, 'A Historical Introduction to Comparative Education', *Comparative Education Review*, III (February 1960), 6–13; and the same author's 'An Historical Survey of American Educational History', *Paedogogica Historica*, XI (1962), 5–21. See also Stewart E. Fraser and William W. Brickman (eds), *A History of International and Comparative Education: Nineteenth Century Documents*, Glenview, Ill (1968); and by Sol Cohen: 'Sir Michael E. Sadler and the Sociopolitical Analysis of Education', *History of Education Quarterly*, VII (Fall 1967), 281–94; and 'English Writers On The American Common Schools, 1884–1904', *The School Review*, 76 (June 1968), 127–46.

57 But see David B. Tyack, 'The Kingdom of God and the Common School: Protestant Ministers and the Educational Awakening in the West', *Harvard Educational Review*, 36 (Fall 1966), 447–69; Nicholas C. Palos, 'A Yankee Patriot: John Swett, the Horace Mann of the Pacific', *History of Education Quarterly*, 4 (March 1964), 17–32; Earl Pomeroy, *The Pacific Slope: A History of California, Oregon, Washington, Idaho, Utah, and Nevada*, NY (1965); and Moses Rischin, 'Beyond the Great Divide: Immigration and the Last Frontier', *Journal of American History*, LV (June 1968), 42–53.

58 Norman Earl Tanis, 'Education in John Eliot's Indian Utopias, 1646–1675', *History of Education Quarterly*, 10 (Fall 1970), 308–23; Frederic Whitehill and James W. Skelton, 'The Church-State Conflict in Early Indian Education', *History of Education Quarterly*, 6 (Spring 1966), 41–51; Robert F. Berkhofer, Jr, 'Model Zions for the American Indian', *American Quarterly*, XV (Summer 1963), 176–90.

59 Tyack, 'New Perspectives On The History of American Education', 23.

60 And in general see David K. Cohen, 'Education and Race: Research Needs and Opportunities', *History of Education Quarterly*, IX (Fall 1969), 281–6.

61 Eg, Karier, 'Elite Views on American Education', op cit; Michael Wreszin, 'Albert Jay Nock and the Anarchist Elitist Tradition in America', *American Quarterly*, 21 (Summer 1969). See also Frederic Lilge's review of Cremin's

The Transformation of the School, in *Studies In Philosophy and Education*, II (Winter 1961–2), 63–7.

62   John E. Talbott, 'The History of Education', *Daedalus* (Winter 1971), 142.

63   Cohen, 'Education and Race: Research Needs and Opportunities', 281–2.

64   John Higham, 'Beyond Consensus: The Historian as Moral Critic', *American Historical Review*, LXVII (April 1962), 616.

65   J. H. Plumb, 'Perspective', *Saturday Review*, 26 November 1966, 51.

Book Reviews

A History of Western Education, Volume 1: **The Ancient World,** by James Bowen, METHUEN, 1972, pp xix + 395, £4.75.
Higher Education in the Ancient World, by M. L. Clarke, ROUTLEDGE & KEGAN PAUL, 1971, pp ix + 188, £2.25.

These two books, though the periods which they cover coincide, are very different in scope and purpose. Professor Bowen's is the first volume of a general history, this volume covering the period from earliest times until Bede in the West and Byzantium in the East. The treatment is broad and general, and the picture drawn in bold strokes. Professor Clarke's scope is less wide, running from the first century to the end of the ancient world, though his last chapter glances forward to the later survival of the ancient traditions; he confines himself to higher education, and his treatment is precise, detailed and limited to what is strictly relevant to his subject.

There is room for both approaches, but the very width of Professor Bowen's proves a disadvantage. Education is itself a somewhat nebulous term. Professor Bowen rightly stresses its connection with literacy, and there is some interesting material in the first chapter on the origins of writing, and again later on the arrival of the alphabet and the spread of literacy in Greece (though it seems a pity to deal with the alphabet twice, on pp 58 and 72). Professor Bowen is also well aware of the connection between education and the general cultural and historical background. Education does not happen in a vacuum. Unfortunately, he fails to avoid the pitfall of writing an inevitably superficial account of cultural and intellectual developments, interspersed with brief historical interludes, which confuses the educational theme. The brevity of the historical interludes makes them unsatisfactory (and there is at least one inaccuracy; it was Cnossos not Mycenae that was destroyed by the eruption of Thera). There is the same unsatisfactoriness in the treatment of cultural and intellectual developments, for example the pre-Socratics, who are a long way from what went on in school (in spite of Aristophanes' *phrontisterion*, which gets no mention). The educational thread is too often lost in this extraneous material, and the same fault recurs in the bibliographies, which contain too much that is of little educational relevance and surprisingly omit Professor Clarke's *Rhetoric at Rome* and Marrou's *History of Education in Antiquity*. All this is ungrateful and ungracious criticism, and there is much that is good in the book and much that the ordinary reader can learn. But Professor Bowen's object is ambitious: 'If we are to understand education in the fullest sense, as distinct from the more behaviouristic and prescriptive demands of particular learning and teaching situations, then we must study its history for the clarification and explanation which can be so secured'. This is an admirable aim, which Professor Bowen's rather episodic treatment hardly achieves.

By contrast Professor Clarke's book, with its more modest scope, comes much nearer to doing so. Indeed, in his introduction he draws some interesting morals, and is able to do so because of his greater precision and closeness to the educational process. He is less concerned with educational theory than to 'describe what was taught and how it was taught'. He includes under higher education everything after the primary stage, that is to say what we should call the secondary stage, with its emphasis on grammatical and literary studies, its continuation into rhetoric and completion in philosophy. One does not expect fireworks or purple patches from the author of *Rhetoric at Rome*. Professor Clarke writes unpretentiously and allows himself only an occasional reference beyond his subject and an occasional judgement; but he does deliver the goods. After an introductory chapter he proceeds to the liberal arts, the first of the stages covered by his definition, with its heavy bias to grammatical and literary studies, and its concentration (in spite of a formal inclusion of music, mathematics and astronomy) on the art of rhetorical expression. 'Perhaps,' he remarks in one of his rare asides, 'the boys would have profited by a little relief from endless speech making'. Perhaps they would; for as Professor Clarke notes, ancient education was in its own way highly specialised, though perhaps by contrast exempt from the criticism so often made of our own form of specialisation—its products *should* have been able to express themselves in their own language, and indeed both in Latin and Greek, since it was essentially bilingual. Professor Clarke includes some account of the daily routine in schools at this stage and also in the schools of philosophy in the stage which followed. There is an interesting chapter on that stage, reminding us that philosophy was looked on 'as providing moral just as much as intellectual education'. And we are reminded in the next chapter of what we too easily forget, that there were professional schools in medicine, in architecture, and under the Empire, in law. The concluding chapters deal with the coming of Christianity and the survival of the ancient tradition at Byzantium and in the medieval West. The Church was itself, in an important sense, an educational institution, and perhaps for that reason made little attempt to take over the pagan schools 'which continued to flourish' to the end. The ancient tradition had a chequered career at Byzantium. In the West it was eventually absorbed by the Church and the monasteries, but through its literature continued to survive; 'the pagan poets survived the competition not only of Christian poets but also of pagan moralists'. *Higher Education in the Ancient World* will join *Rhetoric at Rome* as a work indispensable for the understanding of ancient education.

University College, Cambridge   H. D. P. Lee

The Diary of Thomas Isham of Lamport (1658–81) kept by him in Latin from 1671 to 1673 at his Father's command, translated from the original by Norman Marlow, with introduction, appendices and notes by Sir Gyles Isham and a preface by Sir George Clark, GREGG INTERNATIONAL, 1971, pp 343, no price stated.

Beginning on 1 November 1671, the fourteen-year-old Thomas Isham kept, as an educative exercise, a Latin diary in which for nearly two years he noted the events of his days. The resulting document is probably unique. As presented here, in a model edition, it is required reading for anyone interested in the seventeenth century. The diary is important because it was written for no other purpose than that of practising the writing of Latin, and that it records everyday events. Thanks to the fact that it has been preserved among the archives of a well-documented family, it has been possible to identify and explain virtually all the people, places and events mentioned in passing, and so to build up a full and richly complex picture of country life as it revolved around the seat of a substantial member of the upper gentry. In his long introduction, Sir Gyles Isham fills in the background history of the family and sketches Thomas's short life subsequent to the diary. It is owing to the finely detailed scholarship and love which he brings to bear on his text, that the book becomes a delight and an inspiration.

For the historian of education, the diary has a more specific interest, since it provides an opportunity to examine closely the development in Latinity of one well-educated youth who was consciously attempting to improve. From the Latin text given here, aided by the unobtrusive but precise notes, something can be seen of the moulding of a Stuart gentleman's prose style. Of other aspects of Thomas's education the diary is less informative; although it notes the stages of his progress through Euclid, it has little to say of the books he read. Thomas's attention was concentrated upon the outside world, but the direct observation that 'Robert, our groom, saw Mr Cook, the schoolmaster at Scaldwell ploughing in his crop' is perhaps more revealing of the circumstances of Stuart education than the list of Thomas's textbooks would have been.

London   A. J. Turner

Classics or Charity? The Dilemma of the 18th-century Grammar School, by Richard S. Tompson, MANCHESTER UNIVERSITY PRESS, 1971, pp viii + 168, £2.76.
Most endowed grammar schools of pre-eighteenth-century origin

were intended by their founders to promote the classics and charity: to teach Latin, or Latin and Greek, freely to local 'poor' boys. Their eighteenth-century dilemma was how to reconcile these two objectives as local demand for Latin and Greek diminished and the demand for English, writing and arithmetic increased. A school that wanted to meet the needs of local charity had to abandon or dilute its classical teaching; if it wanted to survive as a classical school it often had to attract monied pupils who could afford a liberal education (probably fee-paying boarders from a distance) and so neglect its local charitable function. This dilemma is the subject of the present study by Professor Tompson of the University of Utah.

The generally accepted view is that, faced with this choice and with the related problems of inflation, poverty and successful competition from private enterprise, the grammar schools declined. To test this doctrine Professor Tompson has taken a sample of fifteen geographically scattered counties (including London) and has studied their 334 grammar schools, almost half of the assumed total for the whole country in the eighteenth century. For nearly a quarter of these he has found manuscript material—minute books, accounts, correspondence, legal papers—mainly in county record offices. His chief printed source is the thirty-eight volumes of reports of Brougham's Commission to Inquire concerning Charities (1819–37)—'the deepest and most extensive examination of endowed schools ever made'—but he has also used a variety of other parliamentary papers, law reports, and treatises on charities, schools and education.

The results hardly justify the expectations aroused by the author's preface, in which he seems to see himself contributing to a reappraisal of the eighteenth century in the manner of a Namier, a Clapham or an Ashton. His general conclusion is that the grammar schools were much more active and 'progressive' than they were made out to be by Leach and the textbook writers who have uncritically accepted his sweeping condemnations. There was no decay, Tompson argues, because grammar schools changed themselves into something more useful by dropping or curtailing the classics and admitting new subjects, or even by becoming elementary schools. In any case, most schools founded after 1660 were intended to teach English as well as Latin. On the whole, the schools continued to serve their founders' charitable intentions, notwithstanding an increasing tendency to impose fees on local boys and to admit non-local boys as fee-paying boarders.

Attempts to give statistical exactitude over a sample of 334 schools to developments such as the introduction of curriculum changes, the admission of boarders and the imposition of fees carry little conviction because of the many uncertainties and imponderables. If English or arithmetic was being taught by a grammar school master in 1700 how can we be sure that his successor was teaching it in 1710? And what did teaching English or arithmetic mean anyhow? Attempts to classify parents at certain schools according to occupations carry even less conviction because of the arbitrary categories—why should a butcher be classed as 'lower mercantile', a baker as 'manufacturer' and a carpenter merely as 'artisan'? On the other hand, although these matters have been industriously investigated, others no less relevant to the condition of the grammar schools are hardly considered at all: the master's freehold, pluralism, the unaccountability of trustees, the generally admitted decline of other endowed institutions—the universities, the Established Church, the town corporations—with which the grammar schools were closely associated.

Impressive though the bibliography is, there are some omissions. It includes no theses. Since Cumberland and the West Riding are two of the sample counties, one might have expected reference to have been made to Bishop William Nicolson's *Miscellany Account* (Cumb & West Antiq & Archaeo Soc, 1877) and *Archbishop Herring's Visitation Returns* (Yorks Archaeo Soc, 1928–31). Errors are few but the archbishop of York in 1769 was Robert Drummond not Hammond (pp 68, 166) and the 'unidentified correspondent of Christopher Wase' (p 127, n 1) plainly identifies himself in his letter as Samuel Frankland, schoolmaster of Coventry (Bodl MS CCC 390, ii, f 211). Finally, it must be said that Professor Tompson's English does not make for compulsive reading: it is generally flat and pedestrian and is marred by cumbrous phraseology (eg for 'disenrolment' and 'enrolment decline' read 'falling numbers').

Because there is no general account of the eighteenth-century grammar schools this book is to be accorded a welcome, but it falls far short of being the book that we need.

University of Hull   John Lawson

A History of King Edward VI Grammar School, Retford, by A. D. Grounds, ST MARTIN'S PRESS, Worksop, 1970, pp 264 + plates, £2.10.

In the first place the history of any one school commends itself to a readership of those closely involved with it. Further, as Mr Grounds suggests in his preface, each new school history published can both make clearer the national pattern of educational development and seek to contribute to the local history of its own area.

Mr Grounds' history of the school of which he is the senior history master will undoubtedly interest those connected in any way with King Edward VI Grammar School at Retford. They will read in his book a detailed and well-documented account of the varying fortunes of the school through the centuries of its existence. They will see demonstrated the link between these fortunes and the succession of masters appointed to the school. They will find evidence, too, of the influence of actions and attitudes of the local community, particularly the governing body. For three centuries this was the corporation of the borough, by the 1830s a self-perpetuating oligarchy described in scathing terms by the Municipal Corporation Commissioners. They may read in the final chapters, which have a good deal of purely domestic concern, of a school whose ceremonies and activities they know and in which they may indeed have taken part. They may read, too, the names of former pupils well known in their own, or famous in wider, circles.

To accomplish his aim of making clearer the pattern of national educational development, the author of a school history must hope to provide information which may help in answering some of the questions historians of education are currently asking. Such a question concerns the relationship between school and local community. One way in which it can be answered is in terms of the social groups from which the pupils of the school were drawn. For the sixteenth and seventeenth centuries Retford appears to offer little new evidence, but for the eighteenth century, the discovery of a headmaster's diary together with the use of other sources has enabled Mr Grounds to give some useful information. In the following century he is able to give another example of the relationship when he shows the impact of the agricultural depression of the 1870s on a school serving a predominantly farming community. The depression undoubtedly contributed to the failure of the attempt then being made by a scholar headmaster to turn the school into a 'first-grade' one. His hopes of attracting more boarders, of developing further the study of classics, and of sending pupils to Oxford and Cambridge were thwarted in the face of dwindling numbers.

Historians of education—and sociologists too—are interested, for a variety of reasons, in those who taught in schools. John Lawson pointed out in his history of Hull Grammar School that, as yet, there had been no detailed study of teachers in the sixteenth and seventeenth centuries. Such studies are being undertaken: for example a register of schools and schoolmasters in the diocese of Ely by Mrs Elizabeth Key is to be published in the *Proceedings of the Cambridge Antiquarian Society*. Mr Grounds devotes a good deal of his book to the headmasters of the school. The clerical link emerges clearly. All but two were university-trained, mostly at Cambridge. From 1551 to 1719 all, with three seventeenth-century exceptions, were in orders. Seven of the nine clerical headmasters, between 1551 and 1837, held curacies or even benefices with their headmastership, and of the eighteen clerical headmasters in the school's history five resigned to go to parishes. The mastership did not, however, seem usually to be a stepping-stone to higher positions whether in schools or church. The average length of service of the twenty-four headmasters in the 400 years of the school's existence is over seventeen years. In her paper on 'The Schooling of the Peasantry in Cambridgeshire 1575–1700' (*Agricultural History Review*, 18 (1970) Supplement), Dr Margaret Spufford quotes

Mrs Key's findings that many schoolmasters in Cambridgeshire in the sixteenth and seventeenth centuries were young men doing a spell of teaching between graduation and a benefice. But in the same period the average service of Retford headmasters was over eighteen years and of the eight masters involved, six died in office, two comparatively young. The above-average stipend and free house may have helped to keep headmasters at Retford.

The statutes of 1552 proposed the study of Greek in the school's fourth form. This was most frequently an aspiration for, rather than a reality of, the curriculum of a school at this time. Yet the first master appointed under the new foundation had 'a good understanding of and ability to translate Greek'. For the rest of the sixteenth and the whole of the seventeenth century the nature of curriculum and method at the school remains hidden. In his chapter on the eighteenth century, however, Mr Grounds is able to give evidence of the persistence of the humanist curriculum. In the nineteenth century, too, there is an interesting demonstration of the link between curriculum and status. Efforts to create a first-grade school, from what remained stubbornly a local grammar school of the Taunton Commissioners' second grade, turned on maintaining a strong emphasis on classical studies as well as an increase in the numbers of boarders.

In the last two chapters, covering the twentieth century, the historian becomes the school chronicler. Yet there is here, too, an interest in some of the information which Mr Grounds has to offer. The development of ceremony and extra-curricular activities has helped to give a corporate identity to the school that has been particularly characteristic of grammar schools in this century.

This is avowedly a history in which attention is focused on one particular institution. The dimension in time which Mr Grounds adopts means that he must deal with the Retford background in broad terms. The techniques of English local historians, when they become widely applied and devoted to the study of the development of local communities such as Retford, will help to give a greater depth of meaning to the local purpose and function of education and the ways in which diverse schools variously perform it.

At the time when the parliamentary storm was raging over the notorious Retford election of 1826 another schoolmaster, J. S. Piercy, headmaster of the National School, wrote the history of the borough. As all who study the history of Retford must do, Mr Grounds acknowledges his debt to Piercy but he can have satisfaction in the knowledge that he, too, has added something of significance both to the history of the place in which he teaches and to the general body of educational history.

University of Cambridge   T. G. Cook

Church, State and Schools in Britain, 1800–1970, by James Murphy, ROUTLEDGE & KEGAN PAUL, 1971, pp xiii + 152, £1.75.

Dr Murphy broke new ground some twelve years ago with his case study of education in Liverpool at a particularly pregnant point of the nineteenth century. By contrast he covers well-trodden territory in his present book. It is devoted to the same general theme—the religious problem in education—but relates to the national field over a wide period.

The perils of presenting, at student level, a slender volume on such a vast and well-documented topic are obvious. It is all too easy to compress the detail into a tabloid, a sort of Oxo cube of information which repels the student. On the other hand a general sweep, however brilliant the interpretation and analysis, may, by its omission of background, leave the unitiated reader not only breathless but baffled. Dr Murphy has avoided both pitfalls in a work which skilfully combines care for detail with astuteness of judgement. With his mastery of the religious and political background and his grasp of issues he has set his topic firmly in context and has deftly woven together the many strands of his theme into a readable narrative.

The author has drawn on an impressive range of secondary sources and has made systematic use of official publications. He writes with the clarity and confidence of one who has browsed at leisure and savoured his materials. The emphasis of his book is on the origins and early development of the dual system in England during the years of the nineteenth century, when the religious issue dominated education, when it wracked men's consciences, roused mass emotion and divided political parties. Naturally enough, Dr Murphy is concerned with the evolution of opinion, policies and provision. Yet there is another aspect which the contemporary publicists and politicians largely ignored and of which we have little evidence. What was the effect on the children themselves of all the effort expended? As Edmond Holmes wrote sixty years ago in *What is and What might be*, 'It would be well if all who talked publicly about religious education could be sentenced to devote a month to the personal study of religious instruction as it is ordinarily given in elementary schools. At the end of the month they would be wiser and sadder men, and in future they would probably talk less about religious education and think more.' Students could today undertake their own fieldwork and tape recollections of old people to discover for themselves whether they left school with, in Holmes' words, 'a permanent distaste for religion'.

Students will find these early chapters pithy and rewarding and even those familiar with the topic will be stimulated to fresh thought by, for example, Dr Murphy's commentary on the Cowper-Temple clause. Similarly they will appreciate his capacity for swift summarisation, his description, for instance, of the six months' grace awarded to the churches in 1870 as 'a concession, a challenge, and a pledge'.

The work has certain shortcomings. On some of the more recent developments, where the author is restricted in his published sources, his judgements are less sound. He would appear, for example, to underestimate the delicacy of Butler's wartime task. There are also occasional lapses such as the description of F. D. Maurice (p 39) as a High Churchman. Moreover, in a work which claims to refer to Britain, the treatment of developments outside England is surprisingly slight. There is a welcome illumination of the 'Irish System' of the early nineteenth century, but North Britain fares badly and Scotsmen will be startled to read of the Act of Union taking place in 1702 (p 11). Clearly Dr Murphy is on unfamiliar ground when he discusses the extent of the influence on education of the Presbyterian churches after 1872. In fact, though they surrendered their schools, they continued to control teacher training for a further thirty-five years before transferring their colleges to secular authority.

The strength of the book lies in its treatment of the English aspect. In his final chapter Dr Murphy looks fully and frankly at the English present-day scene, where he finds the strength of the denominational schools more apparent than real. By implication he prophecies their run-down in the future. Students will find in his book plenty of material to spark off discussion, and for those who wish to probe further into issues and attitudes the author gives useful guidance in a concluding section. In brief, his book fills a gap in student literature and is a worthy addition to the current series.

University of Keele   Marjorie Cruickshank

History of Education
The Journal of the History of Education Society

A SOCIAL HISTORY OF EDUCATION IN ENGLAND

John Lawson and Harold Silver

This exploration of the history of English education at all times and at all levels, makes an important contribution to our understanding of the changing pattern of education within society. The authors examine the medieval origins of our education system and the transformations wrought on it by successive events such as the Reformation, the Civil War and the Industrial Revolution. They look, too, at the effects of cultural upheavals like the Renaissance, and at the influence of the church, the state, and new social or educational philosophies. The book will prove essential reading for all concerned with the history of education and its effect on education today.

£4.90; University Paperback: £2.40

World Education Series

A new series of concise surveys of the educational systems of significant and contrasting countries. The historical background, philosophy, teaching methods and statistics of education at all levels are covered, present controversies and future innovations being briefly discussed.

Education in East Germany
MINA J MOORE-RINVOLUCRI   £2.95

East Germany's educational system took a new road after 1945, and the alliance of manual and intellectual work for every child and student has been realised even more effectively than in the Soviet Union—an interesting study.

Education in New Zealand
J C DAKIN   28 June, £3.25

New Zealand's system has some interesting distinctive features, all covered here along with special aspects such as Maori and technical education.

Education in Scotland
IAN R FINDLAY   £2.75

Scottish education, with its traditional insistence on the three (or four) Rs has long had a reputation for high quality. How far is this deserved?

The Soviet Union
J J TOMIAK   £2.50

The knowledge of how Soviet education works is a key to better understanding of Soviet life in general. This book will appeal to many readers generally interested in the USSR, as well as to teachers, students and specialists in education.

DAVID & CHARLES
NEWTON ABBOT · DEVON

English Roman Catholics and Higher Education 1830-1903

Vincent Alan McClelland

The effort to come to terms with the larger society within which Roman Catholics had to function is the main theme of this study. The problem can be seen in microcosm in the fight for higher education and in the internal tension and turmoil to which it gave rise. There are three main phases in the context—withdrawal, isolation, and dogged self-help; compromise and modification; and gradual assimilation combined with efforts to retain a community identity. £7.00

University Reform in Nineteenth Century Oxford

A Study of Henry Halford Vaughan 1811-1885

E. G. W. Bill

Vaughan was Regius Professor of Modern History at Oxford from 1848 to 1858, and the leader of a group whose influence on the reform of Oxford University has been insufficiently recognized. He asserted that a principal object of the university was the pursuit of learning, and, owing to his treatment by the Newmanites, believed that it could only be achieved by overthrowing its religious framework. Frontispiece £6.50

Oxford University Press

ROSEMARY O'DAY

Church Records and the History of Education in Early Modern England 1558—1642: A Problem in Methodology

DESPITE widespread current interest in the growth of literacy in the early modern period and in the expansion of secondary and higher education, most of the important work in the area of the development of schools has concentrated, with one or two important exceptions, upon the history of the endowed grammar schools and of the curricula adopted therein. Unquestionably the theory behind the secondary education of the period and the history of the growth of individual schools are vital to both controversies and are in themselves interesting. Nevertheless such studies reflect one part only of the educational scene. There is, for example, a crying need for a study of the growth of teaching as a separate profession and for a history of those schools which were not endowed grammar schools proper—that is, restricted to the teaching of Latin grammar—but which in fact accounted for the large majority of schools in England: other grammar schools, English schools and petty schools.

The way to a study of these schools which does not concentrate upon curriculum has been obscured by several methodological problems. Both Professor Simon in his survey of Leicestershire schools from 1625 to 1640[1] and Mrs Simon in her general essay on municipal schools in Leicestershire prior to 1660[2] attempted such a study and with some considerable success, although their work apparently has not been followed up by other scholars on the local level.[3] Before further studies *are* broached it seems necessary to face more directly the most difficult methodological problem of all—one which Professor and Mrs Simon recognised only implicitly and yet one the significance of which it is essential to grasp before the historian can be in any way certain that the picture of educational development which he constructs is either full or reliable. The historian is forced to use diocesan archives for his research into the development of such schools yet why should ecclesiastical records be *expected* to provide full and accurate information concerning the number, distribution and type of schools in an area? What are the limitations of this available evidence?

The answer to both these questions can only lie in a careful examination of the links between education and the Church and of the episcopal attitude to schools within a diocese. How concerned were the ecclesiastical authorities to record accurate information about education as such? Are the records which survive biased either by their apathy or by their excessive zeal?

Renaissance ideas of education and of its role in society may well have underplayed its religious elements and ecclesiastical connections, yet in post-Reformation England, at least, the links between the schools and the Church were as marked as ever. It is common knowledge that schoolmasters were ecclesiastical officers, often in orders, and held responsible in some sense to the Church authorities. But how superficial were these links which bound the schools to the established Church? How interested was the Church in maintaining its hold upon the education of youth and its supervisory powers over teaching personnel? It seems that historians have too readily assumed this interest and have employed church records too uncritically in consequence.

The work of Locatelli on education in the diocese of Auxerre in the late seventeenth century has pointed to the feasibility of an assessment of clerical control over and participation in education based upon diocesan archives,[4] and has further underlined the need for fieldwork. Locatelli possessed excellent documentation. In 1610 and in 1622 the Bishop of Auxerre drew up instructions concerning the regulation of schools in the diocese: schoolmasters, for example, were instructed to catechise their students weekly. In 1695 a later bishop laid down yet more detailed instructions. Each parish was to have two schools, one for boys and one for girls. In the poorest parishes the vicar or *curé* was to act as master. Parents were enjoined to see that their children attended school until at least the age of fourteen. Significantly, the authority of the *curé* over the teacher was stressed—the *curé* was to render an account of the doctrine and behaviour of the schoolmaster to the bishop. It was laid down that the teaching of Christian doctrine was one of the chief aims of education. By 1698 a standard fee for the employment of a schoolteacher was fixed.[5] Locatelli proceeded to determine to what extent these instructions were enforced in the early eighteenth century. He was able to discuss the effects of poverty, size of parish, geographical situation, and parental and ecclesiastical apathy upon the establishment of this network of parochial schools.

Unfortunately, the historian of education in late sixteenth and early seventeenth-century England finds no evidence of such an organised and explicitly declared attempt as this on the part of the hierarchy to foster the development of educational facilities. The question must be approached from a more oblique angle. This article takes as its starting point the Midland diocese of Coventry and Lichfield. An attempt is made to establish the policy of its bishops regarding the supervision of schools and schoolteachers within its jurisdiction in the period before the Civil War. One cannot assume that such policies were representative of those of bishops elsewhere—other bishops may have displayed far greater vigour and enthusiasm in the control of educational facilities and others more apathy. Nevertheless, the material available appears more than adequate to demonstrate the methodological problems of studying the growth of schools through diocesan archives. It will be made clear that while certain of the deficiencies in the sources were inherent to the system itself, others stemmed from the personal policy or lack of policy of the bishops themselves.

Schoolmasters, whether public or private, were undoubtedly considered part of the ecclesiastical system and were treated as ecclesiastical officers just as were midwives and surgeons. In theory no one might exercise the office of schoolmaster without prior admission and licensing by the ordinary or his surrogates. This rule applied throughout the period 1558 to 1642. It was felt that unlicensed schoolmasters would be either recusant or puritan in religious sympathy and thus potentially dangerous. Undoubtedly, hierarchical concern to maintain control over the schools and their personnel was motivated less by interest in education for its own sake than by this fear of nonconformist influences. The maxim—give me a child until he is seven and I will make him mine for life—was felt by the authorities to hold more than a grain of truth and so schoolmasters were made upon admission (after 1562) to subscribe to the Thirty-nine Articles and to the royal supremacy. It should be emphasised, of course, that a significant proportion of the boys taught in these schools were destined for service in the Church or state.

In theory this system of licensing was the perfect vehicle for episcopal control over education within the dioceses but, in practice, it was deficient in several respects. Even assuming the initial interest of the diocesan, there were notable problems involved in enforcement of the regulation. Lichfield diocese, for instance, was large in area, containing between 388 and 420 parishes,[6] and was possessed of poor communications. Episcopal, or even archidiaconal, control over the four archdeaconries was certainly not immediate and that over peculiar jurisdictions was virtually non-existent. It was a matter of no great skill to evade the eye of the authorities, however vigilant, and teach without a licence, particularly in the more remote corners of the diocese. Although the bishops had the machinery of triennial episcopal visitation at their command, it is clear that returns of unlicensed schoolmasters were both spasmodic and unreliable. Occasionally the visitation articles called for a general inquiry into the number of schoolmasters, licensed or unlicensed, for the purpose of checking upon the extent of licensing but the response even to these specific requests was not great. More usually visitation presentments recorded the name of a schoolmaster only if he had transgressed the rules of licensing as understood by the churchwardens. The decision to present a schoolmaster for such an offence was personal and might be affected by several considerations—simple negligence; sympathy with the offender; or threats or bribes from the offender being perhaps the most important.

Visitation presentments thus provide the historian with an imperfect listing of schoolmasters who had failed to obtain a valid licence or who had committed some other offence under the cognizance of the ecclesiastical authorities. In theory, however, the historian should be able to extract a full list of teaching personnel from visitation call books or *libri cleri*. All schoolmasters, whether serving in petty, English, or grammar schools, were required to appear and exhibit their licences to teach before the visitation court. The surviving *libri cleri* for Lichfield diocese, however, suggest that even licensed masters evaded these rules. The triennial visitation of the diocese held in 1639 records the names of few schoolmasters—twelve in the archdeaconry of Coventry; five in Derby; seven in Salop; and seven in Stafford.[7] When it is appreciated that this number is not even equivalent to the number of separate institutions mentioned it is clear that the list is defective. Moreover, several of the schools referred to in W. A. L. Vincent's own incomplete listing of endowed grammar schools do not appear in this *liber cleri*. That of 1620 also appears incomplete.[8] The court which met at Uttoxeter on 1 September 1620 under the presidency of Robert Master, Vicar-General, declared its intention to view the credentials of all rectors, vicars, chaplains, preachers, curates, schoolmasters and farmers of rectories but although some attempt was made to record the names of teachers within Stafford and Salop archdeaconries the impetus had obviously died when the court reached Derby and Coventry. Schools as important as Derby, Duffield, Monks Kirby, Coventry, Birmingham and Wellington receive no mention whatsoever and others are represented by the name of the headmaster alone.

Why are these listings so incomplete? In the first place, there were financial reasons for failing to appear before the court: officially it cost about threepence merely to exhibit a licence, of which the total amount went to the judge of the court,[9] and it was always possible that other fees would be claimed by lesser officials just as when licences themselves were issued. Certainly the bishop's secretary was accustomed to pocket a sum equal to that gathered by the registrar on the exhibition of curates' licences.[10] A yet greater deterrent was the expense entailed in actually obtaining a licence—in 1620 this stood at ten shillings, of which sum two-thirds went to the judge and the remainder to the registrar.[11] Although the visitation court was customarily held in the chief church of the various deaneries, often situated in the market town, it undoubtedly represented an inconvenience to attend it personally and it was expensive to exhibit one's licence by proxy. There is, of course, also the possibility that the officials themselves were not overly concerned or able to enforce the rule about the exhibition of teaching licences. Their lack of personal knowledge about the remoter grammar schools and English schools and certainly of the transitory establishments which depended upon one man's presence and enthusiasm for their very existence was a real bar to the presentment and consequent excommunication of schoolteachers who failed to appear and exhibit their licences. The excommunication books of the diocese, while they prove on occasion a useful supplementary source, certainly provide no systematic listing of schoolmasters excommunicated for operating without permission or even for failing to show their credentials.[12] How could they when the officials who compiled them had a very imperfect knowledge of who was teaching within the diocese? It may also be significant that it is the headmasters of known grammar schools who appear in the lists rather than the undermasters, or teachers in English and petty schools. Were the ecclesiastical officials, perhaps including the bishop, really interested in establishing control only over the sizeable and therefore more influential schools? Naturally there were exceptions to this; *hypodidasculi* and *pedagogi* are mentioned for some schools although there is reason to believe that many of the other institutions were far larger than might be concluded from the evidence of the *libri cleri* alone.

There is substantial evidence that the hierarchy was in fact far less concerned with teachers in the petty schools and vernacular schools. The Lichfield subscription books for schoolmasters cover only a little of the period in question—only those books for the years 1600–4 and 1632–42 contain significant numbers of schoolmasters' subscriptions— but these indicate that very few petty schoolteachers were licensed by the ordinary.[13] In 1615, however, Ralph Home appeared before the visitation court and obtained a licence to read prayers and teach boys 'the abcd' in Betley, Staffordshire.[14] Twenty-nine subscriptions by licensed schoolmasters were entered into one book between 1635 and August 1642.[15] Of not one of these schoolmasters is it possible to say with any certainty that he was being licensed to keep a petty school, although it appears that some distinction was being made between those men assuming established positions in grammar or free schools in the diocese and those merely being licensed to teach. For example, William Jennings, MA, Vicar of Church Eaton, Staffordshire, was licensed to teach in that parish, or anywhere else in the diocese, in August 1638; Robert Ogdon, however, was admitted to the office of third schoolmaster in Shrewsbury school in September of that year.[16] There is, of course, no reason to conclude that those men who received licences to teach rather than positions in established grammar schools were in fact merely teaching the vernacular. Certainly this cannot be inferred from the manner of subscription—this was normally made in English even by those specifically destined for the grammar schools. It is possible that the ecclesiastical authorities maintained an interest in vernacular as well as Latin schools while concerning themselves very little with petty school education.

What support is there for these suggestions elsewhere? The Leicester subscription books for the slightly longer period 1626–39 yielded sixty-two subscriptions from schoolmasters—four of these were for licences to teach the ABC. Professor Simon noted that the subscription of petty teachers cannot have been seriously enforced and also pointed out that the books contained no subscriptions from women teachers although they are known to have been prominent in these petty schools.[17] Records for the diocese of London for a slightly earlier period suggest that here also the licensing rules were not stringently applied to petty school teachers.[18] The subscriptions exist for the period November 1607 to April 1611:[19] of the fifty-eight subscriptions the great majority were for the teaching of grammar (forty-two) and none were specifically for petty school teaching. On 27 November 1607 David Palmer was licensed to teach English and writing at Watford. In the following March John Milward of Hendon, Middlesex, was admitted to teach the reading of English, 'le Accidence', and writing. Schools for the teaching of accounts and arithmetic also appear—on 14 October 1609 John Fretherne, literatus, was admitted to teach 'artem legendi scribendi computandi ac arithmetican' at St Martin-in-the-

Fields. The more common combination was simply that of reading and writing in the vernacular, and accounts—occasionally the teacher was also licensed to teach *puerilia* or the rudiments of grammar. Rarely are the Lichfield entries as specific—on 16 December 1611 Thomas Burdett subscribed before 'obtayninge licence to teatch chilldren to write cipher reade & caste accompts within the diocese';[20] in 1600 George Whittakers was given a general licence to teach boys the rudiments of grammar and James Rawlen received a licence to the same effect in 1603;[21] in 1604 Roger Stoughton of Shustocke was licensed to teach reading and writing[22]—but it is probably a fair assumption that most of the licences recorded in the diocesan records were for the teaching of grammar, with a fairly small number being for the instruction of children in the vernacular and accounts.

If it can be proved that licensing of petty school teachers was never more than occasionally enforced, can it be assumed that a systematic policy of licensing all other teachers was consistently pursued? An examination of the extant subscription books of the diocese would suggest that the answer is No. Although these books cover long stretches of the period in question—in blocks from 1600–4; 1610–14; 1614–18; 1618–32; and 1632–42—they contain very few subscriptions by schoolmasters.[23] The largest numbers survive for the years 1600–4 (23); 1620–2 (16); 1629–32 (14); and 1635–42 (29): for the years 1610–14 there was one subscription for a licence and one obtained from a suspected recusant schoolmaster; the years 1614–24 yielded only six entries; eight subscriptions were taken between 1624 and 1626 but there were no subscriptions for teaching licences at all between early 1626 and 1629 or between 1632 and 1635. There might be several explanations for this rather patchy distribution. Three of the significant blocks of subscriptions occur in loose enclosures to the main subscription books which in themselves contain very few references to schoolmasters. These enclosures consist mainly of subscriptions taken before the issuing of licences to curates, readers, public preachers, and schoolmasters whereas the main series of subscription books contain subscriptions taken before ordination or institution. This could mean that licensing subscription books were always kept entirely separate from the others and that the lack of overlap between the two series is merely coincidental. It may be that some schoolmasters obtained licences at the visitation court which were recorded entirely separately. On the whole, while it seems evident that the subscription books present an incomplete picture of licensing within the diocese because of the absence of books for several years at the beginning of the period, it would seem that the blocks of subscriptions for licences which appear represent the spasmodic attempts of the officials to tighten up on licensing rather than the sole survivals of a separate series of documents. This seems to be supported by the fact that a contemporary official thought it worth-while attaching the loose sheets to the main subscription books.

There is, indeed, direct evidence of fluctuations in episcopal policy regarding licensing. Bishops normally included amongst their visitation articles an inquiry into the distribution and behaviour of schoolmasters. Few of these were particularly original either in content or phraseology. Article 14 of Bishop William Overton's articles for the visitation of 1584 ran:

> Whether you have a schoolmaster in your parish, and whether your schoolmaster teaching publicly or privately be of good and sincere religion and conversation; and whether they be examined and allowed by the ordinary or his officer in that behalf; and whether any living given towards the erection or maintenance of any school be witholden back, or otherwise any ways employed?[24]

This had a close parallel in the articles for St David's in 1583[25] and indeed there is ample evidence that bishops commonly modelled their articles upon those employed in other dioceses. In the same year (1584) Overton and his chancellor, Becon, introduced 'Certain Advertisements' to govern ordinations, presentations, inductions, excessive fees and the control of schoolmasters within the diocese.[26] Although these were in fact a practical application of articles issued by the Privy Council in 1583 they were very thorough-going and owed much to Becon's reforming enthusiasm. The third of these advertisements expressed the view that 'the perverse obstinate untowardness of divers young gentlemen in religion doth argue a manifest and most intolerable corruption in their bringing up, and in schoolmasters'. In response to this threat Overton determined to tighten his control on the licensing machinery. Throughout the period it was common to issue a licence which admitted the candidate to teach in a specific parish or anywhere else within the ordinary's jurisdiction. The implications of this practice for episcopal control over teachers are obvious—when a schoolmaster had once obtained a licence he could move freely from parish to parish without the need for review of his licence and the ordinary had no chance to revise his original decision. Overton, therefore, ordered all schoolmasters to 'bring in their licences before to them granted the third day of the first month next after the visitation' to the Bishop, or his Chancellor, or his Chancellor's deputy, assisted by several preachers,

> to whom if they do not sufficiently allow their ability for learning, their soundness for religion, their honesty for conversation by learning and testimony of such as are well known to the bishop, then to be displaced and inhibited to continue their teaching any longer within this diocese.

Should they receive the approval of the examiners they were to receive instructions to examine their pupils in the catechism at least once a quarter and to ensure that scholars in their care attended church regularly. Perhaps most important of all, it was ordered that,

> no schoolmaster [was] to have or enjoy any general licence throughout the whole diocese uncertainly, but to teach in that particular place whereto he shall be allowed, and the licences contrary to that order to be reformed.

There is evidence that Overton and his officials sought, to their cost, to put these advertisements into general use within the diocese and there is every reason to believe that schoolmasters were commanded to appear at Lichfield for examination in 1584. The policy, however, must have been shortlived. The subscription book which survives for the years 1600 to 1604 contains several issues of general licences.[27] In late September and early October 1604 four licences were issued, all of a general nature, and only two of the recipients were graduates. It is true, however, that this bishop still issued specific licences to some schoolteachers, presumably where there was reason to doubt their qualifications either from the scholarly or religious point of view.

Later bishops of the diocese issued licences of different types. In the time of Bishop Robert Wright (1632–43) the most common form was admission to teach in a specific institution or parish. In 1639 William Overton received licence to teach at Kinnersley, Salop; Thomas Greenly of Cambridge was admitted schoolmaster of Glossop Grammar School; John Cowper 'literatus' was licensed teacher at Arcall Magna Grammar School; John Bett was admitted to teach in Bucknall; and William Bennet was granted permission to teach in Wroxeter.[28] Quite often a specific licence of this type was made rather more general by the addition of the words 'or anywhere in' and a specified district. The latter might be the entire diocese or an archdeaconry within it. On 3 June 1640 William Wales, for example, was admitted to teach in the city of Coventry and elsewhere in Coventry archdeaconry. William Barford, MA, however, was licensed to teach boys at Nuneaton Free School and anywhere in the whole diocese. It might be tempting to conclude that graduates alone were thus privileged and it is true that non-graduates do not figure prominently among the men given general licences but not all graduates were thus privileged, either.

The examination of the Lichfield licences suggests that either the examination administered to schoolmasters prior to their admission was sufficiently rigorous to determine the type of permit granted or that different fees were demanded for different types of licence. A glance at the teaching licences issued in London diocese from 1607–11 will perhaps throw further light upon the problem.[29] In the first year (1607–8) a more definite pattern emerges: men admitted to teach grammar were licensed to teach in a specific parish or anywhere in London diocese, whereas men licensed to teach the vernacular were restricted to operating in a specific parish and in the archdeaconry or even the deanery in which this was situated. This rule appears to break down only when the teacher of the vernacular was a student (*literatus*) of one of the universities. Clearly there was some feeling that men without university education required closer supervision than did graduates or students. As it was largely graduates who staffed the grammar schools and non-graduates the English schools it is probable that the distinction between university and non-university men weighed more with the diocesan authorities than did that between the schools themselves.

It seems fair to conclude that, firstly, the machinery at the bishops' disposal for the enforcement of licensing was in several respects unsatisfactory; secondly, that attempts to ensure that all schoolmasters within the diocese were functioning with a licence were spasmodic and often the response to Privy Council or Metropolitical initiative—that of 1584 being inspired by Privy Council articles and that of 1635 following close upon the metropolitan visitation of the dioceses which paid attention to the government of the grammar or free schools;[30] thirdly, that scant attention was paid to the licensing of petty school teachers even when there was tightening of control over other teachers; and fourthly, that the diocesans were aware of the dangers of issuing general licences and made some attempt to control the scope of licences according to the qualifications and conformity of the candidates, always with the proviso that a greater fee might have been demanded for a more general licence and that deficiencies in either respect might be overcome by a sufficiently large gratuity.

If the bishops were not consistent in their enforcement of licensing they seem to have been consistent in their attitude to teaching within the diocese and in the government of individual schools. This interest was motivated by a desire to enforce conformity within the diocese and by the realisation that the schools were the principal vehicle for the education of the clergy. It is the first motive which is most apparent from the diocesan and, indeed, from the school records. In 1616 Anna Hassall was presented at the visitation for teaching boys 'being a recusant' and was excommunicated; at Lapley, a heavily recusant parish, William Pickstock was charged in the same year with teaching boys without licence and being a popish recusant.[31] In 1623 Richard Cox and his wife Alice were presented for keeping a school without permission and for being recusant.[32] The Coyney family of Caverswall were known papists and, therefore, in 1617 Thomas Tully was noted to teach 'pueros private in domum Thomas Coyney ar' ',[33] and in 1629 Gerard Falden was presented for teaching without licence within that parish and being a recusant.[34] In Tamworth in 1616 the schoolmaster,

James Ramsbotham, was accused of teaching the sons of recusants and not making them attend church.[35] The bishops kept their eyes on Ramsbotham and in 1621 bishop Thomas Morton made further inquiry into his pupils and their church attendance. On 30 June 1621 the churchwardens wrote to him as follows:

> According to your Request, And the discharge of our duetyes and office, we have here under written sent you the names of all thos scollers (which are taught by Mr. Ramsbothome) and doe not Come to Churche. . . .
> Francis Smith the age of xiii yeares
> Richard Cassey the age of xiii yeares
> Harry Cassey the age of xii yeares
> John Thisseldon the age of xii yeares
> John Knightley the age of xii yeares
> Gyles Chapman the age of xii yeares
> Edward Chapman the age of ix yeares
> Thomas Wells the age of xiii yeres
> Thomas Freman the age of xv yeares.[36]

It was further reported that Ramsbotham was teaching without a licence and without a degree and for a combination of all these offences he was suspended from his office. If Ramsbotham obstinately ignored the rules regarding licensing for at least five years others were equally determined to evade authority and teach. In 1619 Ralph and Margaret Ford were presented for recusancy and it was said 'she teacheth children and have a maid her name not knowne which cometh not to Church':[37] twelve years later the same couple were presented for recusancy in the parish of Stoke-on-Trent and the churchwardens continued 'Fords wife doth teache schoole'.[38] Unfortunately this is the sole indication that survives in the records that when prevented from functioning in one parish or even in an area recusant teachers moved elsewhere to pursue their vocation. It is none the less interesting and suggests some of the real problems which the bishops met in dealing with nonconformist teachers.

The visitation records not only reflect anxiety concerning recusant teachers: the officials were also concerned to protect the people from Protestant nonconformist influence. In 1618 concern was expressed by the parishioners of Marston near Stafford that Nicholas Waddington

'predicat ac pueros docet sine licentia'[39] and much later, in 1635,
Ralph Harding layman was charged with reading prayers in Thursfield
chapel, Wolstanton 'without licence or toleration' and teaching boys in
the same chapel.[40] He claimed that he was in fact 'tollerated' by the
bishop as a 'lector' but he immediately refrained from teaching
school. In 1636 Nicholas Ashbie, schoolmaster of Belper, was presented at the visitation for negligent coming to church and was
suspected of extreme puritan leanings because he was 'sufferinge his
schollers to breake the glasse windowes', presumably of the church.[41]
Sometimes one is able to trace the possible influence of a schoolmaster
upon his pupils. In 1631 Edward Hollingshead was presented for
teaching school at Rushton chapel of Leek, Staffordshire without
licence.[42] In 1635 Hollingshead obtained a licence to preach from the
court at Lichfield and by 1636 was curate of Brassington, Derbyshire.[43] At the visitation of that year he was presented by the churchwardens in no uncertain terms for incontinency and heresy:

> Mr Hollinshead curat ibidem whoe beinge distracted (as wee verily beleeve)
> sayd he lived incontinently with one Jane Brunt, and further sayd that he was
> dead and buried and that he was the Messias and that whosoever beleeved
> not in him was damned.[44]

The bishops relied upon complaints from the parish officers for information regarding the activities of unlicensed teachers and of
licensed schoolmasters keeping small village schools. They were more
actively concerned that the larger free grammar schools should be
conformably run. Over some of these the diocesan could exercise little
control—the schools at Wolverhampton, Bridgenorth, Gnosall and
Lichfield, for instance, were outside his jurisdiction and such notices
of them as exist in the diocesan records occur in the proceedings of
metropolitical visitation. The bishop of Lichfield was, however, in a
position to intervene in the affairs of certain of the schools in the rest
of the diocese, notably at Stafford and Shrewsbury. A picture of continuous connection with Shrewsbury school emerges from both
school and diocesan archives.

There is no space here for a detailed consideration of the government of this school but a few general trends should be mentioned. The establishment of the school was encouraged by Bishop Thomas Bentham in the 1560s,[45] but it is not until the beginning of the seventeenth century that direct episcopal intervention in the affairs of the school becomes really evident. In 1607 the bailiffs objected to the appointment of one Ralph Gittins to the second master's place.[46] He was suspected by the puritan corporation of popish leanings, based largely upon his association with Humphrey Leach who had been sentenced recently by Archbishop Bancroft for Catholic sympathies. The Headmaster of Shrewsbury ignored the bailiffs' objections and appointed Gittins to the position.[47] The bailiffs retaliated by appealing to Bishop Overton for a licence to prosecute Gittins in the Court of High Commission and this permission was granted.[48] As a result Gittins was imprisoned and suspended from teaching. When Bishop Neile entered the diocese in 1610 he became interested in the Gittins case and took advantage of his position as visitor of the school to initiate an inquiry at Lent 1611. He concluded that none of the accusations against Gittins was proven, petitioned the Privy Council on his behalf and secured his restoration to the second master's place.[49]

Thomas Morton, who became Bishop of the diocese in 1618–19, was a great champion of scholarship and this, combined with the fact that he was an alumnus of St John's Cambridge, with which college Shrewsbury had a traditional connection, explains his vigorous participation in Shrewsbury's affairs. He was much more concerned with Shrewsbury's educational role than Neile had been. In 1626, for example, he became disturbed at the decline of the school's reputation and numbers and took the unusual step of summoning five of the best scholars from the school to test through their performance the 'sufficiency and insufficiency of the undermasters'.[50] Apparently they were found wanting for the second and third masters resigned in the following year. Morton is said to have examined the two replacements rigorously but no trace is to be found of this examination in the diocesan subscription books, although James Brooke, MA and Fellow of Gonville and Caius, the new second master, was ordained deacon after examination by Morton in September 1628.[51] Morton shared the fear of St John's College that Shrewsbury was in need of good leadership and organisation above all else but he also used his influence to establish the fellowships and scholarships for Shrewsbury boys to attend St John's which had been broached in the 1570s.[52]

Shrewsbury was probably atypical in the amount of scope it gave the bishop for intervention but this case is of great interest in demonstrating the willingness of at least some of the bishops to participate in school affairs. Shrewsbury was by far the largest and most famous school in the diocese, some said in the country, and as such presented a challenge. Its masters were potentially more influential than any others in the bishop's jurisdiction—teaching as they did the sons of local nobility and gentry and future clergymen—and so the bishops were amply justified in supervising the government of this school far more closely than others.

Although it may be true that the bishops maintained a steady interest in the internal affairs of certain schools, normally the larger endowed grammar schools, and were anxious to prevent the infiltration of recusant teachers into the schools, it remains apparent that interest in licensing all schoolteachers in the area was spasmodic. This seems to mean that any estimates of the number and size of schools within a diocese must be regarded as a *minimum* rather than as an accurate representation of the growth and spread of schools in an area. Saying this does not detract from the importance of such evidence but may perhaps make the historian more aware of the pitfalls of taking such information at its face value.

Clearly this argument has a much wider than methodological significance. The somewhat casual interest in licensing adopted by the hierarchy was undoubtedly a factor in the emergence of teaching as a separate profession. Although the schools themselves were still orientated towards the education of professional men and, specifically, future clerics, there is little doubt that the lack of a concerted effort on the part of the hierarchy to bring religious education to the fore in the schools and to supervise the government of these establishments allowed secularisation, in effect, almost uninterrupted growth.

The deficiencies inherent in the visitation system made possible only a very imperfect supervision of an area's educational establishments.

University of Birmingham

References

1 B. Simon, 'Leicestershire Schools, 1625–1640', *British Journal of Educational Studies*, iii (1954–5), 42–58.

2 J. Simon, 'Town Estates and Schools in the Sixteenth and Early Seventeenth Centuries', in *Education in Leicestershire: A Regional Study*, ed B. Simon, Leicester (1968), 3–26.

3 A. J. Fletcher, 'The Expansion of Education in Berkshire and Oxfordshire, 1500–1670', *BJES*, XV (1967), 51–9, makes no use of diocesan records.

4 P. Locatelli, 'L'enseignement primaire et les maîtres d'école a la fin du xvii siecle dans la diocese d'Auxerre', *Revue d'Histoire de l'Eglise de France* (1972), 96–106. E. H. Carter, *The Norwich Subscription Books* (1937), deals mainly with the post-Restoration period. S. M. Wide and J. A. Morris, 'The Episcopal Licensing of Schoolmasters in the Diocese of London, 1627–1685', *Guildhall Miscellany* (1967), also has this later emphasis although it is also interesting for the pre-Civil War period.

5 Locatelli, op cit, 103.

6 British Museum, Harleian MS 594, Return of the dioceses in 1563. This includes chapelries of ease, prebendal stalls and peculiar jurisdictions in its estimate of 561 parishes, which is certainly an overestimate.

7 Lichfield Joint Record Office, B/V/1/62, *Liber Cleri*, 1638/9.

8 LJRO, B/V/1/37, *Liber Cleri*, 1620.

9 LJRO, Dean and Chapter Muniments, Jurisdiction Book, Vol XVII, Table of Fees used in the consistory court, c 1620.

10 Durham University Library, Mickleton/Spearman MS, Vol 7, fo 63; cited in *Correspondence of John Cosin*. ed G. Ormsby, Surtees Society, LII (1868), 8.

11 LJRO, Jurisdiction Book, Vol XVII, Table of Fees.

12 LJRO, B/V/2/1–14, 1581–1640 (excluding 1599–1611).

13 LJRO, B/A/4/1; B/A/4A/17; B/A/4A/18.

14 LJRO, B/V/1/31, 23 September 1615.

15 LJRO, B/A/4A/18.

16 Ibid.

17 B. Simon, 'Leicestershire Schools, 1625–1640', *BJES*, iii (1954–5), 47.

18 Wide and Morris, op cit, 393, 395, suggests that these petty schoolmaster subscriptions were made but not recorded formally, due to pecuniary considerations.

19 London County Council Record Office, Vicar General Crompton, 1607–11, DL/C/339.

20 Borthwick Institute of Historical Research, York, Bishop Neile's Subscription Book, 1610—14, R.IV.Be, fo 15v.

21 LJRO, B/A/4/1.

22 Ibid.

23 LJRO, Subscription Books. This is especially true when it is realised that at least 200 parishes were served by a schoolmaster during the period discussed.
24 *Elizabethan Episcopal Administration*, ed W. P. M. Kennedy, Alcuin Club Collections (1924), 27, 165.
25 Ibid, 143.
26 Ibid, 169–70.
27 LJRO, B/A/4/1.
28 LJRO, B/A/4A/18 enclosure.
29 LCCRO, DL/C/339.
30 Wide and Morris, op cit, is interesting on this point. The argument that the imminence of an archidiaconal visitation would cause an increase in the number of licences taken out is unconvincing, simply because both archidiaconal and diocesan visitations were frequent and regular. A new visitation policy as expressed in the printed articles, however, or a metropolitical visitation might very well induce teachers to apply for licences.
31 LJRO, B/V/1/31.
32 LJRO, B/V/1/45, Aldridge entry.
33 LJRO, B/V/1/34.
34 LJRO, B/V/1/51.
35 LJRO, B/V/1/33, Tamworth entry.
36 LJRO, B/C/3/11, 30 June 1621.
37 LJRO, B/V/1/31, Tutbury entry.
38 LJRO, B/V/1/51, Stoke-on-Trent entry.
39 LJRO, B/V/1/31, Marston near Stafford entry.
40 LJRO, B/V/1/55; he was presented on a similar charge at Audley, Staffs in 1631, see LJRO, B/V/1/51.
41 LJRO, B/V/1/59, 1636, Belper entry.
42 LJRO, B/V/1/51, Rushton chapel, Leek entry.
43 LJRO, B/V/1/59, Brassington entry.
44 LJRO, B/V/1/59.
45 M. R. O'Day, 'Thomas Bentham: a Case Study in the Problems of the Early Elizabethan Episcopate', *Journal of Ecclesiastical History*, XXIII (1972), 151.
46 G. W. Fisher, *Annals of Shrewsbury School* (1899), 102–3.
47 Ibid, 103.
48 Ibid, 104.
49 Ibid, 113; also BIHR, R.IV.Be. 8 December 1611, fo 15v.
50 Fisher, op cit, 126.
51 LJRO, B/A/4A/18, 20 September 1628.
52 J. E. B. Mayor, 'Materials for the life of Thomas Morton, Bishop of Durham', *Cambridge Antiquarian Society*, iii (1865), 28–9.

LUKASZ KURDYBACHA

The Commission for National Education in Poland 1773—1794*

THE 'Polish Commonwealth' of the gentry (the *szlachta*) reached in the middle of the eighteenth century the depths of its decline. Disassociating itself at the beginning of the Counter-Reformation from all progressive thought coming from the West, it treated each breeze of healthy ideas with great suspicion, fearing that it might conceal either heretical thought, dangerous to Polish Catholicism, or some masked intention to abolish the 'golden liberty' of the gentry. The gentry, in its drive to ensure its continued ascendancy, had already in the sixteenth century introduced a restrictive economic policy in the towns and subjugated the interests of the peasants to its own. In political life, the gentry assumed an extremely conservative attitude, opposing and preventing any reforms.

Similar symptoms of decline can be easily discerned during this period in the secondary school system, which was mainly in the hands of the Jesuits, whose teaching programmes and education copied the methods used by other religious orders and the secular clergy. These schools taught the young people mainly Latin, overburdened with rhetoric, and kept them busy with elaborate religious ceremonies.[1] The new philosophical trends, however, were completely disregarded: not a word was said about the laws governing nature, discovered by Galileo, Descartes and Newton, no mention was made of Copernican

* Two hundred years ago, in 1773, a number of eminent Poles, actively supported by the King himself, and taking advantage of the dissolution of the hitherto all-powerful Jesuit Order by the Pope, formed themselves into a Commission for National Education (*Komisja Edukacji Narodowej*), and elaborated far-sighted and wide-ranging plans for educating the Polish nation out of its decline. Drawing upon the most advanced ideas and ideals of the Enlightenment, and notably those of the French Physiocrats, the Commission sought to extend educational provision and place it under secular control, as well as to modernise the curricula and improve the supply of teachers.

theory, long since acknowledged by all leading scientists. Young
people were not at all prepared for life, or for the performance of
public or private duties. With the help of carefully selected material
the conviction was inculcated in them that Polish law and public life,
and the social and economic structure, were so perfect that there was
no need to introduce any changes.

In this 'dark Saxon night'—as Polish historians used to call the first
half of the eighteenth century—there could be noticed, beginning in
the 1730s, some tiny sparks, a forecast of a brighter future.[2] The first
move may be credited to King Stanislaw Leszczynski, who was forced
in 1710 to give up the Polish crown. He settled permanently in Lune-
ville in France, where he set up a school for sons of gentry, based on
the latest achievements of science. The alumni of this school, half of
whom were Poles, later attracted attention at the court of the French
king and in the residences of Polish magnates, by the boldness of their
political views and their common sense in economic matters.[3]

Shortly afterwards, the Czartoryskis' party began courageously to
sponsor a comprehensive programme of reforms. This included the
strengthening of the king's power, curbs on the lawlessness of the
magnates and the anarchical tendencies of the gentry, a substantial
growth of the army, the expansion of industry, and measures to alle-
viate the oppression of the peasants. The outstanding Piarist educationist, Stanislaw Konarski, closely co-operating with the Czartoryski
group and maintaining friendly relations with Stanislaw Leszcnzyski,
established a *Collegium Nobilium* in Warsaw, in 1740—the first modern
select college for young gentlemen, the scions of the leading Polish
families, and ten years later he introduced similar reforms in all the
Piarist schools. The foundations were thus laid for modern Polish
pedagogy, basing its principles and goals on the recommendations of
the philosophy and culture of the Enlightenment. The main concern
was the proper education of the new citizens of the Polish state, by
trying to teach them all the achievements of modern science.[4] Though
Latin continued to be taught in these schools, its hold was limited by
placing it on an equal footing with the native language. More stress
was laid on the natural sciences, especially physics, as most useful for

the eventual development of industry. Konarski's students were, above all, to be enlightened citizens, conversant with their own country's past and aware of its contemporary needs, its strengths and weaknesses and also acquainted with the plans for reforming the state prepared by the political party of the Czartoryskis.

The road mapped out by Stanislaw Konarski and the Czartoryskis was soon followed by Stanislaw August Poniatowski, elected King of Poland in 1764. Ever since his studies in England, he had dreamed of turning his state into a constitutional monarchy, after a thorough transformation of its obsolete feudal political system and economic life, in accordance with the postulates put forward by capitalist economic thought. It was also due to his initiative and support that the first scientific and literary magazine began to appear in Warsaw, entitled *Monitor* and modelled on the English magazine *Spectator*.[5]

Of all the achievements of the Enlightenment, greatest interest in Poland was aroused by the philosophical and economic doctrines of the French Physiocrats. Basing themselves on the theory of the superiority of nature and her eternal laws, they were of the opinion that agriculture was the only truly productive activity, and, as 'friends of mankind', they came out in defence of the peasants. In Poland, an economically and socially backward country, the views of the Physiocratic school quickly turned into something like a national, social and economic ideology. Theoreticians of education frequently referred to this school of thought, maintaining that each country had the right to educate its citizens in accordance with its needs.

One also finds this view in the works of Helvétius, René de la Chalotais and Rolland. They all demanded that Latin should yield its traditional priority in the school curriculum to the national language, that laymen should be appointed as teachers and that education as a whole should be subordinated to the state and, in effect, nationalised. The ideas of these writers were quickened by J. J. Rousseau's *Considerations on the Polish Government*, which demanded that in every free country education should be directed by the state authorities and its administration entrusted to a schools council, composed of high officials who would form the 'supreme board of education'.

Although all these theoretical recommendations found recognition among enthusiastic Polish adherents of the thought of the Enlightenment, they were extremely difficult to implement. The main obstacles were, on the one hand, lack of funds, and, on the other hand, fear of an unfavourable reaction on the part of the conservative gentry. Anxious not to antagonise them, King Stanislaw August Poniatowski, within two years of ascending the throne, opened a *Collegium Nobilium* and covered the costs of its maintenance himself; here was something the gentry had asked for in vain from each new king since the sixteenth century. Soon this school became the model of a secular college educating young gentlemen in the spirit of ardent patriotism, training them for public life, preparing them to become good officers or civil servants. Behind all this was the conviction of the necessity of far-reaching reforms in all the backward sectors of Polish life.[6]

A real chance for the creation of a modern national educational system in Poland during the Enlightenment arose only after the *breve* of Clement XIV in 1773, abolishing the Jesuit Order. When they learnt of this, the ablest adherents of Stanislaw August (Adam Czartoryski, Joachim Chreptowicz, and others) hurriedly drew up memoranda demanding the taking over by the state authorities of the entire property of the abolished order and the diversion of its revenues to a completely secular school system, supervised by the king and adapted to the modern needs of Poland. The new system, they considered, should be based on the native language and national culture, and should prepare Polish youth for full participation in public life.[7] Despite all kinds of obstacles and intrigues the Seym (Polish Parliament) created on 14 October 1773 the Commission for National Education, passing a special law to this effect. Thus, for the first time in the history of Europe, a fully secular Ministry of Education was set up by parliament and responsible to this parliament, acting under the supervision of the supreme state authority, and endowed with full legal, administrative and financial independence.[8]

According to the resolutions passed by the Seym all the academies, secondary schools and public schools for young gentry were subordinated to the Commission for National Education. However, despite such a narrowing down of the social scope of the educational activity of the commission, it decided on 10 December 1773 also to promote the parish schools, intended for the poor gentry as well as for children of townspeople and peasants, a decision that exposed the commission later to many charges on the part of the conservative gentry.

The Commission for National Education was composed of four representatives of the higher chamber of parliament and four of the lower chamber. During the course of the twenty years of its activity, the composition of the commission underwent several changes. A total of 23 members attended the sessions of this committee.[9] Though each one was distinguished by his high intellectual attainment and a sympathetic understanding of the prevalent trends of the Enlightenment, not one of them was a teacher. Since it was their aim to create a uniform teaching system, adapted to the exceptionally difficult situation in the country, and since there existed no exemplars to imitate, they resolved at their first session to appeal to all Polish citizens as well as foreigners to send in proposals, plans and advice, to help towards the working out of a system of national education. In response to this appeal eight submissions were received by the commission, from Polish authors and from Dupont de Nemour of France as well as from Borrelli, a member of the Academy in Berlin. All the authors expressed themselves in favour of a universal and even obligatory educational system, but the representatives of the interests of the gentry demanded separate schools for each of the social orders, while others demanded uniform schools for the children of the gentry and the peasants. The majority of the authors of these memoranda proposed plans to organise a three-tier school system, ie elementary or primary schools, secondary schools and universities, simultaneously presenting draft curricula. Some of them emphasised most forcefully the necessity of setting up normal schools for the training of teachers. Due to the ongoing transformation of the Polish economic system from a feudal into a capitalist one, many authors postulated the setting up of appropriate vocational schools (hydraulics, mechanics and economics to be taught at all levels).

The majority of these bold ideas and proposals were incorporated into the 1774 regulations for parish and secondary schools.[10] On the basis of a common curriculum, the parish schools were to educate gentry as well as peasant children and the teachers were instructed not to discriminate in any way whatsoever between the children of peasants and gentry. This programme, side by side with the teaching of reading and writing, based on such up-to-date methods as composing words with the help of mounted letters and visual aids, envisaged the introduction of physical education and general knowledge in the fields of agriculture, horticulture, hygiene and secular moral education.

In the earliest plans of the commission provision had been made for the opening of 2,500 elementary schools in the whole country, one school for every ten villages.[11] However, this plan proved impracticable, due to the lack of funds and of teachers, as well as the reluctance on the part of the gentry to give education to the lower classes. The appeals of the commission to the wealthier gentry, asking for material aid, did not yield substantial results. The clergy, too, was not in a hurry, because it was difficult for them to accept the fact that the Church would be deprived of its monopoly in educating and instructing the youth. Only the Vilna bishop, Massalski, who was a member of the commission, managed after many efforts to organise 330 schools in Lithuania, which were attended by 4,956 children. This achievement, remarkable for those times and in such conditions, began to diminish after 1780, when Massalski resigned from his membership of the commission.

Of more lasting nature were the efforts made by the commission to set up parish schools in other parts of the country. There still exists much documentary material about the opening of parish schools on the landed estates of many magnates, of the wealthier gentry, bishops, etc. But research has yet to ascertain the exact number of schools. We can only say that by 1783 their number had reached 193. The years of effort made by the commission to organise elementary schools gained in 1789 the recognition of the Seym, which made all the parish priests responsible for the maintenance of a school and a teacher in each parish. Heavy fines threatened those who did not fulfil this duty, while special military disciplinary commissions watched over the proper observance of these regulations.

Secondary schools were mainly intended for the sons of the gentry, and their provision constituted the main official duty of the Commission for National Education. During the first years of its activity the commission planned to open 26 secondary schools with a seven-year curriculum and 52 six-year schools with a very similar programme. By 1786 the commission had set up 82 secondary schools with about 15,000 students.

The curriculum obligatory for all these schools was extremely progressive for those times. It was based on Francis Bacon's classification of sciences approved by d'Alembert in his *Discours préliminaire* to the French Encyclopedie (1751). That dissertation enabled the Commission for National Education to depart from the traditional seven liberal arts curriculum and introduce several modern subjects. Among them the most important position was held by the natural sciences. Latin was still taught, largely because the majority of juridical books were written in that language as well as a considerable number of former laws, but it now yielded its primacy to the native language, a policy which was to strengthen attachment to the national culture and was, side by side with the lessons on Polish history and Polish law, to develop patriotic feelings. This emphasis, in turn, served as a basis for a completely secular programme of moral instruction, which in addition to the duties in regard to the family, the neighbours, older people, etc, taught each boy about his civic duties in regard to his fatherland.[12]

Much of the curriculum—for the first time in the history of education in Poland on such a large scale—was given to mathematical and natural sciences, above all to botany, zoology, mineralogy, agricultural sciences, physics, mechanics, hydraulics, chemistry, and elementary medicine and hygiene. The purpose of all these subjects was on the one hand to facilitate the possible development of manufactures, and, on the other hand, to contribute to the growth of a scientific outlook among young people.

In addition to its work on curricula, the commission devoted much attention to the preparation of what may be regarded as the first school regulations in the western world. It laid down rules for the management of the school by rectors (ie principals) and for the work of the teachers, as well as for schools inspectors. It also drew up the outlines of reports about teaching procedures for the teachers, and laid down clear definitions regulating the duties of the owners of private schools for girls. (The commission did not organise separate secondary schools for girls, but supervised the private boarding-schools, taking care that the girls received the proper amount of instruction.)

Since work on the organisation and curricula of the schools took up much of the time of the members of the commission and hampered their political activity, they set up in 1775 a 'Society for Elementary Textbooks', composed of nine outstanding scholars and teachers. This society considered the curricula and watched over their introduction in the schools, arranged inspections of schools, approved and partly prepared textbooks for elementary and secondary schools. It may thus be claimed to have been the earliest 'pedagogical' department of a state educational body, fully conversant with the methods of work of the schools, their tasks and requirements. During the course of its activities it published 27 textbooks, including a textbook on logic, by the well-known French educator Condillac. This was admittedly not a great deal, but the discussion on some of the textbooks went on for several years and was very thorough. The society appended to each textbook full methodological instructions; this was a definite innovation, unencountered in other countries. Thanks to the Society for Elementary Textbooks each school and each class in the school used the same textbooks, which had the approval of the highest educational body, thus guaranteeing a uniform education for all pupils. The idea that textbooks should have the approval of the school authorities became generally accepted by the majority of the countries only in the nineteenth century.

Undoubtedly the most valuable achievement of the Society for Elementary Textbooks was the *Rules of the Commission for National Education*, a collection of important documents, instructions and regulations. This was the first 'code' of its type, regulating the organisation of the schools as well as the work and duties of the teachers.[13]

All the members of the society participated in the preparation of the *Rules*. The results of their work were discussed at a three-day conference of principals and vice-principals of all the schools. Later, school inspectors investigated the weaknesses and shortcomings of the first draft of the *Rules* in each school, which were taken into consideration in preparing the final version, published in 1783. The *Rules* throw a clear light on all problems related to school life—from pedagogic questions to administrative procedures. They laid down the curriculum for each subject and the teaching methods and organisation of the pupils' work. They attempted to prevent the overburdening of the children with homework, by indicating which days should be set apart for homework for the various subjects. They gave advice, with concrete examples, on how to accustom young people to do independent work, and laid down a list of reading matter at home. They devoted much attention to school organisation and the fostering therein of community spirit, and they prepared forms for individual record cards, etc. Each instruction bears witness to progressive thought, in accordance with the recommendations of the leading educational writers of the Enlightenment, fully respecting the individuality of each pupil, together with concern for the future of the state.

The attempt made by the Commission for National Education to work out detailed regulations that would embrace the entire conduct of the principals and teachers was all the more justified since at that time properly-trained teachers were not yet available for the implementation of the new secularised teaching programmes. After having taken over the Jesuit schools, the commission was forced, at least for the first ten years, to employ ex-Jesuits, who were not at all prepared to teach the new subjects, and manifested a rather negative—often openly hostile—attitude towards the secular school and its novel curriculum. The majority of the former Jesuit teachers, cherishing illusory hopes of a restoration of the Order, conducted a discreet propaganda campaign among the conservative gentry against the new programme, calling it 'the Warsaw plague' or 'miseducation'.[14] They charged the commission with endeavouring to destroy the existing social order, and with spreading atheism and unbelief. They also discredited as much as they could the subjects newly introduced into the curriculum, eg zoology and botany, and above all secular moral education, based on rationalism.

The difficulties encountered with the Jesuit teachers convinced the commission even more strongly that the educational directions it recommended for young people could be correctly implemented only by young secular teachers, who had yet to be trained. The greatest difficulty was that neither of the two universities existing in Poland at that time had the proper conditions to perform this task. The older university, active in Cracow since 1364, was completely under the influence of theology and Aristotle's scholastic philosophy, and not at all capable of spreading modern knowledge. Even worse was the situation in the post-Jesuit university of Vilna, which had only one faculty, that of theology and Church law. The commission was therefore forced to carry out a very thorough reform before entrusting the universities with the task of training teachers for the new secondary schools. The task of the modernisation of Cracow University was given to the young Cracow canon Hugo Kollataj, well known for his enthusiastic attitude towards the rationalism of the Enlightenment.[15] He started with the philosophy department. Liquidating the departments of scholastic philosophy and the philosophy of Aristotle, he introduced new departments teaching mathematical and natural sciences, including zoology and botany, natural law and political economy based on the works of the Physiocrats. In the faculty of medicine he organised clinics to specialise in major diseases, and anatomical laboratories. He based the work of the physics department on laboratories and on astronomical observations. His special concern was instruction in the field of applied mechanics to serve the development of industry and for military needs. In order to spread knowledge in this field as widely as possible among the population, the professors had to accept the duty of lecturing every Sunday to all those interested in the subject.

The reforms introduced at Vilna University by the well-known astronomer Poczobut were based on the same principles.[16] Chosen as lecturers were young people, most of whom had studied in France, England and Italy. Many of them soon became famous as outstanding scholars.

The reform of the two universities enabled the Commission for

National Education to proceed with the previously announced 'tiered' school system. In this way the commission for the first time introduced the idea, put forward in England in the seventeenth century by the unknown author of *New Solima*, and restated in France in the eighteenth century by Rolland, namely the subordination of elementary and secondary schools to the universities in each region. In accordance with the proposals of these two authors the entire school system in the Grand Duchy of Lithuania was subordinated to Vilna University, and the schools in the remaining Polish territories to Cracow University. The Rector of Cracow University was the direct superior of the rectors of all the regional schools, and the latter in turn exercised supervision over all the secondary and elementary schools in their areas. In the same way the Rector of Vilna University controlled as the superior authority the rectors of regional schools in Lithuania. General inspectors, elected for terms of two years from among the professors of the two universities, controlled the secondary and elementary schools. Basing themselves on the reports of the inspectors, the two universities prepared annual general reports for the commission, which thus became fully conversant with the work of every school and could issue proper instructions, allot the necessary funds, appoint new teachers and amend regulations.

After completion of the reforms in both universities, the commission opened in Cracow in 1780 training colleges for future secondary-school teachers. Applicants for places at these colleges were either former pupils of secondary schools, recommended by their rectors, or university students. They were submitted to a severe selection procedure, attention being paid to their state of health, morals and manners, diction, etc. Each successful candidate received a very adequate grant. During their five-year course they lived in student hostels and were supervised by one of the professors. Half of the time was devoted to practical pedagogical work in schools and the other half to university lectures and reading. Each alumnus of a teachers' college was entitled after 20 years of work to an old-age pension, amounting to two-thirds of the salary he received during the past few years of professional work.[17]

The dislike of the conservative gentry for the commission and its progressive educational policy, exploded powerfully in 1792, when some members of parliament demanded the liquidation of the commission's school system and the resuscitation of the Jesuits, pleading that they be once again entrusted with the education of all young people. A year later, during the session of the parliament in Grodno, these same conservative political groups demanded a division of the commission into Polish and Lithuanian sections and its subordination directly to the government, so abolishing its autonomy. The department that took over the supervision of the commission was advised to purge the school system of the remnants of any innovatory spirit of 'that plague—so dangerous for every government', as they called it. Since at the same time many teachers were dismissed, the religious orders were once again able to take over the schools.

This act of suppression, instigated at the order of foreign powers, closed an interesting chapter in the history of Polish education. The Commission for National Education, whose educational achievements had grown out of the fertile soil of the progressive socio-political and educational thought of the epoch of Enlightenment, had put an end to the prolonged 'medievalism' of Polish schools, and to the domination of theology over science, and introduced in its place a rationalist philosophy, including research in the natural sciences, based on observation and experiment. The commission gave education and instruction a national character, replacing cosmopolitan Latin with the native language and stressing the culture of the nation and its history. Furthermore, it adapted the educational trends to the political, social and economic needs of the country.

The most original and innovatory step for a Catholic country was the introduction in all schools of secular lessons on morality, which from the beginning aroused deep alarm and gave rise to attacks led by conservative circles, headed by the clergy. The sharp edge of this type of instruction was directed against the bigotry, religious fanaticism and intolerance of the Jesuit schools, as well as against the anti-humanitarianism, obscurantism and self-seeking of the backward gentry.[18]

However, the ultimate significance of the Commission for National

Education, not only for Poland but also for the entire civilised world, was the fact that due to its existence the education of the younger generation was first considered to be one of the main duties of the state. Thanks to the commission, people began to appreciate that the rationally-organised activity of the school was a tremendous force, capable of preserving the existence of the nation through the improvement of all aspects of national life. By liberating the school from the medieval influence of the Church, the creators of the Commission for National Education simultaneously granted the state the right to adapt educational organisation as well as the curriculum to its long-range development plans, which enabled the school to make its contribution to the great historic processes of developing nations.[19]

University of Warsaw

References

1   J. Wybicki, *Życie moje*, oprac. A. Skałkowski. Biblioteka Narodowa, SI, 106 (Kraków, 1927), 9–10.
2   A. Jobert, *La Commission d'Education Nationale en Pologne* (1773–1794) (Paris, 1941), 73–7.
3   S. Leszczyński, *Dispositio in rem nobilium, qui exercentur in Academia Lunevillae* (1740), 26.
4   S. Konarski, *Pisma pedagogiczne* (Wrocław, 1959), s 164–201.
5   R. Kaleta, *Monitor z roku 1763 na tle swoich czasów* (Wrocław, 1953).
6   K. Mrozowska, *Szkoła Rycerska Stanisława Augusta Poniatowskiego* (Wrocław, 1961).
7   J. Lewicki, *Geneza Komisji Edukacji Narodowej* (Warszawa, 1923), 61–73.
8   *Uniwersał Komisji Edukacji Narodowej, Pierwiastkowe przepisy pedagogiczne Komisji Edukacji Narodowej* (Lublin, 1923), 5–9.
9   Jobert, *La Commission d'Education Nationale*, 473–4.
10 *Przepis do szkół parafialnych, Ustawodawstwo szkolne za czasów Komisji Edukacji Narodowej* (Kraków, 1925), 16–23.
11 T. Mizia, *Szkólnictwo parafialne w czasach Komisji Edukacji Narodowej* (Warszawa, 1964), 53, 97.
12 *Przepis Komisji Edukacji na szkoły wojewódzkie*, Ustawodawstwo szkolne za czasów Komisji Edukacji, 24–41.
13 *Ustawy Komisji Edukacji Narodowej* (Warszawa, 1783).
14 *Komisja Edukacji Narodowej 1773–1794, Raporty generalnych wizytatorów* (Warszawa, 1902–15).
15 H. Kołłątaj, *Raporty o wizycie i reformie Akademii Krakowskiej* (Wrocław, 1967).
16 M. Baliński, *Dawna Akademia Wileńska* (Petersburg, 1867).

17 K. Mrozowska, *Walka o nauczycieli świeckich w dobie Komisji Edukacji Narodowej na terenie Korony* (Wrocław, 1956).
18 S. Tync, *Nauka moralna w szkołach Komisji Edukacji Narodowej* (Kraków, 1922), 12–24.
19 *Pierwiastkowe przepisy Komisji Edukacji Narodowej*, 37, 38, 147.

Editor's Note

Professor Lukasz Kurdybacha of the University of Warsaw, founder and former Director of the Institute of the History of Education of the Polish Academy of Sciences, died in Warsaw on 22nd December 1972, aged 65, after an illness bravely borne. Poland's leading historian of education, he was chiefly interested in educational thought and in the secularisation of education in the seventeenth and eighteenth centuries, and his many publications included a valuable monograph on the present theme, *The Papal Curia and the Commission for National Education, 1773–1783* (in Polish), Cracow, 1949, while another book by him on the commission is due to appear later this year.

The Editor is very grateful to Mr. R. Szreter of Birmingham University for his help in preparing this article for publication.

RAYMOND PALLISTER

Educational Capital in the Elementary School of the Mid-Nineteenth Century

In the mid-nineteenth century, the national income level and the state of technical knowledge imposed a severe limitation on the type and quantity of capital equipment available to the teacher. Indeed, investment in the teacher himself and in his training was at a very low level, a large proportion of the teachers being totally untrained. Yet expenditure on teachers was by far the largest part of total school expenditure. Much less was spent on buildings and considerably less on equipment. 'When the payment of a teacher, and a room to keep school in has been provided,' states the *Report of the Commission of Inquiry into the State of Education in Wales* (1847), 'all else is left very commonly to shift for itself'.[1] The largest piece of capital equipment was the building, which at its cheapest could be like the one visited by Inspector John Allen at Llanarth in 1845, 'a poor hovel, mud walls, mud floor, rented at twenty-five shillings a year'.[2] On the other hand many school buildings were relatively expensive and sometimes over-elaborate in design. 'I have seen more than one building', writes Inspector Marshall, in his report of 1850, 'erected after the design of one of the most eminent of living architects, and at a cost exceeding £2,000, in which so little knowledge of essential details is displayed, that, in spite of their imposing appearance, they can only be regarded as very good banqueting halls converted into indifferent school-rooms.'[3] The Central Boys' School at Norwich, as described by Inspector Mitchell in 1850, must have been as near the ideal for that time as one could find.

The [main] room . . . is now eighty feet long by thirty feet broad and twenty in height. It is lighted by four windows on the south side, one on the west, and one on the east, and also by large skylights. . . . The entrance is by two doors, at each side of the west window, this end being in the Tudor style, with some architectural pretensions. A screen separates the closets for hats and cloaks from the schoolroom. A gallery, at the far end, will hold, sitting, a hundred boys. It is nineteen feet four inches wide, the seats being sixteen feet long, and two adits each twenty inches wide . . . [There is also] a classroom, airy and well lighted, and fitted with a gallery to hold fifty boys . . . [and] there are two fireplaces.[4]

But if this standard was usually unattainable, it was relatively easy and cheap to obtain some building or room in which to hold a school. A Sunday schoolroom, an old warehouse or store-room, a good barn, any place which was capable of containing the required number of children would suffice. 'In almost every homestead, or in every village', says Mr C. Whitehead, in 1865, 'there is a stowage or granary, or large room that could be fitted up.'[5] Cheap buildings appealed to many, and indeed there was considerable criticism of the unnecessary ornamentation of some school buildings. 'I would rather see money contributed for the maintenance of the school', comments the Rev Longueville Jones, a Committee of Council Inspector, 'than for the supposed decoration of the building.'[6]

The typical elementary school building, if there was such in the middle of the century, was a single schoolroom, usually twice as long as it was broad, with high windows, and heated by open fire or stoves; an additional classroom was found only in the wealthier schools, or in schools attached to training colleges.

Once the building had been provided and sufficient money set aside for paying the teacher, then investment in equipment could be made. Some form of seating was essential although it was not a prerequisite of a school to have seats for the children, at least not for all the children. Some of the work done in schools was done in a standing position. The National Society method of mutual instruction recommended that part of the middle of the floor of the schoolroom be set aside for pupils to stand reading,[7] while in British schools 'the centre of the room should be occupied by desks and forms, a clear passage of from six to eight feet being reserved for the reading stations'.[8] The gallery, if there was one, was usually designed to accommodate the whole school for simultaneous instruction from the master. Many of the private venture schools had insufficient seating accommodation and some children had to sit on the floor for want of seats. In 1841, it was

Page 149 (above) *Nineteenth-century elementary school classroom;* (below) *elementary school classroom with perspective desks for object drawing (reproduced by permission of the Curator of Beamish Hall Museum, Co Durham)*

See Pallister, 'Educational Capital in the Elementary School', pp 147–58

Page 150   (above left) *teacher's desk and bell* (above right) *Perspective desk; (reproduced by permission of the Curator of Beamish Hall Museum, Co Durham)*

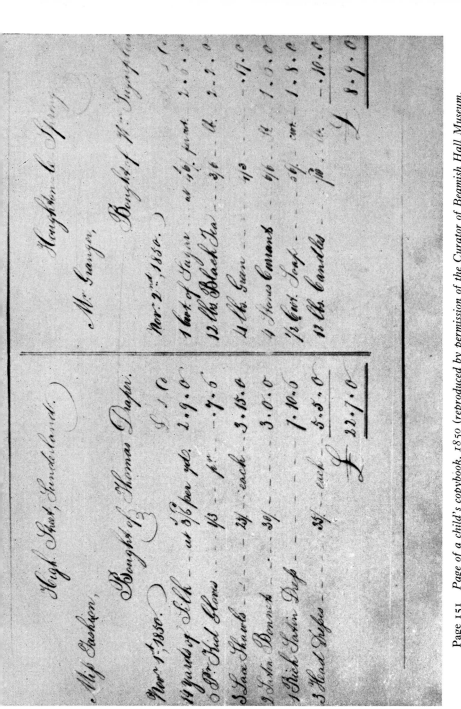

Page 152 (above) *Slate pencil sharpening machine;* (below) *infant's desk and apparatus* (*reproduced by permission of the Curator of Beamish Hall Museum, Co Durham*)

See Pallister, 'Educational Capital in the Elementary School', pp 147–58

reported that in Salisbury 'in some schools, children were required to stand without any opportunity of changing their position for two hours'.[9] Seats were available in church and chapel and in many cases where buildings were hard to acquire these were made use of, but often both the church and the seating arrangements were totally unsuited to the needs of the elementary school. The chapel in which the school at Abergele was held in 1847 was, like most other chapels, 'unsuitable for the purpose. The furniture, with the exception of a small table and a pulpit, consists exclusively of pews. This prevented classification, order, discipline, and system.'[10]

Possibly the cheapest form of desk suitable for writing was the type recommended by the National Society in 1839:

> An inclined plane about ten inches wide, with a horizontal ledge two or three inches wide, to receive the ink at the upper part of it, makes a good desk, and it is best when placed close to the side walls, so that the writer may sit or stand with his face towards them.[11]

The inclined plane, common to most desks in the nineteenth century and highly practical for reading and writing exercises, did not yield to the flat-topped desk until very recent times, when the need for a flat surface suitable for the many other activities of the children in the modern primary school became apparent. Immediately after the institution of the Committee of Council in 1839, specifications for buildings and apparatus were made available to managers of elementary schools, even to the point of specifying the type of wood to be used in the construction of desks. 'The desks and forms are to be of $1\frac{1}{4}$ inch white Christiana deal.'[12] In the 1840s, and for some time afterwards, desks and forms were made as separate units, although often they were fixed to the floor to prevent movement, thereby losing their value as independent pieces of furniture. The British and Foreign School Society in their hints on the erection and fitting-out of schoolrooms recommended that the desks be 9 inches broad and the forms 6 inches broad. Every child would occupy a space of 18 inches on his form, and twenty children would be able to sit side by side on each form. This required each form to be 30 feet in length and each desk the same. On each side, between the ends of the desks and the outside walls was a gangway of 6 feet, thus making the width of the room 42 feet. Its recommended length was 80 feet 6 inches and a room of that size was supposedly able to accommodate 520 pupils in twenty-six rows of desks.[13]

It is in the second half of the century that refinements were introduced. With the introduction of iron legs the desk and seat could be made as one unit (see p 149). Back-rests and shelves were soon added. By the 1880s the more prosperous schools were using two-seater desks, iron-framed, with seat attached and a shelf underneath and a slot at the front for the slate. This was the typical desk of the late nineteenth century and the early twentieth century, and indeed there are still many to be found in use in schools at the present time.

On 7 August 1844, a letter was sent from the Committee of Council to inspectors stating that the committee would pay two-thirds of the expense of providing three or four parallel desks to contain twenty to forty children for simultaneous teaching. Drawings of such desks were later distributed to inspectors. The committee were also prepared to pay two-thirds of the cost of converting desks attached to the wall to make groups of parallel desks in the main body of the room. The desks were to be inscribed 'By grant from the Committee of Council on Education'.[14]

Grants were also available for the purchase of books and apparatus, but these grants were to be made 'only in those cases in which the apparatus will be appreciated and used with skill'.[15] A list of accredited selling agents was also given. Blackboards could be obtained for 5s 6d through an approved agent in 1851; easels made of birch could be had for 10s 6d.[16] Chalk could be bought for 2s a box, or at the cheap rate of 9d a box from the Department of Science and Art.[17] These grants from the Committee of Council and the Department of Science and Art, together with concessionary rates of purchase, led to an improvement in the quantity and quality of aids to the teacher. The better schools were equipped with blackboards and easels, maps, globes, rolls of music, bead frames, reading frames and a plentiful supply of books. Bridge Street School, Darlington, was reported by Inspector Fletcher in 1845 as an excellent school, well furnished 'and enjoying a luxury of apparatus'.[18] Evidence of the increasing range of equipment available to the elementary-school teacher can be seen in the lists of the Department of Science and Art. The following is the list of equipment available to an elementary school for initiating art classes as encouraged by the department in 1855:

> Large compasses 3s od; White chalk (1 gross) 2s od; Slip, two set squares and a T-square 5s od; Letters AOS 3s od; Cronmire's drawing instrument 1s 3d; One set of twelve outlines 4s od; Twelve plates of outlines on canvas 7s od; The same reduced for pencil drawing 1s 6d; Bishop of St. Asaph's outlines 2s 3d; Familiar objects 9d; Box of models £1 2s od; Selection from Dyce's Drawing Book 5s od; Diagram of colour 9d; Total £2 17s 6d.[19]

Where there was a flourishing art class, and there were many in association with the richer elementary schools, one might even find the specially-designed desks for perspective drawing. The student viewed the object to be drawn through the eye-hole of a metal rod which stood in the near side of the desk top, and the object was neatly framed by the upright wood in front (see pp 149–50).

For reading lessons some schools were able to afford reading frames and boxes containing letters, possibly some reading cards and a range of reading books. Books were obtainable through the religious societies and through the government agency at large discounts. Longman and Company held the government agency for some years. Because of bulk purchasing, the government were obtaining on average $43\frac{3}{8}$ per cent reduction on retail prices,[20] and were also able to allow a further reduction of a third on the reduced price to the purchasing schools. The order for books from the government could only be made once every three years and it had not to exceed in value 2s per head of average attendance at the school, or 2s 6d where there were pupil teachers in the school. Despite the ease with which a school could acquire cheap books, there were still many inspected schools without reading books other than the Bible. The Statistical Society of London reported that in one school in Westminster in 1837 there were only two books among sixteen children, all of whom were above five years of age.[21]

Most children would learn to read from the scriptures or from books offering factual material. Much of it was dull to the child. 'I am acquainted with Mrs Trimmer's selections', writes G. Bell, 'and the divers *Historical Questions* published by the SPCK which are all excellent, but to young minds dry and difficult.'[22] Because of economic pressure, geography and history books contained masses of facts put down as concisely as possible, and children could be expected to learn to read from these, besides acquiring either 'cape and bay geography' or the ability to recite 'Billy, Billy, Harry, Ste . . .' for the kings of England. Books of the sort found in elementary schools usually cost less than 2s each, but at a time when it was difficult to find the money to pay the teacher, expenditure on books was regarded as a luxury rather than an essential. *A Manual of English Grammar* by Rev J. M. McCulloch, with 180 pages, sold at 6¼d. Professor Sullivan's *Geography Generalized*, with 146 pages, at 1s 0d.[23] Some textbooks were obviously best-sellers. Out of 175 aided British schools visited by Inspector Joseph Fletcher in 1846, ninety-six used Crossley's *Arithmetic* only, and eighty used Allen and Cornwell's *Grammar*. Sixty-six of the schools had no grammar books and 107 had no books for geography.[24] And the British schools were usually often among the wealthiest of the public elementary schools. In the Roman Catholic schools, which were generally poorer, fewer books were found. 'I have seen two schools', writes Inspector Marshall in 1850, 'in which the only reading book was the New Testament; but this was probably, not so much from choice, as necessity.'[25] It is interesting that in the great majority of even the humblest schools in Scotland, the parents were asked to supply their children with books. This was not unknown in England and Wales, and instances are cited by the inspectors, especially in some of the West Country schools. In these places the children were to buy books at three-quarters of the price fixed by the Committee of Council, either in a lump sum or by weekly payments. The books were forfeited to the school if the child left within twelve months, but if he stayed on then the book became the child's property. When the child moved up to the next class he could sell the books at half price to the school.[26] The renowned Rev R. Dawes was able to persuade almost all parents to provide books. He writes:

During the four years which the school has been at work, I do not think there have been half a dozen cases where the children have not provided themselves with the necessary books.[27] Of a set of small maps, sixpence each . . . sixty-three were bought in a very few weeks.[28]

Written exercises were invariably done on slates with slate pencils; some of the wealthier schools would even be able to afford the mechanical sharpener to go with the slate pencils (see p 152). After exercises were corrected on the slate, the completed work was often transferred, in immaculate style, to a copy-book. Many such copy-books have been preserved by families for future generations to see and admire, and their existence is a testimony to the quality of the presentation of the material in them and the delight that their owners must have derived from them. Most were prized possessions, and we are fortunate that many have survived as visible evidence of the type of work done and the standard of presentation of work at least in the better elementary schools of that time (see p 151).

It is impossible to make generalisations which can give a meaningful picture of the quality of educational capital in schools in the early Victorian period. However, what can be said with certainty, is that there appears to have been a scale of preference for education capital. The building and the teacher were absolutely necessary. After these had been provided, forms and desks were first on the list of furnishings, followed closely by a few reading books. Slates were next, copy-books much later. In the wealthier schools a wider range of reading material would be acquired; then blackboards and easels, chalk, and so on to the more luxurious types of education capital such as drawing apparatus, globes, maps etc. As the century progressed, and as the economy became stronger and richer, what had previously been luxuries became essentials, and what had been rare became common.

Neville's Cross College, Durham

References

1   *Report of the Committee of Inquiry into the State of Education in Wales* (1847), vol 1, 34.
2   *Minutes of the Committee of Council on Education* (hereafter referred to as *MCC*) (1845), vol 1, 110.
3   Ibid, 1850–1, vol 2, 670.
4   Ibid, 270.
5   C. Whitehead, *Night Schools* (1865), 10.
6   *MCC* (1850–1), vol 2, 510.
7   Ibid, 1839–40, 49.
8   *The Manual of the System of Primary Instruction pursued in the Model Schools of the British and Foreign School Society* (1839), 17.
9   Rev Edward Field, *Report on the State of Parochial Education in the Diocese of Salisbury* (1841), 7.
10 *Report of the Committee of Inquiry into the State of Education in Wales* (1847), vol 3, 7.
11 *MCC* (1839–40), 49.
12 Ibid, 142.
13 Ibid, 1846, vol 2, 279.
14 Ibid, 1844, vol 1, 113.
15 Ibid, 114.
16 Ibid, 1850–1, vol 2, 256.
17 Department of Science and Art, *First Report* (1854), 5.
18 *MCC* (1845), vol 2, 236.
19 Department of Science and Art, *Second Report* (1855), 7.
20 *MCC* (1847–8), vol 1, xviii.
21 Statistical Society of London, *First Report* (1837), 15.
22 A letter headed 'Want of good school books on Sacred History and Biography', *English Journal of Education*, vol 1 (1847), 58.
23 *MCC* (1847–8), vol 1, xx et seq.
24 Ibid, 1846, vol 2, 233 et seq.
25 Ibid, 1850–1, vol 2, 667.
26 Ibid, 89.
27 Rev R. Dawes, *Hints on an Improved and Self-Paying System of National Education*, fourth ed (1850), 27.
28 Ibid, 11.

For plates, provided by the author, see pp 149–152

R. D. ANDERSON

French Views of the English Public Schools: Some Nineteenth-Century Episodes

BRITISH and French education have generally gone their separate ways without having much influence on each other. The public schools were the educational institutions of Victorian England which were best known abroad, but they were perhaps especially ill-suited for imitation in France, a country with a strongly-developed system of state secondary education. When French reformers looked abroad, it was usually to Germany, which seemed to have much to teach in the field of scientific and technical education. Yet the English public schools did find some admirers in France, and at least one minister of education—Victor Duruy in the 1860s—made a serious attempt to borrow ideas from them.

Most of the interest, however, was more theoretical than practical, and it was often based on an idealised image of the public schools rather than on first-hand and accurate knowledge. They were cited either to show up some of the defects of French education, especially on the disciplinary side, or to make political points. Admiration of the public schools usually went with political conservatism, and this was one reason why there was resistance to ideas borrowed from them. The subject in fact throws as much light on a certain strain in French political and social thought as on the history of education.

Britain seemed a paradoxical country to outside observers in the early nineteenth century. On the one hand, it provided the world with the model of a modern industrial society, transformed by the energy and utilitarianism of its people and the spirit of enterprise and self-help. On the other, it was a country which had avoided political revolution and where ancient institutions seemed to survive intact. These different aspects gave rise to different forms of Anglophilia, though there was general agreement that the greater 'individualism' of England was what distinguished it from France.

The modern, thrusting side of English life was what attracted the free-trade economists, a small but articulate group in France who were perhaps the leading propagandists for English ideas. They were radical critics of French education, yet they did not appeal to the example of the public schools, which seemed to them relics of a previous age. In fact, the state of English education was rather embarrassing for doctrinaire liberals: despite the absence of state intervention, and the unhindered operation of a free market, England seemed to have a set of schools even more hidebound, classical and out of touch with the needs of the age than the French lycées.[1]

A very different view was taken by the other main Anglophile school, the 'liberal Catholics' who were the nineteenth-century heirs of the aristocratic liberalism of Montesquieu. For them England was attractive as the home of an older social order, of which the public schools formed part. It is among writers of this school that interest in the public schools is most consistently found. Their leader Charles de Montalembert included a chapter on schools and universities in his *De l'avenir politique de l'Angleterre* (1855), and much of what he said was echoed by later French writers on this theme.

This sort of liberalism was essentially an upper-class affair, strongest among those who felt that their class had been excluded from power since the July revolution of 1830. They accepted liberal political ideas, but they rejected the social consequences of the French Revolution— the bourgeois character of nineteenth-century France, and the whole system of the 'career open to talents' which the lycées founded by Napoleon symbolised. They admired England because there liberty was combined with continuity and with the influence of a traditional governing class, and they hankered after a 'decentralisation' in France which would restore effective power at the local level to the landed class.[2] In England, it was thought, the public schools sustained the power of that class and trained it for public duties, instilling into their pupils that combined respect for tradition and liberty which seemed to be an English secret. A more theoretical reason for approving of the public schools—and of Oxford and Cambridge, which attracted some attention in the 1850s because of the controversies over their reform—was their independence and autonomy. They were 'intermediate bodies' between state and individual of a type which elsewhere in Europe had vanished.

Even the outward aspect of English schools and universities was a reminder of the survival of the old order. All French visitors were struck by the contrast between the lycées, which occupied dingy and cramped premises in the centre of towns, and the public schools which, as was appropriate for the education of a landed class, were situated either in the countryside or in small country towns. Montalembert, as a romantic medievalist, was entranced by the princely buildings and the monastic calm of the ancient foundations. 'Nowhere in the world are the middle ages still standing and alive as they are at Oxford and Cambridge.'[3]

Anglophiles of all schools—on this point liberal Catholics and liberal economists were at one—held that English public life was distinguished by the spirit of individual initiative and 'self-government', which was contrasted with the passivity and dependence on government supposedly characteristic of the French. It was in the public schools, it seemed, that the English character was formed. Their whole way of life reflected the general spirit of English society, and was based on the principle of individual freedom and responsibility. It was therefore the disciplinary or 'moral' side of English education which attracted most attention. The intellectual training of the public schools was rarely examined,[4] and when it was the conclusion was usually that France had nothing to learn from it. What went on outside the classroom was found more interesting, and a number of themes recur in all French accounts.[5] They centre on the greater freedom enjoyed by the English schoolboy.

Freedom, first of all, to use his time as he wished. While French *lycéens* had their noses to the grindstone for eleven hours or more a day, doing even their personal work under supervision, in England classes were suspended in the afternoon, and boys were responsible for completing their work in their own time. Classes were shorter in England because of the importance of recreation, both organised and informal. English schoolboys roamed the countryside at will, at a time when exercise in the lycées was limited to gymnastics and supervised walks through the town streets.

An aspect of English freedom which astonished French observers was the formation of debating societies and the publication of school magazines. Public schoolboys were encouraged to discuss the burning issues of the day, while the lycées did their best to exclude any mention of religion or politics. There was a good reason for this: in a country of divided opinions, the schools tried to act as national institutions at the service of all. But those who praised the public schools saw this early encouragement of political consciousness as one of the ways in which they helped create the English 'civic spirit'.

The disciplinary system of the lycées had many critics in France. Its military character was a constant reminder of their Napoleonic origins —drumbeats, not bells, marked the divisions of the day. Every movement of the pupils was supervised, and order and silence were expected to reign throughout. To maintain this system, a special class of employee was needed, the *maîtres d'études*. But in the English schools, it was noted, the prefect system was quite adequate for enforcing a looser discipline, as well as being, of course, an illustration of the English principle of giving responsibility at an early age. Another difference was that *lycéens* wore a semi-military uniform, whereas 'in England, school uniform will never be accepted'.[6]

In general, the English system was directed to developing the will, and to encourage self-discipline and the sense of duty. English boys were given freedom, and punished if they misused it. This 'corrective' principle was contrasted with the French 'preventive' system, where the aim was to watch the boy so closely that he had no chance to do wrong. In England young men were introduced gradually to the responsibility of adult life, while in France there was no relaxation of discipline for older boys, so that the transition to adult freedom was often accompanied by violent reaction or personal disturbance.[7]

There was, of course, a less admirable side to public school life, and even the keenest Anglophiles usually had reservations about corporal punishment (forbidden in the lycées) and fagging. Excessive concentration on games, too, was usually criticised, though the French picture of the public schools was formed before athleticism reached its peak in the late Victorian era.

How much practical effect was the English example likely to have on French schools? An indirect influence may perhaps be seen in the growth of Catholic secondary schools. It was the liberal Catholics, led by Montalembert, who campaigned for the removal of legal restrictions on these schools, a campaign culminating in success in 1850, and they certainly had the idea that the Catholic schools could do for the French upper class what the public schools did for the English gentry. As it turned out, the schools which flourished after 1850 did have something in common with the public schools: they were often in the countryside, they gave more attention to games than the lycées, and they tended to place the formation of character above academic achievement. But this was probably due more to a similar clientele and to the independent traditions of the Jesuits and other teaching orders than to any conscious imitation.[8]

For English ideas to influence the state schools was more difficult. The fact that the public schools were obviously privileged and expensive institutions created prejudice against them. The average educated Frenchman believed that since 1789 France was 'democratic', while England remained 'aristocratic', and conventional French ideas about English life and character reflected this view. The exclusive public schools seemed to fit into the pattern, and to be inferior on political grounds to the lycées, middle-class institutions with moderate fees, whose very austerity and discipline breathed the spirit of republican virtue.

These points were made by the artist Hippolyte Flandrin, comparing England and France in the official French report on the London International Exhibition of 1862. Education in England, he claimed, consisted of schools for the sons of the aristocracy on the one hand, and schools for the poor, provided on purely charitable grounds, on the other. The needs of the middle classes, and the general interests of society, were neglected. But in France, the state extends its solicitude to every class of society: it ensures free education in the primary schools for the children of the poor; it takes care that the colleges and lycées provide secondary education on terms accessible to modest fortunes; and finally, for every class, education and instruction are steps by which they raise themselves in the social order, and the state encourages their rise and progress.[9]

Across the Channel, Matthew Arnold was commending the French state system for just these reasons, and urging the creation of schools like the lycées in England. Perhaps critics and admirers of the English system both failed to realise how it was already changing in these decades, with the appearance of new schools with modern curricula, of local examinations, and of competitive entry on the French model to the army and the Civil Service.

In 1858 the widely-read *Revue des Deux Mondes* gave its readers a review of *Tom Brown's School Days*, by Emile Montégut. Montégut used the book to make the familiar criticisms of the French disciplinary system, and to praise the individualism of the public schools, which taught 'the great lesson that life is a series of obstacles which we have to know how to overcome'.[10] This review was itself fiercely attacked in the teachers' periodical, the *Journal général de l'instruction publique*. The article expressed the resentment of teachers at constant criticism by the 'partisans of the English system', and defended French traditions on grounds of high principle. The individualism of the public schools was 'egoistic' and patrician; the more disciplined life of the lycées taught the virtues of equality and respect for merit, and was essential to the university's mission of inculcating the spirit of national unity and respect for the principles of 1789.[11]

The 'University' was the French term for the whole body of teachers. They formed in fact an organised corporation, and one which was both conservative in its educational views and proud of its democratic social function. French teachers generally came from the lower middle class—they were not 'gentlemen' like English public-school masters. They were very conscious of the way the lycée helped the poor but talented to get on in life, and claimed that within its walls differences of rank and wealth were ignored. All this made them suspicious by nature of innovations from England.

This was soon discovered by Victor Duruy, who as minister of education in 1863-9 took a serious interest in such innovations. Although himself formerly a teacher, Duruy was a remarkably open-minded man, and an energetic reformer who was prepared to consider ideas from any quarter. It was he who commissioned the first official report on secondary education in England. Two commissioners were sent to Britain, Jacques Demogeot, who taught literature at the Sorbonne, and Henry Montucci, professor at a Paris lycée and a modern language expert. They were to inquire into both schools and universities, and the two volumes which they published in 1868-70 are a very impressive achievement. Their inquiries were far more thorough than Matthew Arnold's in France,[12] and were supported by both documentation and personal observation. The public schools naturally took up much of the space in their volume on secondary education, but did not monopolise it. They also visited modern schools, described recent trends in policy, and gave an exceptionally thorough account of education in Scotland.

Demogeot and Montucci's judgement of the public schools was cool, and they avoided speculation of an ideological kind. Their professional opinion was that intellectual education was on the whole weaker in England than in France, and in the section of their conclusion headed 'possible borrowings' they concentrated on questions of moral education and discipline. While arguing that the French system as a whole should be maintained because it suited French society and the French character, they thought its harshness might be modified.

In particular they commended the use of prefects or monitors and the 'tutorial system', by which they meant a house system in which the housemaster also acted as a tutor, as at Eton. The adaptation of these ideas, they thought, might provide a solution to the perennial problem of the *maîtres d'études*: there was always difficulty in recruiting men for this thankless and ill-paid job, and the moral influence of those likely to be attracted by it was dubious. Demogeot and Montucci also recommended shorter class hours, more freedom for pupils in arranging their work, and more recreation, although they deplored the athletic excesses which they found in some schools.[13] They found mild forms of corporal punishment acceptable, but they condemned flogging: 'It is astonishing to see English teachers removing a garment which the prudery of their language hesitates even to name.'[14]

'The formation of characters with a manly stamp, that is the first principle of pedagogy with our neighbours, and we have to admit that they have a better understanding than we do of the education of the will.' That was the lesson of Demogeot and Montucci's report for Ernest Lavisse.[15] It was a concept of education with which Duruy was in general sympathy, but perhaps what interested him more about English methods was that they seemed to suggest answers to some of the practical problems which he faced. In the 1860s, the barrack-like regime of the lycées was increasingly coming under attack. The old liberal idea that it sapped the spirit of individual initiative was now reinforced by a new concern about health. Excessive constraint and long class hours were, it was alleged, undermining the physical vitality of the nation's youth and threatening the degeneration of the race. These arguments were put forward in a book with the expressive title *L'Education homicide*, by the Catholic poet Victor de Laprade. It was the English above all, said Laprade, who understood the principle of *mens sana in corpore sano*.[16]

Two main lines of reform seemed indicated. One was to reduce the burden of work on children, and here the more relaxed English approach seemed to have lessons.[17] The other was to modify the boarding and disciplinary system. Some reformers, like Ernest Renan, wanted the lycées to give up boarding altogether; others, with the English example in mind, urged the moving of the schools to the countryside.

These drastic remedies were beyond Duruy's power, but he did try to humanise the system, and took ideas from Demogeot and Montucci's report for his experiments.[18] These went furthest at two pilot institutions connected with his reform of 'special secondary education' (a modern alternative to the classics): the lycée at Mont-de-Marsan (Landes), which was to specialise in this type of education, and a new school at Cluny for training teachers in modern subjects. At Cluny, the rural siting of the school (in the old monastery) was itself an English innovation: 'Does not Cluny recall Harrow, Eton, Oxford, Cambridge, etc?' asked the principal hopefully.[19] Other innovations were that discipline was enforced by *commissaires* chosen from among the pupils instead of *maîtres d'études*, and that the principal, like an English headmaster but unlike the head of a French lycée, was a teacher as well as an administrator. Demogeot himself inspected the school to check that these arrangements were on the right lines.[20]

At Mont-de-Marsan, the innovations affected the arrangement of classes. They included one-hour classes, giving more time for recreation (in the lycées the class period lasted two hours), and 'setting' pupils according to their strength in individual subjects.[21] In 1868, Duruy incorporated these ideas in a programme of reforms suggested for general application, and added another English idea, allowing optional subjects in examinations.[22] On all these points, he closely followed Demogeot and Montucci.

Duruy fell from power before he could carry out this programme, but there was another experiment with shorter hours at the lycée of Versailles, where in 1868 periods were reduced to an hour and a half. This experiment, however, was not well received by teachers and officials.[23] Another English-inspired innovation at Versailles was that boys were allowed to talk during meals.

The reaction of the teachers to English ideas had been shown in 1864, when Duruy circulated a questionnaire bearing on various points to local administrators and heads of schools. One question asked whether senior pupils might be given 'a sort of monitorial power'; another suggested introducing 'exercices athlétiques' (a footnote explained that the expression was taken from the English) such as *paume* (the French version of tennis), dumb-bells—and cricket. The answers to the circular were fairly sympathetic to the idea of more exercise, but outdoor games were in practice ruled out because of the lack of playing fields.

The monitorial system, however, was decisively rejected. The general feeling was that 'these institutions from across the Channel have no application for Frenchmen, who are born with the feeling of equality and with a horror of espionage, whatever name it goes under'.[24]

The reference to espionage and the appeal to the university's tradition of equality occurred frequently, and several replies made the point that English customs were valid only for an 'aristocratic' society. As always, resistance to English examples was based on the instinctive feeling that the ethos of the public schools was in conflict with the principles on which modern France was organised.

Duruy was perhaps the only French minister of education to have been an enthusiast for cricket. Some of his ideas, however, were brought forward a second time by his friend Jules Simon, who was minister in 1870–3. Simon's ambitious programme of reforms included a strong emphasis on health and recreation, and he showed an interest in both monitors and the 'tutorial system' as answers to the boarding problem.[25]

Like Duruy, Simon met much opposition, and lost office before he could carry his ideas through. In any case, the times were no longer propitious for reforms of this kind. After France's defeat in 1870, Germany rather than England was the model for reformers, and it was rifles rather than cricket bats which they sought to place in the hands of schoolboys. The great educational reforms of the 1880s left secondary education relatively unchanged, and such debates as there were centred on the struggle between the classics and science rather than on the 'moral' side of education. Only in the twentieth century, when sport began to be properly developed in the lycées, might English influence be discovered again.

Yet there were still some Frenchmen who took an interest in the public schools, and it is worth looking at two of them, Edmond Demolins and Baron Pierre de Coubertin. Perhaps significantly, both men were themselves educated by the Jesuits, and their intellectual roots were in the liberal Catholic school. One of the links was the Catholic social thinker Le Play, who cited Montalembert's description of the public schools, and like him praised their autonomous management of their affairs;[26] Le Play was one of the creators of modern 'corporatist' theory.

Edmond Demolins was a disciple of Le Play. In 1897 he published a book celebrated in its day, *A quoi tient la supériorité des Anglo-Saxons*.

Like the earlier liberals, Demolins attributed the superiority of the English to their spirit of self-reliance, but he clothed this idea in the new vocabulary of social Darwinism: the 'struggle for life' and the survival of the fittest were the principles on which English society was based. Demolins's arguments also had a racial tinge, and he saw the Anglo-Saxon race as France's great rival because it was threatening her influence all over the world. He was one of the small and untypical group of Frenchmen who wanted France to become a world rather than a European power and to create a settler empire.

Demolins believed that the individualism of English education played a vital part in forming the pioneering spirit, and the English character in general, linking this with an elaborate theory about 'particularist' (eg England) and 'communitarian' (eg France) societies. But it was not the older public schools which interested him. He had met Dr Reddie, one of the pioneers of British progressive education, and he included in his book a short description of Reddie's school at Abbotsholme.

Unlike most admirers of the English schools, Demolins moved from theory to practice. He sent his own son to another progressive school, Bedales, and himself founded a school on similar lines in France, the *Ecole des Roches* (which still exists) in Normandy. Demolins's next book, *L'Education nouvelle* (1898), was a kind of extended prospectus for this school, and it contained a very full description of life at Bedales.

The progressive schools were of course no more typical of English education than the colonial settler, carving a living from the virgin soil in rugged independence, was typical of English life. Yet Demolins fits into the tradition which we have been discussing, for he admired Bedales for just those features which had always appealed to the public schools' French admirers—the freedom given to pupils, the emphasis on outdoor activities, the cultivation of moral responsibility, the prefect system, the friendly relations between masters and boys. Only the teaching of manual crafts at Bedales struck a new note. From an outsider's point of view, the permanent features of the English tradition were more striking than the differences between public and progressive schools.[27]

In any case, the older schools themselves were still attracting attention. Pierre de Coubertin is best known as the founder of the modern Olympic Games, but he was also an Anglophile, and conducted a campaign based on the English example for the introduction of sport in French schools.[28] Jules Simon was president, and Victor Duruy a member, of his 'Committee for the propagation of physical exercise in education'.

In 1888 Coubertin published his *L'Education en Angleterre*. This was mainly a survey of the leading public schools, and it had few reservations about their way of life. Like Demolins, Coubertin praised English education for producing 'free men and strugglers' and cultivating 'moral energy'. He too attributed England's colonial success to this training, and openly approved the elitism of English education. 'Intellectually as well as physically, the idea of selection dominates English education; everything seems organized with an elite minority in mind.'[29] He condemned the way in which the lycées encouraged excessive social mobility (*déclassement*), and he wanted them to follow the English path by raising their fees and making entry more competitive.

Coubertin was perhaps the only French observer to enter fully into the mystique of public-school sport. Sport, he argued, encouraged the competitive spirit, it taught boys to command and to obey, and it left them too exhausted to think of sex. 'Why has cricket always been so disdained by us? It is a splendid game, of the highest interest, which exacts discipline and gives birth to team spirit (*esprit de corps*).'[30] Coubertin deplored pure athleticism divorced from moral ends, but he also disapproved of the tendency which he found in the schools to put more emphasis on academic attainments. He thought Arnold's compromise between scholarship, religion and gentlemanliness an ideal more in tune with the English character.

Professor Eugen Weber has recently shown how Coubertin's cult of virility was part of the tangled roots of modern right-wing thought.[31] We have seen how French admiration for English public schools was consistently linked with an aristocratic and liberal form of Catholicism. But we can also see how this strain in French thought had changed in the years that separated Montalembert from Coubertin. An old-fashioned concern for aristocratic privilege had turned into a modern elitism, and romantic nostalgia for the institutions of the ancien régime had given way to a philosophy of competition and conflict from which a far more effective attack on democracy might be launched. Much of what was said in favour of the public schools was intended, directly or indirectly, as a critique of the liberal tendencies of French society in the nineteenth century. Perhaps the French teachers were right to see a threat to the spirit of 1789 behind what were on the surface purely educational proposals, and were expressing more than their national prejudice and professional spirit of routine when they met suggestions based on English practice with suspicion and resistance.

University of Edinburgh

References

1   C. Clavel, *Oeuvres diverses* (Paris, 1871), ii, 279–81, 296 (a liberal economist's reflections on Oxford).
2   Cf T. Zeldin, 'English Ideals in French Politics during the Nineteenth Century', *Historical Journal*, ii (1959), 48–9.
3   C. de Montalembert, *Oeuvres polémiques et diverses* (Paris, 1860–8), ii, 341. Cf similar reaction in a report on Oxford by P. Lorain, *Séances et travaux de l'Académie des sciences morales et politiques*, 2nd series, viii (1850), 98. Another admirer of the English universities was the liberal bishop and theorist of upper-class education F. Dupanloup, *De la haute éducation intellectuelle* (Paris, 1855–66), ii, 498.
4   Perhaps because even official visitors found headmasters very reluctant to let them observe lessons: J. Demogeot & H. Montucci, *De l'enseignement secondaire en Angleterre et en Ecosse* (Paris, 1868), iii–vii.
5   One of the fullest and best known was in H. Taine, *Notes sur l'Angleterre* (1872). Taine's views were fairly neutral. For an enthusiastic liberal Catholic account, see C. de Franqueville, *Les Ecoles publiques en Angleterre* (Paris, 1869).
6   P. de Coubertin, *L'Education en Angleterre* (Paris, 1888), 112.
7   E. Marguerin & J. Motheré, *De l'enseignement des classes moyennes et des classes ouvrières en Angleterre* (Paris, 1864), 87–9 (an official report, mainly about other types of school); E. Renan, *Oeuvres complètes*, ed H. Psichari (Paris, nd), i, 540 (a lecture of 1869).
8   It is perhaps odd that the public schools, whose religious bias was consciously Protestant, should have appealed so much to French Catholics. But the whole 'Christian gentleman' side of the Arnoldian ideal was rather passed over by French commentators.

172   *History of Education*

9   *Exposition universelle de Londres de 1862. Rapports des membres de la section française du jury international*, vi (Paris, 1862), 5–6. Information about primary schools was available in E. Rendu, *De l'état de l'instruction primaire à Londres* (1851), which painted a gloomy picture.

10   *Revue des Deux Mondes*, 2nd period, xvi (1858), 380. *Tom Brown's School Days* was translated in 1875, by when it was hardly an accurate picture of public-school life. It was reprinted nine times down to 1911.

11   Aubertin in *Journal général de l'instruction publique*, xxviii (1859), 82–3, 92–4.

12   As was pointed out by a reviewer in *The Quarterly Review*, cxxv (1868), 473–90.

13   J. Demogeot & H. Montucci, *De l'enseignement secondaire en Angleterre et en Ecosse* (Paris, 1868), 592 ff.

14   Ibid, 43.

15   E. Lavisse, *Lycée Impérial Napoléon. Distribution solennelle des prix. Discours . . .* (Paris, 1869), 15. The historian was then a young teacher, and had served on Duruy's personal staff.

16   V. de Laprade, *L'Education homicide*, new edn (Paris, 1868), 114.

17   J.-B. Fonssagrives, *L'Education physique des garçons* (Paris, 1870), 130–2.

18   Correspondence in the archives shows his direct interest in the report.

19   F. Roux, *Histoire des six premières années de l'Ecole normale spéciale de Cluny* (Alès, 1889), 14.

20   Ibid, 29–30, 70, 72.

21   *Bulletin administratif du ministère de l'instruction publique*, new series, vii (1867), 311–13; Archives Nationales F17 8702, Duruy to mayor of Mont-de-Marsan, 27 April 1866.

22   *Bulletin administratif*, new series, ix (1868), 325–9.

23   *Revue de l'instruction publique*, xxviii (1869), 835–6.

24   Reply of inspecteur d'académie of Saône-et-Loire to circular of 16 July 1864, Archives Nationales F17 6846. For others see F17 6843–9, replies to questions IV 12 and V 4.

25   J. Simon, *La Réforme de l'enseignement secondaire* (Paris, 1874), 205–24, 250–9.

26   F. Le Play, *La Réforme sociale en France* (Paris, 1864), i, 421–4.

27   Cf W. A. C. Stewart, *The Educational Innovators. II: Progressive Schools 1881–1967* (London, 1968), 70–3.

28   Described in his *L'Education anglaise en France* (Paris, 1889).

29   P. de Coubertin, *L'Education en Angleterre. Collèges et universités* (Paris, 1888), 45.

30   Ibid, 299, and cf 53–5. See also Demolins on the moral virtues of cold baths, *L'Education nouvelle* (Paris, nd), 67.

31   E. Weber, 'Pierre de Coubertin and the introduction of organised sport in France', *Journal of Contemporary History*, v (1970), no 2, 3–26.

HAROLD SILVER

Education and the Labour Movement: A Critical Review of the Literature

THIS survey is concerned, not with the provision of education for the working class or with the whole range of Radical movements, but with working-class movements from the end of the eighteenth century, and with what became the organised Labour movement. It is concerned with the relations between this movement and all aspects of education —educational ideas, institutions and acts, the education of children and of adults. It attempts to trace the growth and direction of historical interest in this bridge area, and to indicate some useful material.

Only a few historians have in any sustained way explored the links between education and the Labour movement. Many Labour historians have commented briefly on the educational interests of Labour organisations; some historians of education have made passing reference to contributions by working-class organisations. The bibliography at the end of this survey includes, therefore, both major work on parts of this field, and work offering more limited insights.

The Roots of Historical Interest
Interest in this area was made possible by the work on Labour and Radical history which, from sporadic beginnings in the 1870s and 1880s, became more substantial in the following three decades. The first volume of Holyoake's *History of Co-operation* appeared in 1875, and was followed by a number of books on socialism with an historical content, including Hyndman's *Historical Basis of Socialism in England* in 1883. In the 1880s and 1890s the Fabians produced a large number of tracts with an historical content. Thomas Kirkup's *History of Socialism* appeared in 1892, and the Webbs' *History of Trade Unionism* in 1894 (going through five impressions by 1902). Work on specific historical aspects followed, including two American books on Char-

tism in 1916 (by Faulkner and Rosenblatt) and two more in England in 1918 and 1920 (by Hovell and West). Other directions were indicated by J. Holland Rose's *Rise of Democracy* (1912), A. W. Humphrey's biography of the trade union leader Robert Applegarth in 1913, and H. N. Brailsford's *Shelley, Godwin and their Circle* in 1914.

Particular interest centres on the work done on Robert Owen during this period. This work, tracing the contribution of Owen and the Owenites to the growth of working-class consciousness and institutions, really dates from A. J. Booth's *Robert Owen, the Founder of Socialism in England* in 1869; it was revived and extended, so far as education was concerned, in Fabian writings and culminated in Frank Podmore's great biography of Owen in 1906.

With the exception of this work on Owen, interest in education tended to be slight or non-existent (for example, there is little on education in the Webbs' *Trade Unionism* and virtually nothing in Hyndman's *Historical Basis of Socialism*). Nevertheless, the history of radicalism established in this writing was to influence the major publications on the history of education that were produced after the First World War. For example, Charles Birchenough's *History of Elementary Education*, first published in 1927, used such sources (including Cobbett, and the books by J. H. Rose and H. N. Brailsford). J. W. Adamson's *English Education 1789–1902*, published in 1930, used the autobiographies of Thomas Cooper and William Lovett, G. D. H. Cole's biography of Owen (1925), and the work of A. E. Dobbs. Frank Smith's *History of English Elementary Education* (1931), also used Cooper and Lovett, Hovell's *Chartist Movement*, and Dobbs.

The catalyst in bringing the history of education into such a relation with that of Labour and Radical movements was adult education, most strikingly between 1906 and 1925. The nature of the adult education movement inevitably provoked interest in the histories of working-class movements, adult education and economic and social ideas. Central to the embodiment of this interest in a systematic historical form were Albert Mansbridge and A. E. Dobbs.

Mansbridge's contribution was mainly autobiographical: accounts of the Workers' Educational Association appear in a number of his works through to 1940. A paper which he published in two different forms in 1906 and 1907 was, however, of wider importance. In the Co-operative Wholesale Societies' *Annual* for 1906 he published 'A survey of working-class educational movements in England and Scotland'; the following year, using some of the same material but extending it, he published 'Working men and continuation schools' in Michael Sadler's *Continuation Schools in England and Elsewhere*. The 'survey' was a somewhat muddled account of education by and for the working class, focusing mainly on the Co-operative movement. Trade union educational efforts had been incoherent and 'fugitive'; only the Co-operatives among working-class bodies had developed an educational policy that was 'comprehensive' and 'sustained'. In the second version of the paper he thought that the trade unions were now doing more in education, partly owing to the influence of the trades councils. He pointed to wider working-class efforts, by the Social Democratic Federation, the Fabian Society, the Clarion Clubs and Socialist Sunday schools. His main emphasis remained on the work of the Co-operative movement.

Mansbridge explained the reason for writing his 'survey':

> The record of working-class educational experiments in England and Scotland has never yet been written, and, in view of the fact that working-class effort generally is becoming more pronounced . . . it would appear that the time has arrived for a survey of these experiments.[1]

He continued to demonstrate this historical awareness, but at this point the interest shifts to A. E. Dobbs. Dobbs became a fellow of King's College, Cambridge, in 1908. Soon afterwards, 'at the suggestion of Albert Mansbridge, he embarked on a history of English popular education in modern times, with particular reference to movements of democratic origin or tendency'.[2] This appeared as *Education and Social Movements 1700–1850* in 1919 (but had been completed in 1914); an intended second volume never appeared. Dobbs's impressive book arrayed the economic, social and cultural changes of the seventeenth and eighteenth centuries, and looked in detail at the later period, with 'the growth of political and trade organisations which were a product of social unrest, and in which sections of the working class are found here and there struggling to evolve their own forms of instruction and to express their ideals'.[3] Dobbs's range of sources was not wide, but the book was an important departure. In it the relationship between adult education and Dobbs's historical consciousness comes out clearly. At one point he reflects that it is in 'the religious movements of the period and the economic and political consequences of the Industrial Revolution, that we must seek the origin of those ideas of democratic government which have entered so largely into adult education in recent times'.[4] At another point he suggests that 'class-teaching with an element of discussion, which forms a recognised complement to the lecture in modern schemes of higher education, finds its origin in one of the most characteristic aspects of voluntary enterprise . . . the formation of societies for "mutual improvement" '.[5] The book ends with a discussion of the WEA, as having 'drawn together a variety of movements'.[6]

In 1920 Dobbs contributed an 'historical survey' to St John Parry's *Cambridge Essays on Adult Education*, discussing public opinion and education in the early nineteenth century, working-class and extension movements, trade union and Co-operative educational work, the Club and Institute Union, adult schools, the WEA and residential adult education. Dobbs had inaugurated a period of major importance in the writing of the history of this network of relationships, as can be seen from a calendar of some of the publication events of 1919–25.

1919
A. E. Dobbs, *Education and Social Movements 1700–1850.*
Adult Education Committee, Ministry of Reconstruction, *Final Report*. Mansbridge, Tawney and Frank Hodges were members of this committee. The report contained an excellent historical review of nineteenth and twentieth-century developments, and expressed its debt to books by Dobbs, Hovell and the Webbs, the autobiographies of Lovett and Samuel Bamford, P.A. Brown's *French Revolution in English History* (1918), and others. Adult education, it explained, had drawn inspiration 'from churches and chapels, from the achievements of physical science, from the development of cheap

literature and of a popular press, from Co-operation and Trade Unionism, from Chartism and more recent political developments.'[7] Max Beer, *History of British Socialism* (which was also to buttress some of the education history written in the following decade).

1920

A. E. Dobbs, 'Historical Survey', in R. St John Parry, *Cambridge Essays in Adult Education.*

Albert Mansbridge, *An Adventure in Working-Class Education* (an account of the WEA from 1903 to 1915).

A reprint of William Lovett's *Life and Struggles*, with an introduction by R. H. Tawney. This reprint was symptomatic of the growing interest in the Chartists. Hovell and West had been little interested in the educational projects of Chartism, but Tawney considered them more enlightened than anything introduced since.

Basil A. Yeaxlee, *An Educated Nation.* This included a short history of 'early efforts and ideals in adult education', leaning heavily on Dobbs and the 1919 report.

1921

Workers' Educational Trade Union Committee, *Report on Educational Facilities for Trade Unionists.* This, like many other national, regional and local reports of the WEA and its offshoot, the WETUC, showed a marked interest in recent changes affecting the trade unions and educational activities.

1923

W. H. Draper, *University Extension: a survey of 50 years 1873–1923* (commenting on working-class support for the extension movement, and the creation of the WEA).

1924

T. W. Price, *The Story of the Workers' Educational Association from 1903 to 1924.* More wide-ranging than Mansbridge's *Adventure*, this traced the working-class origins of the extension movement, including the trades councils ('but it was with the Co-operative Movement chiefly that relations were established').[8] It included a chapter on 'The WEA and the working-class movement'.

J. F. and Winifred Horrabin, *Working-Class Education*. This distinguished between two strands in working-class adult education—the 'extension' movement and the 'independent' movement, and traced the history of the latter, 'not only for working-class-controlled education, but for an education of a different *kind*'.[9] It described the creation of the Plebs League and the Central Labour College, and discussed trade union support for the College and the National Council of Labour Colleges.

H. J. Twigg, *An Outline History of Co-operative Education* (the period from 1917 to 1924 was covered in another pamphlet published by Twigg in the same year on *The Organisation and Extent of Co-operative Education*).

1925

Margaret T. Hodgen, *Workers' Education in England and the United States*. This contained excellent summaries of Owenite and Chartist educational efforts, later developments in university extension, the foundation of Ruskin and the WEA, and the rival 'independent' organisations.

Basil A. Yeaxlee, *Spiritual Values in Adult Education*. This two-volume dicsussion extended his 1920 work and contained a full description of the main nineteenth and twentieth-century adult education movements, and their roots in popular movements. It drew heavily on Mansbridge, Podmore, Beer, Cole, Twigg and the Hammonds.

By the middle of the 1920s, therefore, a corpus of historical work on education and the Labour movement—mainly dealing with adult education—had become available. From this point it would be possible to trace both the education history that followed Birchenough's 1927 *History of Elementary Education*, and the growing field of Labour history. Apart from general works such as G. D. H. Cole's *Short History of the British Working-Class Movement* (the first volume of which

appeared in 1925) and the influential *Age of the Chartists* (1930) by
J. L. and Barbara Hammond, there appeared other works on specific
aspects of Labour history. W. A. Dalley's *Historical Sketch of the
Birmingham Trades Council* (1927) was an early example of local
Labour history which discussed educational issues. In the 1920s and
1930s historians of national trade unions (for example the woodworkers and miners) referred to union involvement in education.
Books on local and national Co-operative history (for example, Liverpool Co-operation and the CWS) continued the previous interest.

From these starting points we can now look at some of the themes
in the nineteenth and twentieth centuries that have attracted historical
attention.

Early Nineteenth Century

Some of the history of early working-class movements has been well
charted, though their educational ideas and impact have been fully
explored in only a few directions. The work of Dobbs was greatly
extended by Brian Simon in *Studies in the History of Education 1780–
1870* (1960). Two chapters on 'The workers' movement and education'
covered working-class radicalism, Owenism, Chartism and independent
working-class educational efforts. This, and Simon's work on the later
period, is the outstanding modern contribution to this field. Other
general works include R. F. Wearmouth's *Some Working-Class Movements of the Nineteenth Century* (1948), important for a discussion of the
tradition of 'class meetings' in early working-class movements, and
W. H. G. Armytage's *Heavens Below* (1961), which traces the background of utopian ideas and social ideals in these movements.

Of the more recent work on Robert Owen and working-class
Owenism that most explicitly concerned with education is Harold
Silver, *The Concept of Popular Education* (1965), which analysed the
work of Owen and the educational aims and practice of Owenism, including in the trade union and Labour exchange developments.
Stewart and McCann, in *The Educational Innovators 1750–1888*
(1967), included a good chapter on 'The followers of Owen: working-
class educators and utopians', though it is less concerned with working-

class educators than the heading suggests. Studies of Owenism and education have included Sidney Pollard's on William King (1959) and John Salt's on Isaac Ironside (1971), the latter of which discusses the local impact of Owen on educational thought.

Education and the Chartists is a field that has been less fully mapped. The early histories ignored the theme almost totally. Hovell's main contribution, for example, was to summarise *Chartism*, Lovett and Collins's 1840 programme, and recommend it 'to all students of English education'.[10] Faulkner's study of *Chartism and the Churches* (1916) contained an account of Chartist publications and their educational influence, and there are scattered references in such books as G. D. H. Cole's *Chartist Portraits* (1941) and John Saville's *Ernest Jones* (1952). Biographies of some Chartist leaders are understandably little concerned with education, but it is disappointing that the local work in the *Chartist Studies* (1959) edited by Asa Briggs did not take up the theme. One exception to this mainly negative picture is L. C. Wright's *Scottish Chartism* (1953), which is good on the Chartist churches and press, and the 'strong educational bias' of the Scottish Chartists. One of the best sources for Chartism and education remains the Chartist autobiographies, mainly Lovett's and Thomas Cooper's. A thesis by R. Alun Jones entitled 'Knowledge Chartism' (1938) covers much of the educational interest expressed by the WMA and in Chartist programmes—principally Lovett's, and discusses Christian Chartism and the Chartist halls.

Only recently has serious attention been given to Dobbs's theme of the educational and cultural role of working-class publications and political activity. The most important discussion is in E. P. Thompson's *Making of the English Working Class* (1963), with a section on 'radical culture' and an analysis of the replacement of pre-industrial community structures, and of changing working-class consciousness. This is also the approach in Eileen Yeo's 'Robert Owen and Radical Culture' (1971); Gwyn Williams's pamphlet on *Rowland Detrosier* (1965) also gives a sense of the range of political, religious, anti-religious and educational activity. Histories of the fight for an unstamped press tend to have been too 'technical' to offer a clear picture of its cultural impact: the most useful have been Wickwar's *Struggle for the Freedom of the Press* (1928) and Patricia Hollis's detailed map in *The Pauper Press* (1970). Some, but inevitably little, work has been done on working-class libraries, including in Mabel Tylecote's *Mechanics' Institutes of Lancashire and Yorkshire before 1851* (1957), and especially Thomas Kelly's *Early Public Libraries* (1966). In general, however, historical work on the informal agencies of working-class education and culture in this period has been limited.

Later Nineteenth Century
Like his work on the earlier period, Brian Simon's *Education and the Labour Movement 1870–1920* (1965) is an invaluable survey of the whole field. It covers the educational activities of the Socialist organisations of the 1880s and after, university extension, and attitudes in the Labour movement to the school boards and the 1902 Act. Another (unfortunately unpublished) general survey is W. P. McCann's thesis, 'Trade Unionist, Co-operative and Socialist Organisations in Relation to Popular Education 1870–1902' (1966), which provides all that the title promises, including the trade unions and the NEL, some ephemeral working-class organisations, the working-class movement and the school boards, and Labour and Socialist attitudes towards secondary and technical education, and the 1902 Act. Edmund and Ruth Frow's *Survey of the Half-Time System in Education* (1970) cuts across the field in the same way, being concerned with the attitudes and campaigns of the SDF, the ILP, the trade unions and the teachers.

The research has been insufficient for us to have a clear picture of the trade unions' relations with education in the late nineteenth century. Studies of *national* trade unionism have offered only isolated clues on such themes as technical education and evening classes. Histories of individual unions are relatively unhelpful, the best served being the woodworkers, because of Applegarth's interest in education, and the efforts of the Carpenters and Joiners to provide technical education for its members (see Humphrey's *Applegarth* and Higenbottam's history of the ASW). Some regional studies of miners' trade unionism provide information: J. E. Williams's *Derbyshire Miners*

(1962), for example, mentions union support for the Chesterfield and county technical education committees in the 1890s. Of greater importance has been the work on trades councils, especially since the 1950s. For example, K. D. Buckley's account of *Trade Unionism in Aberdeen 1879 to 1900* (1955), indicated attitudes to such things as textbooks, school fees, the school leaving age, school board elections, and technical and secondary education. The same range of interests emerges from Ian MacDougall's edition of *The Minutes of Edinburgh Trades Council 1859–1873* (1968).

The most important trade union studies from our point of view here, however, have been of Manchester and Hull. Leslie Bather's thesis, 'A History of Manchester and Salford Trades Council' (1956) contains details of representation on the school board, interest in topics like playgrounds and gymnasia, technical education and evening classes, and a United Education Party, in which the trades council, the ILP, Progressives and teachers put forward a programme for the 1900 school board election. Raymond Brown's thesis, 'The Labour Movement in Hull 1870–1900' (1966) offers the fullest picture of the range of interests of a trades council, with a detailed treatment of the Hull Trades Council's approach to educational issues, local and national. It describes, for example, the promotion of school board election candidates from 1874 (successfully from 1883), demands for improved education and a free library service, the use by the council of a TUC check-list of questions (including on education) for general election candidates in 1885, and an extremely important 23-point programme for education issued by the trades council in 1895. Other studies like Brown's would improve our picture of this period, and histories of school boards in the context of local political and social movements would do the same. For Hull, for example, there is also a thesis by Terence Cluderay (1968) on the school board, which mentions the 'Labour candidates' and the 'brave plan' of 1895. Most local studies of school boards, however, have so far shown little interest in local political and popular movements.

Apart from the studies by Simon and McCann, there is little on the educational interests of the Socialist organisations of the last two de-

cades of the century, except for the Fabians. Such work as Tsuzuki's
on Hyndman (1961) and Eleanor Marx (1967) and Nethercot's on
Annie Besant (1961) contain limited references. David Rubinstein's
account of the 1888 London School Board election in 'Annie Besant
and Stewart Headlam' (1970) is a detailed account of one of the salient
episodes of the period. Given the importance of education to Fabian-
ism there is surprisingly little in Margaret Cole's *The Story of Fabian
Socialism* (1961), but there is a good section in A. M. McBriar's
Fabian Socialism and English Politics 1884–1918 (1962). The outstanding study is Edward Brennan's thesis, 'The Influence of Sidney
and Beatrice Webb on English Education, 1892–1903' (1959), which
describes how the Fabians provided the Progressive Party in London
with an educational policy, Sidney Webb's work on the Technical
Education Board, and the way the majority of the Fabians were out of
step with the Labour movement over the 1902 Education Act.

On the Co-operative movement in this period, Twigg covers such
topics as the growth of Co-operative education committees, classes and
lectures. The educational work of the Rochdale Co-operators was
described by Holyoake in the 1893 edition of his history of the Rochdale pioneers, and by A. Greenwood in a pamphlet on *The Educational
Department of the Rochdale Equitable Pioneers* (1877). The latter, the
fullest account of any educational venture by a working-class organisation in the nineteenth century, gives detail of, for example, expenditure, numbers of books and issues, catalogues, reading rooms, lectures
and science and art department classes. More recent work on the history of Co-operation either takes in a wide span of the nineteenth and
twentieth centuries, as for example G. D. H. Cole's *Century of Co-
operation* (1944), or is concerned with the twentieth century.

There is little specifically on working-class adult education in this
period, interest tending to focus on the early nineteenth century and
then on the twentieth-century developments after the foundation of
Ruskin and the WEA. The extent of the work done in the 1910s and
1920s is evident from the publication by R. C. Rowse in 1933 of a
bibliographical guide—*An Introduction to the History of Adult Education*. Two books of central importance published since that date have

covered the whole nineteenth and twentieth-century period—J. F. C.
Harrison's *Learning and Living 1790–1960* (1961), and Thomas
Kelly's *History of Adult Education in Great Britain* (1962). N. A.
Jepson's thesis on the university extension movement between 1873
and 1902 (1955) contains a discussion of working-class involvement,
and Labour movement financial and organisational contributions.

Twentieth Century
There has been considerable historical interest in working-class adult
education in this century. In addition to the work by Harrison and
Kelly (and in Simon's *Education and the Labour Movement*), there have
been studies of the two 'wings' of the movement. The Horrabins'
record of 'independent' working-class education was continued by
J. P. M. Millar in 'Forty Years of Independent Working-Class Education' (1949), and the Horrabin terminology and theme were pursued
by Ruth Frow in a thesis on 'Independent Working Class Education
with Particular Reference to South Lancashire, 1909–1930' (1968).
This dealt with Labour College activities, tensions between the Central Labour College and regional needs, and trade union support for
the NCLC. Nothing of substance has been written on the history of
the Labour movement's relations to Ruskin, but on the 1909 strike and
the rival foundation there is Craik's *Central Labour College 1909–24*
(1964). T. A. Jackson's autobiography, *Solo Trumpet* (1953) discusses
his experience as a Labour College lecturer from 1919. Contributions
such as these to the history of adult education are important, since an
official history of the NCLC has long been promised but does not yet
exist, and since the NCLC's work and influence in the inter-war years
has been seriously under-estimated in much of the writing from the
WEA standpoint.
    Material on the history of the WEA and of working-class support
for university extension has been written by Robert Peers (1928), and
S. G. Raybould (1949). Mary Stocks wrote a fifty-year history of the
WEA (1953) with a section on the trade unions. Trade union support,
through the Workers' Educational Trade Union Committee from
1919, featured in all this work. Historical interest in the WEA and

related activities has also been at local or regional level, including Thomas Kelly's *Outside the Walls* (1950), which looked at the relationship between university extension and the Labour movement in Manchester, and R. A. Lowe's work on North Staffordshire, notably 'The North Staffordshire Miners' Higher Education Movement' (1970). Lowe's thesis on adult education in the Potteries and the founding of Keele University (1966), Drusilla Scott's *A. D. Lindsay* (1971), and other works, have related the Labour movement and adult education to the foundation of the university at Keele. D. J. Booth's sociological study of the WEA in New Milton in the 1960s (1972) contains important historical chapters on the early history of the WEA nationally, indicating political and ideological forces which shaped its development.

Trade union involvement in adult education is the theme of some other work on the WEA and WETUC. *Trade Union Education with Special Reference to the Pilot Areas* (1959) by Clegg and Adams reported on WEA efforts to improve its work among trade unionists. S. G. Raybould's 'Changes in Trade Union Education' (1959) described a post-war trend in trade union interest away from general education towards 'technical' trade union training. A. J. Corfield, in *Epoch in Workers' Education* (1969) traced the history of the WETUC from its beginnings through the Iron and Steel Trades Confederation in 1919; a feature of the book was its account of changing teaching methods and courses.

The history of twentieth-century trade unionism contains surprisingly little about attitudes to educational developments. Histories of national unions sometimes refer to members' attendance at WEA, NCLC or other classes. Some, such as Bundock's *Story of the National Union of Printing, Bookbinding and Paper Workers* (1958), discuss controversy about affiliation to the WETUC or the NCLC; others, including Fox's *History of the National Union of Boot and Shoe Operatives* (1958), discuss more fully union attempts to promote the education of their members. Regional histories of the miners, as we have seen, make a contribution: Williams's *Derbyshire Miners*, for example, describes support for adult education, and the arrangement of courses with Nottingham and Sheffield universities.

The main published work on the educational policies of the Labour Party, Labour governments and Labour-controlled councils, has been since 1967. There is no historical work on the Communist Party or other Socialist, Marxist or revolutionary groups which discusses educational policy. Only two books published before 1967 are of interest in connection with the Labour Party—G. D. H. Cole's *History of the Labour Party from 1914* (1948), which has scattered references to Labour policies on education, and the two pre-war governments, and Fred Blackburn's biography of George Tomlinson (1954), with some ingenuous description of his period as Minister of Education. Of greater importance is an unpublished thesis by Jack Schofield on 'The Labour Movement and Educational Policy 1900–1931' (1964), covering the 1902 Act, child health and welfare, the half-time system, the 1918 Act, post-elementary and technical education. It is mainly a study of the policy documents of the constituent bodies of the Labour movement.

The Left Book Club, launched in 1936, was an educational force of considerable importance. John Lewis's history (1970) emphasises that 'it demanded, and sought to give *understanding*'.[11] This detailed account of the publications, lectures, discussion groups and the political-educational movement in general parallels for this period the work on the early nineteenth-century working-class press and culture.

Gerald Bernbaum's *Social Change and the Schools 1918–1944* (1967) discussed the interplay of economy, social class, political and educational policy and provided a new, synoptic view of the period, and of Labour policies in particular. D. W. Dean's article on the failure of the Trevelyan Bill (1969), and his thesis of the previous year, pin-pointed the sorts of internal disagreements and hesitations Labour in office had to face. Also in 1969 appeared an article by J. M. Collins on 'The Labour Party and the Public Schools', and Rubinstein and Simon's *Evolution of the Comprehensive School 1926–1966*, which covered ground similar to Bernbaum's, but with a more specific focus, and extended the discussion into the post-war period. Michael Parkinson's *Labour Party and the Organization of Secondary Education*, the following year, was more concerned with educational politics, and was kindly but critical towards the Party's record. Benn and Simon's *Half Way There*, also in 1970, was a 'report on the British comprehensive school reform'; it was not a history, but the chapter on 'Circular 10/65 and English empiricism' looked (more critically than Parkinson) at the Labour government's record. In the same year Batley, O'Brien and Parris, in *Going Comprehensive*, produced an important account of differences in local Labour Party policies, action and doubts about comprehensive reorganisation in Darlington and Gateshead (the only comparable study was one by Peschek and Brand in 1966 on *Policies and Politics in Secondary Education: case studies in West Ham and Reading*). A political study of a different kind was Maurice Kogan's conversations with Anthony Crosland (and Edward Boyle), published as *The Politics of Education* (1971), discussing the relations of Crosland as Secretary for Science and Education in 1965–7 to the parliamentary Labour Party and Transport House, circular 10/65 and the Public Schools Commission.

If further synthesising work is to be possible in the history of education and the Labour movement it is clear that contributions such as these from sociologists and political scientists, as well as more substantial local studies, will have an important part to play.

Centre for Science Education, Chelsea College,
University of London

References (see bibliography for publication details)
I am grateful to a number of people who have made valuable comments and suggestions in connection with this survey, particularly Roy Lowe, Phillip McCann, David Rubinstein and Brian Simon. Help was also given by members of a seminar group of the History of Education Society, at which an early draft of this paper was discussed.

1 Mansbridge, 'Survey of Working-class Educational Movements', 261.
2 Obituary in King's College, Cambridge, *Annual Report*, November 1958. I am grateful to Mr A. N. L. Munby for this reference.

3   Dobbs, *Education and Social Movements*, 240.
4   Ibid, 141
5   Ibid, 171.
6   Ibid, 251.
7   Adult Education Committee, *Final Report*, 9.
8   Price, *Story of the Workers' Educational Association*, 14.
9   Horrabin, *Working-Class Education*, 40.
10 Hovell, *Chartist Movement*, 207.
11 Lewis, *The Left Book Club*, 64.

Bibliography: Education and the Labour Movement. Compiled by Harold Silver

Chronological divisions are arbitrary, but may make this bibliography more manageable than a single list. Some works overlap the periods; in some cases they are repeated, in others included only in the section to which they mainly refer (full publication details are given only on first mention). Works in the 'general' section cover all or a major part of the period since the beginning of the nineteenth century; these references are not repeated in subsequent sections. Place of publication is London unless otherwise stated. Details of editions other than the first are given only where a later edition contains useful additions. The bibliography is not exhaustive. The intention has been to include material that is essential in a given field, or that may indicate additional bibliographical sources or lines of advance.

I General

Adamson, John William, *English Education 1789–1902* (Cambridge, 1930). Especially ch VI—'The workman's self-education', and ch XIII—'The compromise of 1870 and the Cross Commission'.

Armytage, W. H. G., *Heavens Below: utopian experiments in England 1560–1960* (1961). Phase II—'The Owenite apocalypse', and Phase III—'The heyday of experiment'.

Beer, M., *A History of British Socialism* (1919; 1940 edn with additional chapter).

Cole, G. D. H., *A Century of Co-operation* (1944). Contains chapter on 'Co-operators and Education'.

——, *A Short History of the British Working-Class Movement 1789–1947* (1925–7; 1948 revised edn). Scattered references, eg Owenite education, trades councils and school boards.

Dobbs, A. E., 'Historical survey', in Parry, R. St John, *Cambridge Essays in Adult Education* (Cambridge, 1920). Covers eg early nineteenth century, trade unions and co-operation, extension movement, WEA, residential education.

Harrison, J. F. C., *Learning and Living 1790–1960: a study in the history of the English adult education movement* (1961). Especially for Owenite, radical and self-help movements in early nineteenth century, university extension, WEA (Leeds in particular), NCLC in Yorkshire.

Hodgen, Margaret T., *Workers' Education in England and the United States* (1925), Chs on early working-class search for education, Chartism, late-nineteenth, early-twentieth century adult education.

Horrabin, J. F. and Winifred, *Working-Class Education* (1924). Chs on 'The pioneers, 1789–1848', 'The philanthropists, 1848–1908' and 'The proletarians, 1908–1924'. Detailed description of 'independent' working-class education movement.

Kelly, Thomas, *A History of Adult Education in Great Britain* (1962). Especially for early political Radicals, adult and night schools, late nineteenth-century Co-operative education, and ch 15—'The universities and working-class organisations'. A second edition (1970) contains a section on workers' education in the 1950s and 1960s.

——, (ed), *A Select Bibliography of Adult Education in Great Britain* (1952; 1962 revised edn). Section III—'History and organisation of adult education'.

Reconstruction, Ministry of, Adult Education Committee, *Final Report* (1919). Ch I—'History of adult education since 1800, appendix I—'Survey of adult education'. Sections on Chartism, Co-operation, North Staffordshire miners. Invaluable. An abridged version was published as: *A Design for Democracy* (1956), with an introduction, 'The years between' by R. D. Waller.

Rowse, R. C., *An Introduction to the History of Adult Education* (1933). Pamphlet, bibliographical guide in three sections on the beginnings, 1850–1924, and after 1924.

Sadler, M. E. (ed), *Continuation Schools in England and Elsewhere* (Manchester, 1907). Contains Mansbridge, 'Survey' (see below); also other references to working-class bodies and further education.

Twigg, H. J., *An Outline History of Co-operative Education* (Manchester, 1924). Sections on early Co-operation, 1844–69, congresses after 1869 and education committees, other working-class bodies 1898–1914, Co-operative Educational Fellowship and Co-operative College.

Yeaxlee, Basil A., *Lifelong Education: a sketch of the range and significance of the adult education movement* (1929). Includes 'Prophets and pioneers in the nineteenth century', and 'The movement in our own time'.

——, *An Educated Nation* (1920). Chs on 'Early efforts and ideals in adult education' and the period before and after the First World War.

——, *Spiritual Values in Adult Education: a study of a neglected aspect* (1925), 2 vols. Yeaxlee's most substantial contribution. Two chs in vol I on nineteenth-century background and 'main movements', and one in vol II containing detailed recent history.

II   Early Nineteenth Century

Birchenough, Charles, *History of Elementary Education in England and Wales from 1800 to the Present Day* (1927; 1938 third edn). In relation to early Radical history and Chartism.

Black, A., 'Education before Rochdale', two articles in *The Co-operative Review*, vol XXVIII, no 6 (1954), and vol XXIX, no 2 (1955). For early Co-operators and Halls of Science.

Booth, Arthur John, *Robert Owen, the Founder of Socialism in England* (1869).

Especially ch V—'Early history of co-operation', and ch VI—'Society of Rational Religionists'.

Brown, W. Henry, *A Century of Liverpool Co-operation* (Liverpool, [1930]). For Owenite Co-operators and education.

Cole, G. D. H., *Chartist Portraits* (1941). Mainly for Lovett.

——, *The Life of Robert Owen* (1925; 1930 edn).

Cole, Margaret, *Robert Owen of New Lanark* (1953).

Cooper, Thomas, *The Life of Thomas Cooper. Written by himself* (1872; 1971 Leicester edn, with introduction by John Saville). For Chartism and working men's self-education.

Dobbs, A. E., *Education and Social Movements 1700–1850* (1919). Still one of the most fertile sources for early nineteenth-century working-class and Radical movements and ideas of all kinds.

Engels, Friedrich, *The Condition of the Working Class in England* (1845, first English edn 1887). Comments on educational activities of trade unionists, Socialists and Chartists.

Faulkner, Harold Underwood, *Chartism and the Churches: a study in democracy* (New York, 1916). Material from Chartist press and elsewhere about education, libraries, publications and lecturing and their educational effect.

Garnett, R. G., 'E. T. Craig: Communitarian, Educator, Phrenologist', *The Vocational Aspect*, vol XV, no 31 (1963). Particularly for Manchester Co-operation and the Ralahine community and education.

Harrison, J. F. C., *Robert Owen and the Owenites in Britain and America* (1969). Short section on Owenite educational interests, and one on working-men Co-operators.

——, *Utopianism and Education: Robert Owen and the Owenites* (New York, 1968). Selections, with introduction. Only slight references to working-class Owenism.

Hollis, Patricia, *The Pauper Press: a study in working-class radicalism of the 1830s* (1970). For working-class politics and attitudes, and educational impact of press.

Holyoake, George Jacob, *The History of Co-operation* (1875–9; 1906 edn). Section XXVII—'Social policy of co-operative societies'.

Hovell, Mark, *The Chartist Movement* (Manchester, 1918). References to Chartist churches and schools, mainly for Lovett and Collins 1840 programme.

Howell, George, *A History of the Working Men's Association from 1836 to 1850* (Newcastle upon Tyne, [1971]), with introduction by D. J. Rowe. Details of educational aims, activities, Holborn Hall classes; repeats some of the Chartist documents in Lovett's *Life and Struggles*.

Jones, R. A., 'Knowledge Chartism. A study of the influence of Chartism on nineteenth century educational development in Great Britain' (Birmingham MA thesis, 1938).

Kelly, Thomas, *Early Public Libraries. A history of public libraries in Great Britain before 1850* (1966). Includes working-class self-help libraries, and section on 'the growth of working-class literacy'.

Lovett, William, *Life and Struggles of William Lovett in his Pursuit of Bread, Knowledge and Freedom* (1876; 1920 edn with introduction by R. H. Tawney). Contains many important Chartist documents relating to education.

Pankhurst, R. K. P., *William Thompson, 1775–1833. Britain's pioneer socialist, feminist and co-operator* (1954). Mainly for the Co-operative movement and education.

Plummer, Alfred, *Bronterre: a political biography of Bronterre O'Brien 1804–1864* (1971). For unstamped press and background of Owenite and Chartist ideas.

Podmore, Frank, *Robert Owen: a biography* (1906). Still one of the most substantial and valuable studies of Owen, Owenite ideas and education.

Pollard, Sidney, 'Dr William King of Ipswich: a co-operative pioneer', *Co-operative College Papers*, no 6 (Loughborough, 1959). For *The Co-operator* and Co-operative interest in education.

Rose, J. Holland, *The Rise of Democracy* (1912). Early attempt to chart Radical, Owenite and Chartist ideas, including on education.

Rose, R. B., 'John Finch, 1784–1857. A Liverpool disciple of Robert Owen', *Transactions, Historic Society of Lancashire and Cheshire, vol 104* (1957). Educational activity of Liverpool dockers, 1830s; Co-operative and Socialist interest in schools and Hall of Science.

Salt, John, 'Isaac Ironside 1808–1870: the motivation of a radical educationist', *Brit. J. of Educ. Studies*, vol XIX, no 2 (1971). For Sheffield Chartism, Owenism and Hall of Science.

Saville, John, *Ernest Jones: Chartist* (1952). Extracts from Jones and 1851 Chartist programme, including education.

Silver, Harold, *The Concept of Popular Education: a study of ideas and social movements in the early nineteenth century* (1965). Ch IV—education and working-class political reformers, Owenite Co-operators, labour exchanges and trade unionists. Ch V—education and Owenites, Halls of Science and Chartists.

——, 'Owen's Reputation as an Educationist', in Pollard, Sidney, and Salt, John (eds), *Robert Owen: prophet of the poor* (1971).

——, *Robert Owen on Education* (Cambridge, 1969). Selections with an introduction.

Simon, Brian, *The Radical Tradition in Education in Britain* (1972). Introduction traces tradition from Godwin to Lovett, with extracts from leading figures— plus William Morris.

——, *Studies in the History of Education 1780–1870* (1960). The most important survey of early nineteenth-century working-class and Radical movements in relation to education. Especially chs IV–V, on the workers' movement and education—working-class Radicalism, Owenism, independent alternatives to mechanics' institutes, Chartism.

Smith, Frank, *A History of English Elementary Education 1760–1902* (1931). An early social history of education, with some context of radical, especially Chartist, ideas.

Bibliography

Stewart, W. A. C. and McCann, W. P., *The Educational Innovators 1750–1880* (1967). Section on 'The followers of Owen: working-class educators and utopians'.

Thompson, E. P., *The Making of the English Working Class* (1963). For working-class and Radical culture and the range of popular organisations and ideas.

Tylecote, Mabel, *The Mechanics' Institutes of Lancashire and Yorkshire before 1851* (Manchester, 1957). Some description of independent working-class activity in opposition to the institutes; connections between adult education, Chartism and trade unionism.

Vaughan, Michalina and Archer, Margaret Scotford, *Social Conflict and Educational Change in England and France 1789–1848* (Cambridge, 1971). Section on 'working class educational thought'.

Wearmouth, Robert F., *Some Working-Class Movements of the Nineteenth Century* (1948). For 'class meetings', Radical political groups, Chartism.

Wickwar, William H., *The Struggle for the Freedom of the Press 1819–1832*.

Wiener, Joel H., *A Descriptive Finding List of Unstamped British Periodicals 1830–1836* (1970). Valuable, well-annotated bibliography of over 550 items.

Williams, Gwyn A., *Rowland Detrosier: a working-class infidel 1800–34* (York, 1965). Education as a field in which 'working-class infidels and believers . . . could work together'. Workmen's clubs, natural history society.

Wright, Leslie C., *Scottish Chartism* (Edinburgh, 1953). Good on Chartist churches, press, policies for education.

Yeo, Eileen, 'Robert Owen and Radical Culture', in Pollard, Sidney, and Salt, John (eds), *Robert Owen: prophet of the poor* (1971). Important for 'alternative culture' of Owenite Socialist and Chartist movements.

III   Late Nineteenth Century

Bather, Leslie, 'A History of Manchester and Salford Trades Council' (Manchester PhD thesis, 1956). Especially for school board, trades council representation, 1900 United Education Party programme.

Brennan, Edward J. T., 'Educational Engineering with the Webbs', *History of Education*, vol I, no 2 (1972).

——, 'The Influence of Sidney and Beatrice Webb on English Education, 1892–1903' (Sheffield MA thesis, 1959). Especially ch II on Fabians, Progressive Party and LCC; ch VI, up to and including 1902 Act.

——, 'Sidney Webb and the London Technical Education Board', *The Vocational Aspect*, vol XI (1959), vol XII (1960), vol XIII (1961). Webb's educational policies and work, left-wing criticism of his scholarship policy, 1902 Act and Fabian Society.

Brown, Raymond, 'The Labour Movement in Hull 1870–1900, with special reference to new unionism' (Hull MSc thesis, 1966). Relationship to school board, sponsorship of university extension lectures, 1895 education programme, campaigns for technical education, libraries.

Bryher, Samson, *An Account of the Labour and Socialist Movement in Bristol* (Bristol, Pt I, 1929; Pts II and III and combined volume, 1931). Socialist success in 1889 school board election (includes programme).

Buckley, Kenneth D., *Trade Unionism in Aberdeen 1878 to 1900* (Edinburgh, 1955). Trades council and school board, interest in fees, textbooks, leaving age, technical and secondary education.

Cluderay, Terence, 'The Hull School Board—its task and its achievement' (Hull MEd thesis, 1968). Labour candidates, 1895 trades council programme, Progressive Party 1898.

Cole, Margaret, *The Story of Fabian Socialism* (1961). Slight references to school boards and events up to 1902.

Corbett, John, *The Birmingham Trades Council 1866–1966* (1966). Education and 2nd (Birmingham) TUC, support for NEL, 1900 school board election —association with Socialist bodies.

D.[alley], W. A., *An Historical Sketch of the Birmingham Trades Council, 1866–1926* (Birmingham, 1927). Campaigns for free, compulsory education; school board representation from 1894.

Davis, W. J., *The British Trades Union Congress. History and recollections* (vol I, 1910; II, 1916). Scattered information on policy and debates, including half-timers, school boards, free education, evening classes.

Fraser, William Hamish, 'Trades Councils in England and Scotland 1858–1897' (Sussex PhD thesis, 1967). References in pt IV, ch I ('municipal affairs') and pt V, to libraries, school boards.

Frow, Edmund and Ruth, *A Survey of the Half-time System in Education* (Manchester, 1970). Campaigns by SDF, ILP, trade unions, NUT.

Frow, E. and Katanka, M., *1868 Year of the unions* (Edgware, 1968). Technical education interests of Manchester and Birmingham unions.

Greenwood, A., *The Education Department of the Rochdale Equitable Pioneers. Society Limited: its origin and development* (Manchester, 1877). Details of funds, book stock and issues, catalogues, reading rooms, lectures, Science and Art Department classes, educational equipment.

Hamling, William, *A Short History of the Liverpool Trades' Council 1848–1948* (Liverpool, 1948). Mentions school board elections, 1880s interest in University College evening lectures and extra-mural department.

Higenbottam, S., *Our Society's History* (Manchester, 1939). Carpenters' and Joiners' support for NEL, technical education for own members from 1860s.

Holyoake, G. J., *Self-Help by the People. The history of the Rochdale Pioneers 1844–1892* (1858; 1893 extended edn). Detailed picture of educational and cultural activities.

Howland, Robert Dudley, 'Fabian Thought and Social Change in England from 1884 to 1914' (London PhD thesis, 1942). Slight discussion of Webbs, technical education board, 1902 Act.

Humphrey, A. W., *Robert Applegarth: trade unionist, educationist, reformer* (Manchester, 1913). Ch VIII—'Technical instruction: the carpenters' classes'; ch IX—the NEL.

Jepson, N. A., 'A Critical Analysis of the Origin and Development of the Oxford and Cambridge University Extension Movement between 1873 and 1902, with special reference to the West Riding of Yorkshire' (Leeds PhD thesis, 1955). Mainly section II, chs on extension and the working class, factors influencing recruitment of working-class support, relations of lecturers and union leaders, local committees, finance.

Lowe, R. A., 'The Development of Adult Education in the Potteries with special Reference to the Founding of a University in the Area' (Keele MA thesis, 1966). First four chs discuss nineteenth-century adult education, workmen's clubs, mutual improvement societies, adult schools and halls, university extension.

Judges, A. V., 'The Educational Influence of the Webbs', *Brit. J. of Educ. Studies*, vol X, no 1 (1961).

McBriar, A. M., *Fabian Socialism and English Politics 1884–1918* (Cambridge, 1962). Good section on 'The Fabians and education in London'.

McCann, W. P., 'The Trades Guild of Learning', *The Vocational Aspect*, vol XIX, no 42 (1967). 1870s, trade unions and members' education.

——, 'Trade Unionist, Co-operative and Socialist Organisations in Relation to Popular Education 1870–1902' (Manchester PhD thesis, 1960). Full account of trade union and Socialist bodies, in relation to the NEL, school boards, technical and secondary education, higher-grade schools, evening classes, 1902 Act.

——, 'Trade Unionists, Artisans and the 1870 Education Act', *Brit. J. of Educ. Studies*, vol XVIII, no 2 (1970).

MacDougall, Ian (ed), *The Minutes of Edinburgh Trades Council 1859–1873* (Edinburgh, 1968). Lectures, evidence to Endowed Schools Commission, evening classes, technical education, 1872 Education Act, libraries.

Mansbridge, Albert. 'A Survey of Working-Class Educational Movements in England and Scotland', *Co-operative Wholesale Societies Ltd. Annual for 1906* (Manchester, 1906). Mainly for detailed account of Co-operative support for evening and continuation education.

——, 'Working Men and Continuation Schools', in Sadler, M. E. (ed), *Continuation Schools in England and Wales* (Manchester, 1907). As above, but wider reference to late nineteenth-century Socialist organisations.

Nethercot, Arthur H., *The First Five Lives of Annie Besant* (1961). For Radicals, Socialists and 1888 London school board election.

Pollard, Sidney, *A History of Labour in Sheffield* (Liverpool, 1959). Local Labour organisations, school board, libraries.

Postgate, R. W., *The Builders' History* (1923). Chapter on 'The servile generation' discusses Liberalism, education and the unions from the 1860s.

Rubinstein, David, 'Annie Besant and Stewart Headlam: the London School Board Election of 1888', *East London Papers*, vol 13, no 1 (1970).

Simon, Brian, *Education and the Labour Movement 1870–1920* (1965). Like the author's book on the earlier period, indispensable. Detailed analysis of Socialist organisations, clubs, discussions, lecturing, Socialist Sunday schools; extension movement; TUC, ILP, SDF and school boards, child welfare, secondary education.

Summers, David Fowler, 'The Labour Church and Allied Movements of the Late Nineteenth and Early Twentieth Centuries' (Edinburgh PhD, 1958). Vol I describes movement from 1891, Sunday lectures, social and range of educational activities, support from ILP, Fabians. Vol II contains detailed tables, lists of lecturers, topics, large number of extracts.

[Tate, George], *London Trades Council 1860–1950: a history* (1950). Mentions joint committee with London school board teachers, support for free, compulsory, non-sectarian education, evidence to Cross Commission.

Thompson, Paul, *Socialists, Liberals and Labour: the struggle for London 1885–1914* (1967). Scattered references to school board, educational views and programmes.

Tsuzuki, Chushichi, *H.M. Hyndman and British Socialism* (1961). References to SDF education programme, school board elections.

——, *The Life of Eleanor Marx 1855–1898: a socialist tragedy* (Oxford, 1967). Mainly for Aveling's lecturing, London School Board, educational causes.

Webb, Sidney and Beatrice, *The History of Trade Unionism* (London, 1894). Mentions Applegarth and the NEL, 1888 London school board election, trades councils and school boards, education codes.

Williams, J. E., *The Derbyshire Miners: a study in industrial and social history* (1962). References to trade unionists and school board elections in 1890s, support for technical education committees.

IV   Twentieth Century

Adams, F. J. *et al, Education in Bradford since 1870* (Bradford, 1970). References to WEA and Socialist Sunday schools.

Amalgamated Union of Building Trade Workers, *Our Next Step Education* (nd [1922?]). Pamphlet for NCLC joint education scheme: history of 'Labour and education', especially Ruskin, WEA and the Labour College ('education of a special kind, based on the working-class point of view').

Arnot, R. Page, *The Miners in Crisis and War: a history of the Miners' Federation of Great Britain (from 1930 onwards)* (1961). Mentions miners' support for raising school leaving age.

——, *South Wales Miners: a history of the South Wales Miners' Federation (1894–1914)* (1967). S. Wales miners at Ruskin, role in Plebs League and foundation of Central Labour College.

Banks, Olive, *Parity and Prestige in English Secondary Education* (1955). Especially for Labour movement and secondary education for all, tripartism, public schools, 1930s and 1940s.

Barker, R. S., 'The Educational Policies of the Labour Party, 1900–1961' (London PhD thesis, 1968). See following. Thesis has similar pattern, more detail and quoted material.

——, *Education and Politics 1900–1951: a study of the Labour Party* (Oxford, 1972). Education policies of Labour governments 1924, 1929, Labour discussions of public schools, adult education, Teachers' Labour League, comprehensive school policy. Some on ILP and Fabians; mainly Labour in parliament.

Batley, Richard, O'Brien, Oswald and Parris, Henry, *Going Comprehensive: educational policy-making in two county boroughs* (1970). Important account of Labour and comprehensive schools policies in Darlington and Gateshead, 1950s and 1960s.

Benn, Caroline and Simon, Brian, *Half Way There: report on the British comprehensive school reform* (1970). Ch 3—'Circular 10/65 and English empiricism', for a critical study of Labour government action.

Bernbaum, Gerald, *Social Change and the Schools 1918–1944* (1967). TUC and Labour Party policies towards education, Fisher Act, 1924 Labour government, Hadow, secondary education.

Blackburn, Fred, *George Tomlinson* (1954). Ch XIII describes period as Minister of Education, 1947–51: public schools, Durham closed shop dispute.

Booth, Desmond John, 'The Emergence, Development and Prospects of the Workers' Educational Association, with special Reference to the Southern District and the New Milton WEA Branch' (Southampton MPhil thesis, 1972). Ch I, 'the emergence of the WEA: Mansbridge, co-operatives, local committees, MacTavish and trade union movement, WETUC, opposition from NCLC'. Ch II, 'the evolution of the WEA Southern District'. Ch III and onwards, New Milton branch in 1950s and 1960s. Appendices include speeches, articles, syllabuses, reports.

Bryher, Samson, *An Account of the Labour and Socialist Movement in Bristol.* 1906 meeting in support of Will Thorne's bill for free secular education (nine-point bill in full).

Bundock, Clement, J., *The Story of the National Union of Printing, Bookbinding and Paper Workers* (Oxford, 1958). Union controversy 1938–41 over affiliation to WEA or NCLC.

Carr-Saunders, A. M. *et al*, *Consumers' Co-operation in Great Britain* (1938). Mainly 1935, but some background, including the Co-operative College from 1919.

Clegg, H. A., *General Union: a study of the National Union of General and Municipal Workers* (Oxford, 1954). Financial support from 1928 for WEA and NCLC, and for union officers on courses in 'modern industrial developments'.

—— and Adams, Rex, *Trade Union Education with Special Reference to the Pilot Areas: a report for the Workers' Educational Association* (1959). Pilot developments from 1954 among trade unionists; glances back to WETUC, Ruskin, Central Labour College, trade union education schemes of 1950s.

Cole, G. D. H., *A History of the Labour Party from 1914* (1948). References to Labour policy on education, including first two Labour governments.

Cole, Margaret, *The Life of G. D. H. Cole* (1971). Contact WEA from 1912, director of tutorial classes London University—connections WETUC,

NCLC. Ch XIII—Countess of Warwick's Easton Lodge scheme in 1920s to found Labour College.

Collins, John M., 'The Labour Party and the Public Schools: a conflict of principles', *Brit. J. of Educ. Studies*, vol XVII, no 3 (1969).

Coltham, S. W., 'Adult Education for North Staffordshire Mineworkers: a survey of developments from 1953 to 1958', *Rewley House Papers*, vol III, no 7 (1958–9).

Corfield, A. J., *Epoch in Workers' Education: a history of the Workers' Educational Trade Union Committee* (1969). Antecedents, creation 1919, Iron and Steel Trades Confederation, followed by post office, railway clerks and other unions, NCLC rivalry, methods, pilot areas, courses for shop stewards. TUC centralises and finances courses from 1964. Extensive statistics 1930–63.

Craik, William W., *The Central Labour College 1909–29: a chapter in the history of adult working-class education* (1964). Ruskin, secession, the college, the NCLC, role of the trade unions, take-over of NCLC by the TUC 1964.

Dean, D. W., 'The Difficulties of a Labour Educational Policy: the failure of the Trevelyan Bill, 1929–31', *Brit. J. of Educ. Studies*, vol XVII, no 3 (1969).

——, 'The Political Parties and the Development of their Attitude to Educational Problems 1918 to 1942' (London MPhil thesis, 1968). Chs on Labour Party and 1918 Act, economies 1919–23, dual system, Hadow, Trevelyan, school-leaving age, secondary education, public schools, teachers.

Draper, William H., *University Extension: a survey of fifty years 1873–1923* (Cambridge, 1923). References to foundation of the WEA, support for extension movement from mill hands and miners.

Elvin, Lionel, 'Ruskin College, 1899–1949', *Adult Education*, vol XXI, no 4 (1949). Trade union leaders and Ruskin, decline of WEA–NCLC controversy. Slight, but one of few things written.

Fox, Alan, *A History of the National Union of Boot and Shoe Operatives 1874–1957* (Oxford, 1958). Good section on interest in trade union education from 1920s; representation on TUC Education Advisory Committee and WETUC; financial support for members on courses and summer schools; scheme with NCLC from 1936.

Frow, *A Survey of the Half-time System in Education*. SDF shifts attention to school meals, 1905; successful end to half-time campaign 1918.

Frow, Ruth, 'Independent Working Class Education with Particular Reference to South Lancashire, 1909–1930' (Manchester MEd thesis, 1968). Nineteenth-century development of 'independent working class education'; Plebs League in the North-West, Labour College movement and the NCLC in South Lancashire, trade union support; substantial appendices.

Fyrth, H. J. and Collins, Henry, *The Foundry Workers: a trade union history* (Manchester, 1959). Slight references to apprentice training, WETUC courses, summer and day schools.

Garside, W. R., *The Durham Miners 1919–1960* (1971). Union support for WEA classes, scholarships for miners to Central Labour College, competitions, prizes. Adverse effect longer working day after 1926.

Hall, B. T., *Our Fifty Years: the story of the Working Men's Club and Institute Union* (1912). Circulating library, association with WEA and Ruskin.

Higenbottam, *Our Society's History*. Union offers prizes for technical drawing, support for WEA and NCLC.

Jackson, T. A., *Solo Trumpet: some memories of socialist agitation and propaganda* (1953). Ch 6, 'Further north': appointment as lecturer, North-Eastern Labour College, 1919; movement for 'independent working class education'.

Jones, John Cynfyn, 'The Labour Movement in Relation to Secondary Education 1902–1924' (Leicester MEd thesis, 1965). Labour movement and 1902 Act, Board of Education policy, higher elementary schools, free places, reconstruction plans 1914–18, 1918 Act, economy measures, secondary education for all.

Kelly, Thomas, *Adult Education in Liverpool* (Liverpool, 1960). Pamphlet contains section on 'university extension and the WEA'.

——, *Outside the Walls. Sixty years of University Extension at Manchester, 1886–1946* (Manchester, 1950). Links with WEA, Co-operative movement, trades councils.

Kidd, Archibald T., *History of the Tin-Plate Workers and Sheet Metal Workers and Braziers Societies* (1949). References to interest in apprentice technical training (Glasgow Tin-Plate Workers), support for Ruskin (Union of Tin-Plate Workers) and NCLC (Sheet Metal Workers and Braziers).

Kogan, Maurice (ed), *The Politics of Education: Edward Boyle and Anthony Crosland in conversation with Maurice Kogan* (Harmondsworth, 1971). Crosland as Secretary for Education and Science, 1965–7; relations to Party education group, Transport House, CASE; 10/65, Public Schools Commission.

Lewis, John, *The Left Book Club: an historical record* (1970). From 1936, monthly books, *Left Book News*, meetings and campaigns, reprints, educational series, lectures, specialist groups, New People's Library; ends 1948.

Lowe, John, *Adult Education in England and Wales* (1970). WEA, NCLC, trade unions, Co-operatives, working men's clubs, National Co-operative Education Association.

Lowe, 'The Development of Adult Education in the Potteries'. Chs V–XI cover tutorial classes, North Staffs Miners' Higher Education Movement, WEA Labour and Keele University, WEA–extra-mural relations. Statistical appendices.

——, 'The North Staffordshire Miners' Higher Education Movement', *Educational Review*, no 22 (1970). From 1911 to merger into WEA district 1920–1.

Malbon, Gladys, 'Adult Education in North Staffordshire and the Foundation of the University College at Keele', *Rewley House Papers*, vol III, no 3 (1954–5).

Mansbridge, Albert, *An Adventure in Working-Class Education, being the story of the Workers' Educational Association, 1903–1915* (1920).

——, *The Kingdom of the Mind: essays and addresses 1903–37* (1944, introduc-

tion by Leonard Clark). Contains reprint of 'Working Men and Continuation Schools'.
——, *The Making of an Educationist* (1929). Booklet, slight references to TUC, CIU and Co-operative Union support for WEA.
——, *Margaret McMillan*, prophet and pioneer (1932). ILP 1893, election to Bradford school board 1894; mainly personal work, but references also to London and Radicals, and WEA.
——, *The Trodden Road* (1940). Pt I, autobiographical, summarises his earlier writing on 'labour and learning', also later WEA and extension work.
——, *University Tutorial Classes* (1913). Slight references to Rochdale and Longton classes, 1907 Oxford conference, trade unionists, Labour councillors.
Manzer, Ronald A., *Teachers and Politics: the role of the National Union of Teachers in the making of national education policy in England and Wales since 1944* (Manchester, 1970). Discusses relations to TUC.
Marsden, Dennis, 'Politicians, Equality and Comprehensives', in Townsend, Peter, and Bosanquet, Nicholas (eds), *Labour and Inequality* (1972). Summarises and criticises Labour's record; sections on Labour's policies to 1964, controversies, comprehensive reorganisation.
Mendelson, J. et al, *Sheffield Trades and Labour Council 1858 to 1958* (Sheffield, nd). Protest against militaristic teaching after First World War; support for WEA and NCLC; leading role of Sheffield NUR.
Millar, J. P. M., 'Forty Years of Independent Working-Class Education', *Adult Education*, vol XXI, no 4 (1949). Plebs, Labour College, NCLC, trade union links, TUC support after Second World War.
Oxford and Working-Class Education: being a report of a joint committee of University and working-class representatives on the relation of the University to the higher education of workpeople (Oxford, 1908; 1909 revised edn). Includes details of Labour movement representation on 1907 committee; Labour support for Ruskin and extension movement.
Parkinson, Michael, *The Labour Party and the Organization of Secondary Education 1918–65* (1970). Mildly critical, detailed account of all aspects of Labour Party policies and action, in and out of government.
Peers, Robert, 'Adult Education', in J. Dover Wilson, *The Schools of England* (1928). For the Extension movement and WEA.
Peschek, David and Brand, J., *Policies and Politics in Secondary Education: case studies in West Ham and Reading* (1966). Especially 1950s and 1960s, developments in Labour policy.
Pollard, Sidney, *A History of Labour in Sheffield*. WEA, Sheffield Labour College, NCLC.
Price, T. W., *The Story of the Workers' Educational Association from 1903 to 1924* (1924). Short, effective account of early Labour movement support, especially the Co-operative movement. Formation of local classes, Advisory Committee on the Education of Working Women, and ch VII—'The WEA and the working class movement'.

Raybould, S. G. (ed), *Trends in English Adult Education* (1959). Contains 'Changes in trade union education'—good account of developments in WETUC, NCLC and trade union education, including correspondence courses; educational work of the ETU and the NUM.

———, *The WEA. The Next Phase* (1949). Especially for changes in 1930s and 1940s in social composition of students, attendance, subject popularity. Statistical appendix.

Redfern, Percy, *The New History of the CWS* (1938). Includes brief but good account of support for WEA, NCLC, Co-operative College and other educational activities.

Reid, F., 'Socialist Sunday Schools in Britain, 1892–1939', *International Review of Social History*, vol XI, pt I (1966). Connection with ILP and SDF politics and positivism, Cinderella Clubs, Crusaders, propaganda and educational activities.

Reid, J. H. Stewart, *The Origins of the British Labour Party* (Minneapolis, 1955). Discusses Labour attitudes over 1906 Provision of Meals Act and amending acts.

Rose, B. J. and Marshall, R. L., *The Co-operative College: a commemoration 1919–1969* (Leicester, 1969). Brief pamphlet account of origins and move to Loughborough 1945.

Rubinstein, David and Simon, Brian, *The Evolution of the Comprehensive School 1926–1966* (1969). Mainly on the period after 1945, criticism of selection in 1950s, local developments, the evolution of Labour policy, 10/65.

Ruskin College, *The Story of Ruskin College, 1899–1949* (Oxford, 1949). Brief pamphlet, some references to trade union support, Central Labour College and NCLC. Revised 1968 edition adds nothing on Labour movement.

Schofield, Jack, 'The Labour Movement and Educational Policy 1900–1931' (Manchester MEd thesis, 1964), 2 vols. Discusses the Labour movement and 1902 Act, child welfare, half-time system, 1918 Act, post-elementary and technical education. Detailed study of policy documents of Co-operative Union, TUC and Labour Party (also ILP, Fabians, British Socialist Party).

Scott, Drusilla, *A. D. Lindsay: a biography* (Oxford, 1971). ILP education classes and interest in education. Ch 4—'Adult education', good, but no source references. Labour and Keele.

Simon, Brian, 'Classification and Streaming: a study of grouping in English schools, 1860–1960', in *Intelligence, Psychology and Education: a Marxist critique* (1971). Useful clues on the Labour Party and secondary education for all.

———, *Education and the Labour Movement 1870–1920*. Early twentieth-century campaigns by Socialist organisations, Marxist study groups, WEA, Central Labour College, Plebs, NCLC.

Smith, H. P., 'Edward Stuart Cartwright: a note on his work for adult education', *Rewley House Papers*, vol III (1949–50). Organising secretary Oxford tutorial classes committee from 1912, co-operation with WEA, organisation of WEA districts and joint committees, 1919 Report, North Staffs Miners' Higher Education Movement.

——, *Labour and Learning* (Oxford, 1956). Mainly a study of Oxford–WEA relations; also Ruskin, Plebs and Labour Colleges.

——, 'A Tutorial Class makes History', *Adult Education*, vol 31 (1958–9). Longton class history, WEA, Mansbridge, Tawney, SDF, North Staffs Miners.

Stocks, Mary, *The Workers' Educational Association: the first fifty years* (1953). Especially ch 7—'The struggle for the trade unions'.

Thomas, D. Lleufer, *University Tutorial Classes for Working People* (1916). Short section on Wales WEA, especially 1907–10, collaboration of Co-operative societies, trades councils and some miners' lodges; trade union opposition to relations with Oxford extension movement.

Thompson, Donna F., *Professional Solidarity among the Teachers of England* (New York, 1927). Section on 'Alliance with Labor organizations'— nationally and locally.

Tropp, Asher, *The School Teachers: the growth of the teaching profession in England and Wales from 1800 to the present day* (1957). References to relations between the NUT, TUC and Labour Party.

Twigg, H. J., *The Organisation and Extent of Co-operative Education* (Manchester, 1924). Expenditure, classes, students, 1917–23.

Ward, Lionel Owen, 'An Investigation into the Educational Ideas and Contribution of the British Political Parties (1870–1918)' (London PhD thesis, 1970). Discusses Labour movement and free and compulsory education, child labour, school leaving age, teacher training, school management. Ch 8, 'Education and party opinion in 1918'.

Whitbread, Nanette, *The Evolution of the Nursery-Infant School* (1972). Slight but useful references to ILP, Fabians, WEA, trades councils, TUC and Labour Party.

Williams, *The Derbyshire Miners*. Miners' relations with extension movement, WEA, Ruskin, NCLC; support for Chesterfield Technical College, Sheffield University mining department, and schemes for miners at Nottingham University College and Sheffield University.

Workers' Educational Association, *Adult Education after the War* (London, [1942]). Good account of adult education and Labour movement support since 1919. Historical section also reprinted separately as

——, *Workers' Education in Great Britain: a record of educational service to democracy since 1918* (1945).

Workers' Educational Trade Union Committee, *Report on Educational Facilities for Trade Unionists* (1921). Changes in trade union educational interests since 1899 (appendices on rural workers, seafarers, women workers, Labour College, Ruskin, Scottish Labour College, WEA).

Book Reviews

The Inns of Court Under Elizabeth I and the Early Stuarts 1590–1640, by Wilfrid R. Prest, LONGMAN, 1972, pp xii + 263, £4.00.

W. R. Prest has produced an important study of the development of the four Inns of Court under Elizabeth and the early Stuarts. The book is a specialist monograph, being based upon the author's Oxford D.Phil thesis, but unlike many such works it is by no means parochial in its significance. Its interest for the historian of education is two-fold. It presents a coherent statement of the development of legal education from the fifteenth century onwards, commenting upon the virtues and inadequacies of the system of instruction employed; and it seeks to place the history of the Inns within the wider historical context of the educational revolution.

Dr Prest, working from the premise that the Inns 'must be seen as dynamic organisms changing through time, not static entities', does sketch for the reader their institutional and administrative framework, but he devotes more space to demonstrating the place of the Inns within society. He goes far towards explaining the inadequacy of the description 'third university' when applied to the early modern Inns of Court. Although the Inns served an important educational function they were in many ways more akin to residential clubs (or trade unions) than to university colleges. The examination of the size and social and regional composition of the Inns is a valuable contribution to an understanding of the nature and significance of the educational boom of this period. He shows the Inns as socially or financially exclusive institutions which, far from intensifying narrow regionalism, actually provided 'a unifying common experience for the natural magistracy of the nation'.

Two chapters are devoted to the purely educational role of the Inns
—as regards both the vocational preparation of would-be lawyers and
the liberal education of non-professional students. The argument lends
vigorous support to the view that the educational revolution was one
of numbers rather than content. Dr Prest's verdict is that, although the
oral exercises stipulated were well suited to the training of lawyers, the
teaching function was grossly neglected. Attempts to simplify legal
training and provide supervision and guidance for students were few
and rendered useless both by practical administrative difficulties and
the objections raised by narrow vested interests within the profession.
Similarly, no special course was constructed for the introduction of the
non-professional student to the rudiments of law or for his more liberal
education. Dr Prest comes to the conclusion that whereas the *laissez-
faire* system allowed the student to pursue whatever extra-curricular
activities he chose, it left everything to personal initiative—providing
freedom to study but no advised programme of study. The prominence
of the Inns in intellectual and cultural life owed more to the geographical location of the Inns (in London, near the court) and to the
fact that here were drawn together representatives of the well-born,
literate class, than to encouragement from within the societies themselves. Nevertheless, the Inns helped 'to diffuse the artistic and intellectual effervescence of Elizabethan and early Stuart London throughout the land'.

Dr Prest has avoided most of the possible pitfalls. His conclusions
are not pushed beyond what the evidence will support; his tables and
statistics are clearly presented and useful. It is probably fair to say that
the defects of this work are largely those imposed by the evidence. It
is to be regretted that more space was not devoted to the structure and
development of the legal profession itself, as demonstrated by the
records of the Inns—especially as vested interests played an important
part in preventing reforms in vocational training. More detail on the
relationship between the Inns of Court and the Inns of Chancery
would have been welcome. Dr Prest appears to have concentrated upon
records kept centrally in London or the USA. He could probably have
made good use of the papers of Thomas Lord Coventry in the Bir-

mingham Reference Library, which contain much material pertaining to the Inns of Court.

University of Birmingham   Rosemary O'Day

Popular Education in Eighteenth Century England. A Study in the Origins of the Mass Reading Public, by Victor E. Neuburg, WOBURN PRESS, 1971, pp 200, £2.75.

The eighteenth century is one relatively unexplored by historians of education and any attempt to clarify issues and trends within the period merits a sympathetic interest. Mr Neuburg's book is not so much concerned with education as with popular literature and the emergent capacity of the lower orders to read. As such it is part of the tradition of works by R. K. Webb and R. D. Altick although it is inferior to those predecessors.

Mr Neuberg begins with various familiar contemporary arguments against the education of the poor and their counter-arguments. He then surveys some careers of schoolteachers and pupils which suggest that poor children in the eighteenth century could learn to read. In the best chapter in the book he considers the provision of literature for teaching children to read, notably Thomas Dyche's *Guide to the English Tongue* and others, concluding from their many editions that they were widely used. Having established the existence of school reading-material he discusses adult tracts, the SPCK, and reading in the army. This chapter contains the best interpretative idea in the book, an attempt to examine how far men were surrounded by printed words in everyday situations that would stimulate a desire to read. He then briefly considers chapbooks, which he regards as of great importance, and religious tracts. He concludes that a working-class literature was coming into being and that this was helping to form a political consciousness.

Interesting at this programme is, the book fails to leave the reader totally satisfied owing to two main faults; first, a highly impressionistic approach to crucial parts of the evidence, and second an imbalance which destroys what should have been a forensic climax in the later chapters. Impressionism hazes the first two chapters, which are most directly about education. In the first the reader is presented with details of two opposing attitudes, but little clear idea as to whether one viewpoint was superseding the other and whether changes in, say, population, industry, religion, and the availability of labour and skills, were of educational significance. These lacunae are more crucial in Chapter 2, where it is essential to the argument to establish that the education of the poor was good enough to raise literacy sufficiently to create a new breakthrough phenomenon—'the origin of the mass reading public'. The discussion of education on which we are invited to accept this proposition consists of seven references to good teachers offset by five references to bad ones, and eleven disparaging comments on the low state and competence of teachers offset by sixteen references to people who learned to read in some fashion and who wrote reminiscences. The reader may consider that on the balance of this evidence and its presentation it would be impossible to come to any meaningful conclusion on the point at issue.

Mr Neuburg's almost deliberately anti-quantitative, non-analytical approach also leads him to dismiss too easily evidence that might have helped his case, namely the computing of literacy trends through marriage registers. While rejecting this potentially fruitful—and the most feasible—approach as 'only partial' he adopts a definition of literacy (the ability to read a book or a page) for which he understandably finds it so impossible to find any evidence as to render his chapter on literacy stillborn. He is able to find one excellent piece of data for one London school where 74 per cent of boys between 1767–1810 could 'read' but recognises that this is scarcely sufficient to establish a point about levels and movements in reading capacity for England for the whole period.

These defects in the argument about education and literacy would not matter if the author could press home his circumstantial evidence that there was a large body of literature which the masses actually read. But the chapter on chapbooks is the shortest, a mere seven pages on the books and two on the trade; the following chapter, on tracts, also has eleven pages and is chiefly about the Methodists, concerning whom it is, concluded, paradoxically, that the lower classes did not read their literature anyway. The extended discussion of this popular literature, the real *scène à faire* of the book, never materialises; a catalogue list of some printers and sellers in the appendix is no substitute for it. The brevity and thinness in this area probably arises from Mr Neuburg's wishing to avoid repetition of his extended essay on chapbooks published in 1968. Accordingly the book does not fully succeed, either as a discussion of popular education or of popular literature.

The book is pleasantly readable and one hopes Mr Neuburg will eventually give us that fuller study of chapbooks which is still needed and for which his expertise is specially suited.

University of East Anglia   Michael Sanderson

The Changing Curriculum, edited by Malcolm Seaborne, METHUEN, for the History of Education Society, 1971, pp x + 100, £1.50.
There is an old guessing game—now a psychiatric pastime—in which one player says a word, and his opponent has to cap it with another, complementary word. Thus, if the first says, 'Fish', the second replies 'Chips'. The odds are long that if someone in the world of education was posed the word, 'Curriculum', he would reply, 'Reform'. We are firmly wedded to the belief that the curriculum is a dynamic entity: we expect that any curricula with which we are concerned will change greatly in content within our lifetimes. But this is a recent belief. By and large, one of the striking features of English education has been its remarkable ability down the centuries to resist curricular change at all levels. Hence, the history of the curriculum in England is mainly a study of wordy battles whose practical outcome was seldom more than limited. But this makes it especially important to discover, when changes do occur, what factors have been involved in producing the shift.

These two aspects—the negative and the positive—are clearly reflected in the present collection of six articles (by R. R. Bolgar, C. Webster, W. H. G. Armytage, H. C. Morgan, W. H. Brock and E. G.

Edwards) which deal with aspects of curriculum change from the Renaissance to the twentieth century. The resultant unity of feeling is enhanced by the fact that four out of the six articles refer especially to scientific and technical curricula. This is surely no coincidence. The claims of science were always large, and its supporters often vociferous. During the nineteenth century, scientific subjects helped spearhead curricular diversification at all levels. On the other hand, educational reformers rarely thought of science as an isolated element to be introduced into the curriculum. Rather they would see it as one of a variety of subjects, all of which were to be accepted. The growing importance of science as a proper subject of study was matched at the end of the nineteenth century by a corresponding acceptance of other subjects. It is a perhaps unavoidable defect of a collection of articles by various hands that wider relationships of this sort are left to one side.

The main reflection induced by the present volume is that the history of educational curricula has more than its fair share of received opinions that need a new and detailed critical examination. Some of these opinions are, indeed, examined by these authors; others slip through. Let me give two examples. Payment-by-results examinations are referred to twice, both times disparagingly. This is undoubtedly the normal attitude; but on what is it based? I suspect that a detailed investigation of payment by results might easily show that it was actually beneficial in many of its effects. Again, two of the articles explicitly, and others implicitly, deal with the idea that there exist networks of influential people—here scientists—who keep in close touch, and act as unified groups to exert pressure and further their own interests. Now the concept of scientific networks has come under attack recently from sociologists. Sociological investigations of the contemporary scientific scene seem to show that the network concept is only meaningful in certain circumstances. Otherwise the people making up the network, by any reasonable definition of interconnection, are found to include most of the scientists alive today. Are the networks discerned in the articles under review meaningful networks or not? Indeed, can one define a meaningful network from an historical study, as one can from a contemporary investigation?

There are certain minor defects in the presentation of some of these articles—such as infelicities of phrase. (For example, was the sentence, 'For the Lunar Society of Birmingham was but one of many such groups in France and Germany', really intended?) There is one major defect that is no fault of the authors—a printer who takes a fiendish delight in inserting spaces in the middle of words. But it is far more important that these articles are interesting, and do provoke thought. In the area of curriculum studies that is a virtue of great price.

University of Leicester

A. J. Meadows

Education and Politics 1900–1951, by Rodney Barker, OXFORD UNIVERSITY PRESS, 1972, pp viii + 173, £3.

This is an interesting and useful study of one aspect of the Labour Party during the first half of the present century. Dr Barker has not attempted to trace or to set out the many aspects of the party's education policies but has rather sought to examine the way in which opinion and policy developed on the issues connected with secondary education and the light which this throws on the development of the party. The examination is thorough and has been based largely on original sources. Transport House papers and the personal papers of R. H. Tawney and C. P. Trevelyan have been extensively used.

The story of the emergence as party policy of the need for the establishment of common or comprehensive secondary schools is central to this volume. The party only became fully committed to this aim in 1951 and even after that date many of the party's leading figures showed little enthusiasm for it. Many Labour-controlled local authorities were continuing to build new grammar and modern schools well into the sixties. From the opposing standpoint Lord Butler has commented that it was by the later 1960s that the 'future of the grammar schools had been turned into a political football through the obsessive insistence of the Labour Party on a doctrinal rather than an empirical approach' to comprehensive secondary schooling. The first major educational programme issued by the party in 1914 called for the raising of the school-leaving age, the abolition of fees in secondary schools and more day-continuation schools—aptly described by Dr Barker as virtually repeating the existing Liberal government's proposals. The gradual improvement of the existing services and a steady widening of their availability to poorer children together formed the basis of Labour's official educational policies until the fall of the Attlee government in 1951. The movement of opinion within the party on the issue of comprehensive schooling is carefully analysed.

In view of the importance which the Labour Party has more recently attached to the need to take steps to end the exclusiveness and 'social divisiveness' of the public schools, it is remarkable how little part they played in the party's educational thinking both before and after World War II. They 'lay completely outside its experience and hence outside its ambitions'. The endeavours of some members of the Headmasters' Conference to find a way to obtain public money for their schools in the early years of the war led eventually to the appointment of the Fleming Committee and this in its turn caused both the party and the TUC to give more thought to their attitude to these schools. Yet after 1945 both Ellen Wilkinson and George Tomlinson at the Ministry of Education—and the party generally—were too preoccupied with more urgent matters in the maintained schools to devote time or energy to the public schools during the six years of post-war Labour rule.

The reform of the school curriculum is shown to have been of no interest to the party. Throughout this period it accepted the existing character of the curriculum and did not seek to formulate and impose schemes of education for a socialist commonwealth. The greatest activity shown was an occasional flicker of interest in the role education might play in promoting citizenship. Virtually the only administrative step taken was when a few of the more pacifist Labour-controlled local authorities placed bans on the formation of cadet corps in their schools. Although the author does not make the point, it has come to be part of the tradition in this country that control of the school curriculum rests mainly with members of the teaching profession: the wisest politicians might well be those who do not put themselves at cross purposes with the teachers' associations by presuming to tell teachers what to teach.

University of Leeds

Peter Gosden

The History of Education in Ghana, by C. K. Graham, FRANK CASS, 1971, pp 218, £3.50.

The origins of educational administration and practice in Ghana lie long before her boundaries were drawn in the three stages of 1874 (Gold Coast Colony), 1901–2 (Ashanti and the Northern Territories) and 1914 (Part of Togo). Subject to many European influences, before Britain established her dominance, the variety of origins is considerable.

Administrators and ministers of religion from several European nations set up the first schools to offer European-style education on the Gold Coast in the forts and trading settlements of the seventeenth and eighteenth centuries. In the nineteenth century British, German, Swiss and French missionary societies established school networks. Two of these (the British Wesleyan and Swiss/German Basel) were extensive, and grew initially among tribes giving no allegiance to any overseas power. The British administration provided a few schools in the coastal towns too, and, after 1874, made grants to the missions. In the twentieth century the colonial administration assumed even more power, controlling financial support and influencing deeply the philosophical bases of educational work.

In an unbalanced book Dr Graham gives a short but adequate account of schools before 1800, devotes most of his effort to the nineteenth century (129 pages), and gives only 37 pages for a chapter of terse notes on the period 1901–57. Even within the nineteenth century the treatment is uneven, for while British and Wesleyan policy in Cape Coast and its surrounding area is thorough and detailed, the account of Basel Mission work is compressed and treatment of the Bremen and other ventures scanty. References, notes and bibliography all reflect this imbalance and there is a particular lack of use of source material in German.

This defines the limits of the book's interest: it is in educational growth in Cape Coast and its hinterland. This theme is drawn from rich source material, made painstakingly available in extensive notes and a full bibliography. Its especial value is its exposition of the interplay of European provision and African response. The missionary and trader opening up their respective fields are one dimension of the story only; local people responding as catechist, teacher and clerk, to seize the openings generated by Christian and commercial enterprise, are another. Even the initiative in establishing schools lay not only with the European but sometimes with a local community who built a school house and then sought a teacher. But well-intentioned European schemes for agricultural education elicited no such response, foundering upon a deeply-held belief that to farm under supervision was akin to slavery and abhorred as such. So it was that academic education leading to the status and rewards of European occupations caught the African imagination and gave the response upon which the nineteenth-century educators developed their schools.

The interdependence of British government and Wesleyan enterprises, the education of women and girls, and provision for teacher education in the Cape Coast area, are also described in some detail. Here, however, Dr Graham is on the whole covering ground already worked over by other scholars, notably Bartels.

As an attempt to give an account of 'the growth and development of the European type of education in the Gold Coast from the first contact with European civilisation to independence' the book is a disappointment. In the narrower specialist field, however, Dr Graham adds usefully to our knowledge and understanding.

Doncaster College of Education   David C. A. Bradshaw

History, Sociology and Education, edited by T. G. Cook, METHUEN, for the History of Education Society, 1971, pp 64, £1.40.

The conflict between sociology and history was sired by academic exclusiveness out of Anglo-American empiricism. Its lack of relevance to practising historians, more concerned with ideas, techniques and modes of analysis that will help them in their task of answering specific historical questions (however large), has not deterred publishers from snatching at essay collections pertaining to the supposed controversy. The recent book by Hofstadter and Lipset may confuse quantification and techniques with the sociological discipline, but it is a large and portentous book. The slim volume under review here is a more modest product, containing four papers read at the History of Education Society's conference in 1970. T. G. Cook explains in his preface the purpose of the conference, which was 'to engage in an enquiry into the relationships between the history and sociology of education by inviting notable practitioners of sociology to discuss the aims and methods of their discipline and to demonstrate these methods in operation in historical situations'. It is, however, difficult to justify the publication of the papers as a book. Possibly, after the artificial controversies of the conference era have died away, a historian will attempt a sociological explanation of the situation in the 1970s where academic societies demanded not only a periodical, generally justifiable, but also the hard-cover publication of their conference proceedings. These papers might have been interesting to hear, and they should have provoked some interesting discussion, but they really do not stand up to a careful reading.

Half the book is devoted to papers by Gerald Bernbaum and Kenneth Charlton in which they speculate about the relationship between sociology and history. Professor Charlton has some intelligent and, at times, subtle observations to make, but pervading the whole is an outdated tone of complaint. 'In insisting on being so self-consciously theoretical the sociologist is in danger of losing contact with the world of men and women, their doubts, their fears, their aspirations and their follies, and on occasions their plain cantankerousness, if not bloodymindedness, in their determination to avoid doing the expected thing.' He moves towards the only serious grounds for arguing that there is some theoretical conflict between sociology and history *as disciplines*, that they work from different methods of explanation, but it is a difficult position to maintain in general terms, and the result is a vague complaint about conceptual theories being imposed on 'the evidence of the past'. One completes reading Professor Charlton's essay rather unclear as to what the argument is about, but quite clear that there is an argument going on.

Mr Bernbaum has more of interest to say. He argues with much relevance that 'it is impossible to conduct the debate in terms of historians utilising, in a haphazard fashion, a selection of techniques borrowed from the social sciences, or of sociologists culling details from the research monographs of historians with which to demonstrate the validity of their theoretical perspectives'. In the second part of his paper, however, he does just that, losing sight of the real distinctions between conceptual apparatus, technique, methodology and theories, and showing how now one, now another of the sociologist's weapons can be deployed to the advantage of the historian. If the essay is loose in aim, it is interesting in its observations, particularly when he draws upon the apt analogy of econometric history.

Professors Kelsall and Musgrove provide the case studies referred to by Mr Cook. They are not good advertisements for the new hybrid discipline. Professor Kelsall's discussion of the growth of competition by examination in civil service appointments, and his useful demonstration of the effects of the introduction of interviews in the 1920s, are traditional history with the blinkers on. Perhaps the role of the sociologist might at least be to remove the blinkers? The real problem is that Professor Kelsall never sees that the ideas whose impact he is discussing—the competitive ideal, the concept of intellectual merit as the sole basis for selection, the belief that this merit is measurable—are themselves historically determined and need to be placed within a framework of historical explanation if the process is to be understood. What remains is a mundane piece of historical reconstruction, little connected with a debate on sociology and history, except in that it makes the reader very aware that a good sociologist would never have left unasked some of the very important questions that Professor Kelsall ignores.

Professor Musgrove presents himself as a sociologist studying the bureaucratisation of education, and concerned with history for comparative reasons. His paper certainly gives one some idea of what a sociological approach has to offer many historians—the use of systematic hypotheses, the careful and precise outlining of questions, the seeking of answers to questions rather than just interesting data. It was clearly an excellent lecture, full of ideas and anecdotes. In a book it is flimsy and insubstantial, a collection of not very deep thoughts rather than an argument. His concern is bureaucracy in education—which seems to Professor Musgrove to mean the public schools—and he focuses his attention upon the internal structure of these schools with little reference to the society in which they existed and to which they in some way responded.

The importance of any conceptual and technical apparatus is the questions which it leads the historian to ask, and the means it provides for answering them. If we are looking for a simple relationship between sociology and history, it is here perhaps that we might begin our search. But the search is not an important one. This book reads as if historians have not been drawing on developments in sociology for a long time, finding approaches, questions, concepts, techniques, and so on. The book is concerned with a controversy which, if it exists at all, is relevant only in the form of generalised argument. The battle will only cease as more good historical work is written that takes advantage of the liveliness of contemporary sociology. A critical reading of either Michael Anderson's *Family Structure in Nineteenth-Century Lancashire* or Thernstrom and Sennett's *Nineteenth-Century Cities* will teach the reader far more about how sociological methods can inform historical research than he will learn from this flimsy book of essays. What is more, he will be intellectually excited.

Emmanuel College, Cambridge   Geoffrey Crossick

The Rise of a Central Authority for English Education, by A. S. Bishop, CAMBRIDGE UNIVERSITY PRESS, 1971, pp ix + 313, £4.20.

Studies in the Growth of Nineteenth-Century Government,
edited by Gillian Sutherland, ROUTLEDGE & KEGAN PAUL, 1972,
pp viii + 295, £3.75.
Education in Evolution, by John Hurt, RUPERT HART-DAVIS, 1971,
pp 286, £2.50.

The smooth and well-articulated machine which Mrs Thatcher
directs has been created in the twentieth century, from the administrative fractions amalgamated by the Board of Education Act of 1899—
the Educational Establishment of the Privy Council Office, the Department of Science and Art, and the educational wing of the Charity
Commissioners. After 1856 the first two were nominally joined in the
Education Department, and its political head, the Vice-President of
the Committee of Council on Education, was both a Charity Commissioner and responsible for approving the commission's educational
schemes. The functions of the three departments overlapped, all being
involved to varying degrees in both elementary and secondary education. Yet in origin, powers and outlook they were far apart; they were
financed by different parliamentary votes, and recruited and organised
their staffs differently. They showed towards each other as much
suspicion as co-operation. Points of contact aggravated rather than
resolved tension.

Dr Bishop's book outlines the growth of these three institutions, and
their changing powers and tasks, down to 1899. He unravels complica-
tion with frequent skill and fluency, and gives to undergraduates a
shrewd and sensible guide to a maze which has often baffled them. Yet
the book is somewhat disappointing. The range of questions asked, and
sources exploited, is narrow. Comments on the context of educational
development are few, and sometimes unconvincing—as is, for example,
the claim that as a 'general rule' progress occurred during Liberal
ministries, and stagnation when Tories were in power. The 1846
Minutes and the 1902 Act were generated by Conservative governments, and the 1870 Act could not have been carried without Conservative support: on the other hand, the 1862 Revised Code was produced by a Liberal government and reflected distinctively a tenacious
and unimaginative set of Liberal social attitudes.

Dr Bishop draws rather uncritically on unreliable secondary sources. His view of the Education Department under Lingen owes too much to Kekewich's autobiography, inaccurate and overcharged with re-crimination, and written many years after the events it purports to describe. The praise of Kay-Shuttleworth as a man of 'human warmth . . . genuinely interested in the education of children' seems to derive from Frank Smith's outdated biography, and though part of the truth, fails to acknowledge the sad complexities of his unbalanced personality, the ruthlessness and narrow sympathies that made him such a success-ful Poor Law Inspector, his inability to delegate responsibility or to achieve a cordial working relationship with his colleagues at the Privy Council Office, and his habit, shared with so many Victorians, of senti-mentalising the playful innocence of the children of the poor, while regarding the school chiefly as an instrument to shape and sculpt them into deferential, dutiful and submissive adults.

The main sources used are the parliamentary papers; much of the book summarises the reports of royal commissions and select com-mittees. Often they make the same point, time and again, about Britain's technical backwardness or the foolish overlap of departmental duties, so that the book suffers in places from redundancy, and a jerky, lumpy narrative. Moreover, such sources, though guides to the broad outlines of departmental growth, often fail to reveal in a precise and proximate way the nature and quality of administration, or why a particular form of bureaucratic organisation was chosen from many possible, or who was really responsible for creative innovation in government. For exact answers to these questions it is necessary to quarry the manu-script records of the departments, their officials, and politicians. Dr Bishop rarely consults such sources. When he does, there is a great gain in depth and sharpness of focus: the account of the creation of the Education Department in 1856, deriving partly from PRO material, is far more informative than the account of the origin of the Committee of Council in 1839, for which not even the papers of Kay-Shuttle-worth and Russell were used.

The dozen essays that Dr Sutherland has edited are concerned with the growth of the Civil Service. All but one began as contributions to a

Past and Present conference in 1969, and have the qualities perhaps
inevitable in such collections: an unevenness of weight and merit, the
solidity of some contrasting with the tentative content or unclear
structure of others. The two papers on the Education Department are
among the best—substantial and penetrating studies, by Dr Richard
Johnson and Dr Sutherland, of its senior personnel, before and after
1870. A clear message of the collection is the danger of over-generalisa-
tion. There was little positive direction of the Civil Service as a whole
till this century. Treasury control was almost entirely negative; that is,
it could merely try to stop increases in expenditure. Even then it found
it hard to defeat large proposals, especially when advanced by important ministers or departments. Subject to little external impulse
towards uniformity, or towards continuing efficiency and drive,
departments were quite dissimilar in their fortunes.

Dynamic phases occurred at different times and in response to
different impulses. In the first half of the century the clerks of the
Home Office defeated the not very strenuous efforts to reform its
obsolete structure, so that when the Home Secretary acquired new
functions such as control of factory inspection fresh out-departments
were created for them, outside the framework of the old office. At the
same time the Colonial Office was transformed by the evangelical zeal
of James Stephen: its structure was reorganised, a systematic routine
established; above all, it became a potent instrument for innovation in
colonial policy. But after Stephen retired in 1850 it had little impetus
to change either itself or the colonies: it stagnated till this century.

Kay-Shuttleworth was the Stephen of the Educational Establishment of the Privy Council Office. But though each had an energising
religious faith, Kay-Shuttleworth's was much more complicated and
idiosyncratic, its exact nature puzzling contemporaries and being
obscure still; in addition, his creative powers and attitudes had other
roots, unshared by Stephen, in Utilitarianism, and his experience as a
doctor and a Poor Law official. His productive decade at the Privy
Council Office was followed by twenty years of relative standstill under
Lingen: there was great physical expansion, and much bureaucratic
efficiency; a vast amount of paperwork was intelligently processed and

waste inhibited by draconian internal audit. Lingen 'cut his Treasury teeth' in the Education Department. His only significant contribution to fresh educational policy, however, was his enthusiastic elaboration of the Revised Code, partly in response to the pressures of Gladstone and Lowe.

Dr Hurt's book overlaps considerably the others under review, but is at once narrower and shorter in scope, and more intensive in treatment, than Dr Bishop's, though with a rather similar avoidance of highly relevant sources. Dr Hurt examines closely the Education Department (more properly the Educational Establishment of the Privy Council Office) before 1870, detailing the complex system of grants developed between 1833 and 1860, the attempts to cope with a shortage or surplus of teachers, the growth of the departmental bureaucracy. A main theme is the continual conflict between the churches and the department over the control and direction of elementary schooling. Much new material is offered on the ways in which the voluntary societies and their school managers manipulated the grant regulations to their advantage: but the attitudes of each side to the other are not explored in sufficient detail; the profusion of speeches, memoranda, books, pamphlets and journals generated by early Victorian education controversy remains largely untapped. Despite his exemplary thoroughness on some topics, Dr Hurt does not even exploit fully the parliamentary papers and the archives of the department on which he mainly relies: an important point of friction between State and Church—the 'rights of conscience' of non-Anglican pupils in National schools in the 1840s and 1850s—is not mentioned.

Dr Hurt defends the Revised Code of 1862. He regards it as a largely successful attempt to replace inefficient and excessively religious instruction, conducted by indolent teachers and subsidised by a system of grants too open-ended for the state to control, with effective, largely secular instruction, fostered and revealed by objective tests of the 3Rs, and paid for on their results. Dr Hurt admits that curricula narrowed after the code, but blames the teachers for cramming children for the examinations and ignoring the administrators' counsel to teach unexaminable subjects too. He shows a surprising lack of sympathy for teachers needing to ensure that their very large classes passed their examinations; he exaggerates the faults of the schools before the code, and its beneficial results, and does not mention suggestions of the time for effectual modes of governmental control and subvention that would have been less malignant in their effects than the code. The view from Whitehall is limited: from the schoolroom, or the vicarage, there are others—not less partial, nor always more attractive, but different, and necessary.

Trinity Hall, Cambridge   Peter Searby

The History of Loughborough College School, by Bernard Elliott, Loughborough College School, Loughborough, 1971, pp x + 235, £1.25.

The Cambridge Grammar School for Boys, 1871–1971, by A. B. Evans, Cambridge Grammar School for Boys, 1971, pp 75 + plates, 30p.

Kingswood School in Wesley's Day and Since, by A. G. Ives, EPWORTH PRESS, 1970, pp xvi + 264, £2.25.

The variety of the background of those English academic secondary schools which had their origins before the Great War is wider than often realised. Not all by any means began as endowed grammar schools or 1902 secondary schools. The three schools whose histories are reviewed here illustrate this well.

Cambridge Grammar School, founded in 1871 as a 'Higher Grade School', an early use of the term, was really a rather superior elementary school with some Standard VII and ex-Standard VII pupils. After 1902 it failed to secure Higher Elementary School status, and was classed as an elementary school, although at times it taught French and even Latin. In 1919 it became a Central School, and in 1956 a grammar school.

Loughborough College School originated in 1690 as a girls' charity school, in the early nineteenth century being incorporated within a larger girls' elementary school. A scheme of 1875 turned it into a 'higher class elementary school for boys'. In 1894 a secondary department was added and it became an 'Intermediate School'. In 1909 it was classed as a Higher Elementary School, and during the Great War became effectively a department of (later junior technical school within) Loughborough Technical Institute. In 1921 it became a technical high (grammar) school and in 1967 an upper school under the 'Leicestershire Plan'.

Kingswood School, founded by John Wesley in 1748, was at first open to all (including, for a while, girls) suitable for the type of education it provided—boarding, predominantly classical, and religious. Later it became almost exclusively a school for the sons of Methodist ministers, until in the present century, it again opened its doors to a more general intake. In recent times it has developed into a large well-provided boarding school of national standing with much in common with the older public schools. Yet, because of its continuing Methodist connection and its tradition of providing an education suitable for the 'sons of the Manse', subtly different.

The reviewer of school histories must to be fair take into account the intentions of the authors, for such histories may legitimately be written at different levels for different purposes. Some have as their prime concern a factual record of events and people for a readership of former pupils. The best of these will, if soundly based, nevertheless provide also raw material for those historians with more general and more analytical interests. The histories of Loughborough College School and Cambridge Grammar School are essentially superior works of this kind. Well written, based on a variety of (mainly domestic) sources, informative and detailed, and though largely concerned with answering the question 'What happened?' at times going beyond that. Mr Elliott's work is based on the more exhaustive research; Mr Evans is particularly skilled in bringing alive the periods and people of whom he writes. Excellent as they are in their own way, however, they lack any investigation in depth of the more sophisticated questions currently concerning educational historians and which tend to be answerable only by application of analytical techniques. A study of the changing social structure of the parent body at the Cambridge and

Loughborough schools would, for example have been interesting, as would a disciplined attempt to discover how far the schools acted as engines of social advance. Some detailed examination of school administration (apart from the personal achievements of heads chronologically presented) would also have been welcome.

The Kingswood history is the most scholarly of the three. Based on widespread and exhaustively searched sources it is a work of general concern in its own right. The early history of the school is treated within the wider field of the educational views and work of Wesley and his followers and is thus important for those interested in the influence of Methodism on education and child-rearing during the Industrial Revolution period and before. Later chapters are significant particularly in the context of the growth of the independent boarding school ideal in the nineteenth century and the changing curriculum of such schools.

As Mr Ives approaches the present day, however, his book begins to a degree to fall into the same category as the other two volumes reviewed here. Though all three books rightly underline the importance of individual headmasters in English secondary education, it is doubtful whether the history of a great school in recent times should be interpreted solely in terms of heads as successive reigning monarchs. The intricacies of the financial history of independent schools such as Kingswood, for example, require more systematic treatment than can be provided through the narrative approach.

Such criticisms apart, however, these are worth-while publications. They are by no means the institutional hagiographies such works often were in the past. And the extension of school history writing outside the field of the typical endowed grammar and public schools is to be welcomed.

University of Leeds   W. B. Stephens

English Primary Education and the Progressives 1914–1939, by
R. J. W. Selleck, ROUTLEDGE & KEGAN PAUL, 1972, pp 192, £2.00.
Readers of Mr Selleck's earlier work, *The New Education 1870–1914*,
will turn to his latest with keen anticipation, and they will not be dis-
appointed. True, a fair part of his first chapter is not very obviously
linked with his main theme, being concerned largely with the contributions made by the schools to the war effort from 1914 to 1918. But
thereafter his performance is masterly. He shows that 'the progressives
were not a disciplined army marching, united, on a particular town.
They were a group of travellers who, finding themselves together on
the road, had formed a loosely united band.' He makes no attempt to
expound in detail the views and practices of individual reformers but
undertakes the far more demanding task of demonstrating what some
of these had in common, to what extent some were influenced by
others, where marked divergences existed and, more subtly, how often
a common vocabulary disguised wide differences of opinion. His
treatment of this last is particularly illuminating when he discusses the
varied meanings given to such favourite words as 'freedom', 'individuality', 'play' and so on, though the conclusion which he draws, that
this ambiguity, by concealing differences, gave strength to the progressive movement, is open to doubt: it is arguable that the movement
was often resisted because the more extreme views (on 'free discipline'
and play for example) were often taken by critics to be typical of all.
His analysis of the relation between theory and practice among the
reformers (the practice so often preceding the theory, and then, in
turn, being influenced by it) is convincing, as is his apologia for the
sweepingly confident claims which the earlier progressives found it
possible and desirable to make; though one might ruefully complain
that the tradition thus continued (for it was not unknown to Comenius,
Owen, Bell, Wilderspin and so many others!) encouraged some less
distinguished disciples in the teacher-training world to become
tediously impervious to honest doubt. There is an interesting study of
the influence on opinion (generally helpful or thought to be so) of
Dewey, Freud, McDougall and the students of child development; the
reactions of teachers in ordinary schools are sympathetically considered;

but one misses greatly any account of the attitude of parents.

In short, Mr Selleck provides a wide-ranging and sensitive survey of progressive ideas from different points of view, and he conducts his examination with a welcome absence both of the fervour which so often mars this kind of study and of the heavy irony which can come so easily to those who have avoided the heat of battle and, with hindsight, can deplore the excesses of those more fully engaged. He writes with sympathetic good humour, and as a good historian he tolerates even the intolerant, because so treated they become interesting. His knowledge of his field is impressive and he ranges about it with ease, quoting and selecting instances with compelling relevance. The style is admirably clear and the frequent bubbles of wit arise naturally within it; only occasionally does he labour a point and then, it would seem, because he is unaware that the effectiveness of his first exposition makes a second and a third unnecessary.

University of Liverpool   James Murphy

Index

Abacus, 6–13 passim
Absence from school, causes of (pre-1870), 23–4
Acland, Thomas, 35, 40, 45–6
Adult education and Labour movement, literature on, 173–88
Agriculture, and school attendance, 22, 27–8, 57
American education, history of, 79–96
Arithmetical instruments, 5–18
Arithmetick by Inspection, 5, 6, 8–9
Arithmeticke, Instrument for, 1667, 5–18, 41, 42
Arnold, Matthew, 35, 164, 165, 170
Attendance, school, 19–34, 57
Auxerre diocese, regulation of schools, 1610–98, 116–17

Bailyn, Prof Bernard, 79, 80–1, 82, 85, 87, 89
Bedales, French admiration for, 169
Birmingham Daily Post, on free education (1885), 65
Board schools, numbers of, 1876–85, 58
Books, elementary school (mid-nineteenth century), 154–7
Brackley school, Northants, 39, 51
Brown, George, inventor of arithmetical instrument, 12
Buildings, *see* School buildings
Bunce, J. T., 65
Buxton, Sidney, 75

Calculators, 5–18
Cambridge university examinations, Northants, 40, 45, 46
Capitation grants, 1885, 26–7
Catholic schools:
  and free education (1885), 56–78 passim

in USA, 87
Catholics, French liberal, and English public schools, 163, 168, 170
Catholic Times, on free education (1885), 61, 67, 68
Certificates of merit, 30–2
Chamberlain, Joseph, and free education, 56–78
Chartism, in history of education, 179, 180
Children's Employment Commission, 23
Church records, 1558–1642, 115–32
Church Times, on free education (1885), 62, 65
Class meetings, in history of education, 179
Classrooms in nineteenth-century elementary schools, 148, 149, 153–4
Clipston, former grammar school at, 43, 48
Compton, the Rev Lord Alwyne, 36–7
Compulsory education, Victorian views on, 19–20, 23
Conservatives and free education (1885), 69
Co-operatives, literature on educational policy of, 175, 176 ff, 183
Copy-books, mid-nineteenth century, 151, 157
Corporal punishment, in public schools, 163, 166
Cotterell, Sir Charles, 6ff, 12, 13
Coubertin, Pierre de, 168, 170–1
Cracow university, eighteenth century, 142, 143
Cremin, Lawrence, 79, 81–2
Curricula, Poland, 1773–94, 139
Czartoryskis party, Poland, 134–5